THE ROUGH GUIDE TO

LIVERPOOL

A Fan's Handbook

AN UNOFFICIAL GUIDE

Rough Guide Credits
Editor Mark Ellingham
Design and layout Jon Butterworth, Hazel Brown and Aubrey Smith
Photos Action Images, Empics, Corbis, Mark Leech, Stuart Freedman

Acknowledgments
Dan and Dave thank Stephanie Jones and Chris Hughes for their invaluable
contribution to the project, Mark Williams and Nick Moore for panel items,
Aubrey Smith for pictures. Peter Hooton, Kevin Sampson, Mark Platt, John Pearman,
RAOTL and all contributors to the Liverpool Matchday Magazine 2000-2002.
Dan thanks Davey Liver, Steph, Chris, John & Bernie, Reed, Shaky and Dr Fun.
Dave thanks the superb staff on the Liverpool Matchday Magazine 2000-2002.
Rough Guides thank Carlton Books for granting us a sublicense on this book.

Publishing Information
This first edition published August 2002 by
Rough Guides Ltd, 62-70 Shorts Gardens, London WC2H 9AH

Distributed by the Penguin Group
Penguin Books, 80 The Strand, London WC2R 0RL
Penguin Putnam Inc, 375 Hudson Street, New York 10014, USA

Typeset in Minion and Helvetica to an original design by Henry Iles.
Printed in Spain by Graphy Cems. 416pp.

THE ROUGH GUIDE TO

LIVERPOOL

by
Dan Davies and **Dave Cottrell**

ROUGH
GUIDES

Contents

Reds in review

This is Anfield

Tell you the story...

Fixture this

INTRODUCTION

Imagine it's autumn 1998 all over again. Roy Evans has gone and Gérard Houllier has just taken sole charge of a demoralised team, burdened by the freight of unparalleled heritage and struggling to stay in the Premiership's top 10. What would you think if someone came up to you and told you that, in three years' time, Liverpool would win five trophies in six months, culminating in victory over the reigning European champions? That they'd subsequently march to within six minutes of the semi-finals of the Uefa Champions League at their first attempt?

That by the spring of 2002 there'd be 21 new faces, 13 nationalities and only five familiar names – Owen, Murphy, Carragher, Berger, Heggem – in the squad? Next thing you know they'd be telling you the hopes of a nation rested upon the shoulders of a 22-year-old from Huyton… if only he hadn't gone and aggravated a groin injury in the final game of the season. More to the point, would you ever have supposed you'd be reading a book like this – celebrating a legendary past yet anticipating a perhaps more thrilling future?

When Houllier took complete control for the first time on 14 November 1998, the team to face Leeds United at Anfield was: James, Heggem, Carragher, Staunton, Bjornebye, Thompson, Redknapp, Ince, Berger, Riedle (Leonhardsen), Fowler. On the bench were Friedel, Harkness, Kvarme and Murphy. The manager expressed sadness at the departure of Evans before calling for "lots of effort and total commitment" in his programme notes. "We need new players," he added. "It won't be easy because there aren't too many quality players available, and anybody we do bring in has to be better than what we already have."

It was a formidable undertaking, but it took him just 33 months to transform the Reds from the tactically naive team that took the lead and pressed for a second against Leeds before allowing them to score three times on the break, to the assured, resilient unit that could outwit and withstand the might of Bayern Munich on a late August evening in

Monaco. By the end of season 2001/02, with second place in the Premiership and an automatic return to the Champions League secured, Liverpool were undoubtedly back.

From the start, Houllier insisted his chosen route for the renaissance of English football's finest football club was "a gradual one". But the plan was to build "a better team in terms of quality and quantity, a younger team which is very eager to win things together". At times it's meant being ruthlessly objective – as cult hero Robbie Fowler, former goalkeeper Sander Westerveld and even skipper and long-server Jamie Redknapp would doubtless testify.

All the while there have been glimpses of Houllier's grand plan. On the characters he wants in the dressing-room: "If you look for them there are still players around who, whatever wages they are on, will fight for you once they are on that grass. Yes, you need to have talent, but you also need winners. A Liverpool player must play like a lion, give his all."

And on the unity and collective spirit he fosters: "My team's motivation comes from an everlasting desire to win trophies. The players have a vision that they share with the fans and staff. They trust themselves a lot – there aren't many teams in the Premiership who trust themselves as much as Liverpool do."

On Saturday 13 October 2001, what he could not possibly have foreseen was the illness that almost robbed him of much more than his footballing dream. It was a measure of the faith, resolve, discipline and professionalism he had engendered in his players that they responded so positively under caretaker manager Phil Thompson to a backdrop of unwavering support and the usual full houses at Anfield.

While the boss was away, the Reds refused to lie down in the Champions League, becoming the first British team to win Kiev, qualifying for the second group phase and eventually going 14 consecutive away fixtures unbeaten in Europe.

John Arne Riise continued to prove an inspired signing. Nicolas Anelka was brought in as an exciting if temporary replacement for Robbie Fowler. And Michael Owen reached his 100-goal milestone and was voted European footballer of the year.

While the defeat of Roma upon Houllier's return was perhaps the biggest single highlight of the season, the team's consistently powerful performances in the domestic league were the greatest cause for celebration. Liverpool finished second for the first time in 12 years. On their travels they won 12 and lost just four games. Some sections of the media actually labelled them boring – curious for a side that might have conceded the fewest goals in the Premiership but also scored the fourth most.

It was an achievement that prompted former manager Kenny Dalglish to note, "You don't realise how magnificent the team has been this season until you consider Gérard Houllier wasn't there for a long period – you miss the manager more than any player."

On the eve of a new season, the talk in the press is no longer of daunting tasks but undreamt possibilities. When they write about Houllier today, journalists reach for their Latin phrasebooks and use terms like 'magnum opus' and 'modus operandi' – as if it were improper to describe his supervision of Liverpool's rebirth in everyday English.

Where appropriate, however, you'll find plenty of plain talking in this essential and easy-to-use guide to all things LFC. Much more than just a tribute to one man's faith and vision, it reviews last season's rollercoaster ride game by game with all the stats that matter.

The entire first-team squad, including the summer's latest signings, is profiled – as well as the backroom staff and key Academy personnel. And there's a comprehensive round-up of former Reds still in the game. Then, of course, there's the history – everything you need to know about football's most famous stadium and the managers and players who built a dynasty. The stories, the myths, even the practical jokes.

There's advice and information, too, on tickets, supporters clubs, merchandise, local media, fanzines and websites, food and drink, and travel and accommodation. Plus a definitive guide to the city, its nightlife, fashion and that unique dialect known as Scouse. And looking ahead, profiles of every other club and venue in the Premiership prelude a diary of the forthcoming season with all the key dates, anniversaries and birthdays.

As they've been heard to say on Anfield's legendary Spion Kop from time to time, it's the gear. Enjoy.

Dan Davies and Dave Cottrell
June 2002

SEASON REVIEW
2001/02

AUGUST 2001

Wednesday 8 August 2001 Champions League 3rd qualifying round 1st leg

FC Haka 0   Liverpool 5

Heskey 32, Owen 56, 65, 87, Hyypia 86

Kick-off 7.45pm Olympiastadion, Helsinki **Att** 33,217 **Referee** A Ibanez (Spain)
LIVERPOOL Arphexad, Babbel, Henchoz, Hyypia, Carragher, Berger, Hamann, Gerrard (Murphy 66), Litmanen (McAllister 58), Owen, Heskey (Fowler 72) SUBS Nielsen, Riise, Barmby, Traore
FC HAKA Vilnrotter, Karjalainen (Ivanov 83), Makela, Allto, Vaisanen, Popovits (Ruhanen 70), Torkelli (Pasanen 72), Kovacs, Wilson, Okkonen, Kangaskorpi SUBS Toivonen, Bajic, Ivanov Koivuranta, Pogioli BOOKED Makela

Not knowing the identity of the opposition until the last minute wasn't the ideal preparation for our first foray into the Champions League but in a stadium half filled with local Liverpool fans, Houllier's boys took a decisive first step in the competition with a five-goal hiding of FC Haka. Frustrated by a well-drilled offside trap in the first half, the Reds went in at the interval with just a solitary Emile Heskey goal to show for their efforts. But a second-half hat-trick from Michael Owen and a late fifth from local pin-up Sami Hyypia put the icing on a satisfying evening's work. Champions League here we come.

Vital stats
Shots on target 12 | Shots off target 10 | Owen's hat-trick was his first in European competition

Quote unquote
"I'm pleased because this was our first competitive game of the season. The motivation and desire were there to see." **Gérard Houllier**
"Haka couldn't really live with us after the second goal." **Phil Thompson**
"They reminded me of the Liverpool of old – all the one or two touches, just like they did in the days of Terry McDermott and Graeme Souness." **Keith Armstrong** Haka manager

Man of the match Michael Owen **Atmosphere** Pretty vocal with at least half the Finns in the stadium supporting the Reds.

Sunday 12 August 2001 — Charity Shield

Liverpool 2 — Manchester United 1

McAllister 1pen, Owen 16 — Van Nistelrooy 50

Kick-off 2pm Millennium Stadium, Cardiff **Att** 70,227 **Referee** A D'Urso

LIVERPOOL Westerveld, Babbel, Henchoz, Hyypia, Riise (Carragher 83), Barmby (Biscan 70), Hamann, McAllister, Murphy (Berger 70), Heskey, Owen SUBS Redknapp, Arphexad, Traore, Litmanen BOOKED Murphy, Hamann

MANCHESTER UNITED Barthez, Irwin, G.Neville, Stam, Silvestre, Beckham, Keane, Butt (Yorke 65), Giggs, Scholes, Van Nistelrooy SUBS Carroll, Solskjaer, Johnson, Neville, Chadwick, Brown BOOKED Scholes

A third visit to Cardiff in the space of a few months brought a third victory, a third straight win over the old enemy and a fourth trophy of the year. Steven Gerrard was out injured and Robbie Fowler was dropped after a training ground bust-up with Phil Thompson but the first showpiece game in Britain to be played under a closed roof witnessed a blistering start from Liverpool, who set about United from the opening whistle. Within a minute Danny Murphy had been fouled in the box by Roy Keane, allowing Gary McAllister to stroke home the penalty. Fifteen minutes later and Liverpool's advantage had doubled when Owen left Gary Neville on his arse before sliding the ball past Barthez with his left foot. A fine Westerveld save from Keane preserved Liverpool's half-time lead but United came out strong in the second period. Despite a 50th-minute reply from Ruud van Nistelrooy, fellow Dutchman Westerveld was in no mood to be beaten a second time.

Vital stats
88% pass completion rate for Didi Hamann | 40% possession | 7 shots in total

Quote unquote
"Sander was tremendous and pulled off some stunning saves to keep them at bay. I also think Didi Hamann had an outstanding game in the centre of midfield." **Phil Thompson**
"Ferguson's thoroughbreds remain the benchmark and to defeat them for a third time in succession will intensify the self-belief developed under Houllier." **Henry Winter** The Daily Telegraph

Man of the match Michael Owen **Atmosphere** Loud and proud although the familiar surroundings of the Millennium Stadium seemed a little strange with the roof on.

Liverpool 2   West Ham United 1
Owen 18, 77   Di Canio 30pen

Kick-off 3pm Anfield **Att** 43,935 **Referee** J Winter

LIVERPOOL Arphexad, Babbel (Riise 45), Henchoz, Hyypia, Carragher, Murphy (Redknapp 72), Hamann, McAllister, Biscan (Barmby 56), Owen, Litmanen SUBS Nielsen, Traore BOOKED Carragher

WEST HAM UNITED Hislop, Schemmel, Dailly, Song, Winterburn, Sinclair, Carrick, Moncur (McCann 69), Cole (Courtois 78), Todorov (Defoe 67), Di Canio SUBS Forrest, Soma BOOKED Moncur, Sinclair, Di Canio, Todorov, Dailly

Liverpool started the Premiership campaign in determined fashion and it took only five minutes for Jari Litmanen to release Michael Owen who in turn forced a great save from Shaka Hislop. On 18 minutes Owen made amends by firing past the Hammers keeper after Gary Mac's clever back-heel. A first-half Di Canio penalty levelled the scores after Stephane Henchoz was adjudged to have fouled Todorov but Liverpool quickly regrouped and went back on the offensive. Sami Hyypia, Litmanen and Dietmar Hamann fashioned chances before Owen picked up the ball on the right side of the West Ham penalty area, twisted past two defenders and hammered a low, angled shot past Hislop for the winner.

Vital stats

16 shots on goal to West Ham's 3 | 57% possession | 81% pass completion rate for Michael Owen

Quote unquote

"Jamie Redknapp coming on as a substitute lifted both the crowd and the team and him getting back was pleasing for everyone." **Phil Thompson**

"The difference between the side was one man, Michael Owen. When you play against someone like him, you have to try to restrict the number of chances he has. Today he had only three but he scored with two." **Glenn Roeder** West Ham United manager

Man of the match Michael Owen **Atmosphere** The season started here but not on the Kop it didn't. Must have still been hungover from Dortmund.

Champions League 3rd qualifying round 2nd leg

Liverpool 4   FC Haka 1

Fowler 35, Redknapp 49, Heskey 55, Wilson 84og   Kovacs 44

Kick-off 7.45pm Anfield **Att** 31,602 **Referee** T Hauge (Norway)

LIVERPOOL Arphexad, Wright, Hyypia [Babbel 65], Traore, Vignal, Barmby, Redknapp, Biscan, Diomede, Fowler, Heskey [Litmanen 59] SUBS Nielsen, Murphy, Gerrard, Riise, McAllister

FC HAKA Vilnrotter, Bajic [Koivuranta 80], Karjalainen, Allto, Okkonen, Ruhanen [Innanen 65], Kangaskorpi, Wilson, Pogioli [Ivanov 77], Torkelli, Kovacs SUBS Toivonen, Halonen, Pasanen

BOOKED Kangaskorpi

Liverpool fielded a much changed line-up to complete the job against plucky Haka at Anfield, with skipper Jamie Redknapp making a goal-scoring comeback after 15 months out through injury. A decent crowd took advantage of lowered ticket prices and Liverpool's second string eventually put on a show after being rocked by an unlikely Haka equaliser. Recalled Robbie Fowler, who had kissed and made up with Phil Thompson, headed the Reds in front from a Redknapp corner. Redknapp was then involved in the next two goals, firing home from close range on 49 minutes and unlocking the defence for Heskey to make it 3-1 four minutes later. The popular captain got a hero's reception when he was substituted for Steven Gerrard 19 minutes from time. David Wilson headed into his own net in the closing stages to complete a comfortable 9-1 aggregate victory for the Reds.

Vital stats

Robbie Fowler's 12th goal in Europe put him 3rd in club's all-time scoring chart

Quote unquote

"We fielded a different side because of the lead we held, and it gave us a chance to look at some of the younger players in action. They all took the opportunity well and Grégory Vignal, Djimi Traore and Stephen Wright all enjoyed good games." **Phil Thompson**

"While a scoring return to action spread the broadest smile across Redknapp's face, a telling contribution to the Reds' third meant even more. Spotting Heskey in space, Redknapp swept away 15 months of misery with one leisurely swing of his right boot." **John Edwards** Daily Mail

Man of the match Grégory Vignal. **Atmosphere** Not bad considering the tie was won already. A few old favourites were given an airing – We Love You Liverpool, Oh When The Reds… Fields Of Anfield Road started but not that many knew the words yet.

It's a podium finish for Sami, Robbie, Jamie and co after a formula-one triumph in Monaco

Tuesday 24 August 2001   **Uefa Super Cup**

Liverpool 3   Bayern Munich 2

Riise 23, Heskey 45, Owen 46   Salihamidzic 57, Jancker 82

Kick-off 7.45pm Stade Louis II **Att** 13,500 **Referee** V Pereira (Portugal)
LIVERPOOL Westerveld, Babbel, Hyypia, Henchoz, Carragher, McAllister, Gerrard (Biscan 66), Riise (Murphy 69), Hamann, Heskey, Owen (Fowler 83) SUBS Arphexad, Redknapp, Vignal, Litmanen. BOOKED Hamann
BAYERN MUNICH Kahn, Lizarazu, Linke, Kovac, Sagnol, Thiam, Salihamidzic (Santa Cruz 72), Hargreaves, Giovane Elber, Sforza (Kovac 66), Pizarro (Jancker 66). SUBS Dreher, Kuffour, Fink, Zickler

"We've only won five cups," sang the travelling Kopites in Monaco after Liverpool swept aside the reigning European champions with the best display of attacking football since Gérard Houllier took over. John Arne Riise bagged the opener on 23 minutes, his first for the club, after Steven Gerrard released Michael Owen into space. Oliver Kahn then foiled Owen on 31 minutes before the irresistible Emile Heskey tormented the Bayern defence before dinking the ball over the German international keeper for

17

Emile Heskey tangles with Bayern midfielder Hasan Salihamidzic in the Uefa Super Cup

an exquisite solo goal. Liverpool further extended their lead a minute after the break when Carragher's long ball found Owen who slid the ball under Kahn. Bayern came back into the game with typical determination and scored two goals to set up a nail-biting finish. But there was to be no denying the Reds a famous victory and another trophy for the cabinet.

Vital stats

Liverpool had 8 shots on target to Bayern's 3 | Both sides forced 4 corners | Liverpool conceded 17 fouls in the 90 minutes

Quote unquote

"The lads performed magnificently. They totally dominated the European champions for an hour, scored three excellent goals and produced some brilliant attacking football." **Phil Thompson**

"Liverpool have only won one Super Cup before. So I told the boys this could be the second one, don't miss the opportunity. When this team wants a result, they get it." **Gérard Houllier**

Man of the match Sami Hyypia **Atmosphere** Party time in the stands for the travelling Reds.

Bolton Wanderers 2   Liverpool 1

Ricketts 29, Holdsworth 89   Heskey 66

Kick-off 8pm Reebok Stadium **Att** 27,205 **Referee** G Poll

BOLTON WANDERERS Jaaskelainen, Barness, Bergsson, Whitlow, Charlton, Gardner, Frandsen (Farrelly 69), Warhurst, Nolan (Diawara 82), Hansen, Ricketts (Holdsworth 56) SUBS Banks, Nishizawa BOOKED Charlton, Holdsworth

LIVERPOOL Westerveld, Babbel (Riise 46), Henchoz, Hyypia, Carragher, Gerrard, Hamann, McAllister, Murphy; Owen, Fowler (Heskey 64) SUBS Arphexad, Biscan, Litmanen BOOKED Fowler, Henchoz

Despite dominating from start to finish, the Reds conspired to lose their first match in four and a half months. It was a defeat that contained depressing echoes of previous seasons when Liverpool had followed impressive victories with costly setbacks against less-fancied Premiership opponents. Westerveld had already saved well from Gardner when Ricketts connected to head home for Bolton on 26 minutes. Robbie Fowler squandered a chance to equalise before half time and Owen headed wide just after the interval. Two minutes after being brought on for Fowler, however, Heskey capitalised on fine work by McAllister and Hamann to level the scores. But with Liverpool pressing desperately for the winner their dominance deserved, Sander Westerveld made a critical mistake. Just two minutes remained on the clock when a speculative 25-yarder from Holdsworth somehow squirmed from the Dutchman's grasp and ended up in the back of the net. It was to prove the final straw for Sander and he never played for the club again.

Vital stats

Liverpool had 20 shots on goal to Bolton's 16 | 57% possession | 90% pass completion rate for Steven Gerrard

Quote unquote

"As results go this was as disappointing as they get. It's déjà vu in many ways for us. It's a bit like what happened at the start of last season, so the coaching staff were extremely unhappy at the result." **Phil Thompson**

"Bolton, favourites for the drop, rode their luck to make it three wins out of three. It cost (Liverpool) the chance to take a psychological advantage over their title rivals who have experienced hiccups." **Richard Tanner** Daily Express

"I felt sorry for the players afterwards because it was a harsh return for what had been a very good display on the road against a team who were flying high." **Gérard Houllier**

19

Man of the match Steven Gerrard **Atmosphere** The less said the better **League position** 12th

SEPTEMBER 2001

Liverpool 1
Gerrard 46
86

Aston Villa 3
Dublin 31, Hendrie 55, Vassell

Kick-off 3pm Anfield **Att** 44,102 **Referee** A D'Urso
LIVERPOOL Dudek, Henchoz (Murphy 76), Hyypia, Riise (Vignal 60), Carragher, McAllister, Barmby (Owen 60), Hamann, Gerrard, Heskey, Fowler SUBS Biscan, Arphexad BOOKED Barmby, Carragher, Vignal SENT OFF Gerrard
ASTON VILLA Schmeichel, Delaney, Wright, Mellberg, Alpay, Boateng, Hendrie (Staunton 70), Merson (Hadji 70), Kachloul, Vassell, Dublin SUBS Enckelman, Ginola, Balaban BOOKED Alpay, Mellberg

A week after Owen, Gerrard and Heskey had put Germany to the sword in Munich, Liverpool's all-conquering internationals were brought back to earth with a bump as Aston Villa ran out deserved 3-1 winners over a disjointed and disappointing Reds outfit. Jerzy Dudek made his debut in goal following his transfer from Feyenoord but was powerless to stop Dion Dublin heading Villa's opener from a Merson free-kick. A rollocking at half time saw Liverpool come out with renewed vigour and when Steven Gerrard headed an equaliser a minute after the restart, the game

Reds protest to Andy D'Urso but Steven Gerrard's already received his marching orders

looked there for the winning. But a combination of poor defending and too many sloppy individual performances saw Villa add a second through Lee Hendrie. And then the wheels came right off. Gerrard received his marching orders after a horror challenge on George Boateng and to rub salt in the wounds, Vassell hammered a rising shot past Dudek to make it 3-1 on 86 minutes. Not even seven minutes of injury time was enough to save the hapless Reds.

Vital stats

93% pass completion rate for Didi Hamann | 13 attempts on goal compared to Villa's 6 | 22 fouls conceded to Villa's 18

Quote unquote

"It was an extremely frustrating afternoon for us all round. We knew it wouldn't be easy as it never is when players return from international duty." **Phil Thompson**

"I don't want to be known as some kind of football bad boy, but aggression is part of my game. I regret what happened and will learn from it. I hope I can make it up to the club." **Steven Gerrard**

"It is one of football's great imponderables – how can Liverpool collect gong after gong when the occasion demands, yet make such a pudding of what is supposed to be their bread and butter?" **Paul Joyce** Daily Express

Man of the match Didi Hamann **Atmosphere** Confusion before kick-off as odd timing of YNWA spilt over to game. Never really got going in this one and we just couldn't raise the lads **League position** 15th

Tuesday 11 September 2001	Champions League

Liverpool 1   Boavista 1

Owen 29   Silva 3

Kick-off 7.45pm Anfield **Att** 30,015 **Referee** Kyros Vassaras (Greece)
LIVERPOOL Dudek, Carragher, Henchoz, Hyypia, Vignal, Gerrard, McAllister, Hamann, Murphy (Riise 71), Heskey, Owen SUBS Arphexad, Fowler, Redknapp, Barmby, Biscan, Litmanen BOOKED Vignal
BOAVISTA Ricardo, Frechaut, Turra, Emanuel, Erivan, Petit, Alexandre, Glauber, Sanchez (Pedro Emanuel 59), Duda (Bosingwa 84), Silva (Serginho 79) SUBS William, Loja, Gouveia, Marcio BOOKED Turra, Silva, Emanuel, Glauber, Ricardo, Petit, Pedro Emanuel

Liverpool's first game in the Champions League proper could not have got off to a worse start. While most thoughts were still fixed on the terrible scenes that had unfolded in America that afternoon, it was clear that the minds of Liverpool defenders were also elsewhere. A third-minute free-kick caused mayhem in the home penalty area and the Brazilian Silva capitalised to blast home. Dudek then acrobatically denied Duda to keep Liverpool in the game before Heskey played Owen in behind the Boavista defence to equalise with a superb curling shot. It was the seventh competition in which Owen had scored on his debut. Gerrard then went close with a 40-yard piledriver before half time and again tested the keeper with a free-kick on the hour. But as the play acting from the Portuguese side became more theatrical, Liverpool could not find a way through the massed ranks of defenders. Vignal's shot over the bar was the best effort in a final wave of attacks on the Boavista goal.

Vital stats
8 tackles by Grégory Vignal, the most on the night for Liverpool | 12 attempts on goal compared to Boavista's 13 | 58% of possession

Quote unquote
"Our football was a vast improvement on the Aston Villa game and beforehand we felt it was vitally important for everybody at the club to show an improvement." **Phil Thompson**
"It was an emotional game and we had the best chances. Liverpool were more aggressive but we Portuguese are great warriors – just look at our history." **Jaime Moreira Pacheco** Boavista coach
"I thought we came up against a good Boavista side but I also think we could have won the match." **Sami Hyypia**

Man of the match Grégory Vignal **Atmosphere** Our first European game of the campaign was overshadowed by world events and while the Kop got behind the team it was understandably a little subdued.

Saturday 15 September 2001	Premiership

Everton 1   Liverpool 3

Campbell 4   Gerrard 11, Owen 29 (pen), Riise 52

Kick-off 12noon Goodison Park **Att** 39,554 **Referee** P Durkin
EVERTON Gerrard, Naysmith, Stubbs, Unsworth (Radzinski 46), Weir, Watson, Xavier (Gascoigne 46), Gravesen, Alexandersson (Hibbert 74), Campbell, Ferguson SUBS Simonsen, Tal
LIVERPOOL Dudek, Riise, Hyypia, Henchoz, Carragher, Vignal, Hamann, Gerrard (Smicer 85), Murphy (McAllister 77), Owen, Heskey SUBS Fowler, Arphexad, Wright BOOKED Murphy

More uncharacteristically sloppy defending saw Liverpool trailing again early on in a game they had to win. Kevin Campbell's sharp turn and shot sent the Gladwys Street into raptures but Evertonian joy was short-lived as Steven Gerrard turned on the style in a performance that had the critics

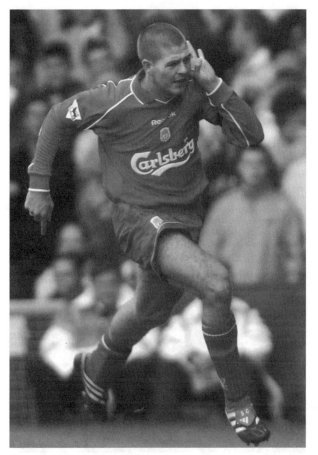

Gerrard's just silenced Goodison Park with a screamer. Now show us your tongue, Stevie

drooling. Stepping past Gary Naysmith in the 11th minute, Gerrard hammered an equaliser from the tightest of angles before letting the Bluenoses in the Lower Bullens know exactly what he thought of them. Owen went on to put the Reds in charge with a first-half penalty following a foul on Heskey and then Gerrard again went close from long range. In the second half, Gazza clattered the man many believe to be his natural heir in England's midfield but was powerless to stop a dazzling solo effort from Riise on 55 minutes. The Norwegian streaked away down the left before finishing with clinical precision. Henchoz cleared off the line from Campbell on the hour and Dudek showed his class with two late stops from the Everton captain. Job done, Goodison gutted, season back on track.

Vital stats

53% possession | 8 attempts on goal compared to Everton's 14 |62% pass completion rate for Steven Gerrard

Quote unquote

"I'm pleased we managed not only to have a good result but a good display of football I think the message is we're getting back to business now." **Gérard Houllier**

"He's 21 and it seems to be happening for him the way it happened for me at Spurs. He's a different class. Like Michael Owen, he's oozing confidence. I'm proud he's English." Everton's **Paul Gascoigne** on Steven Gerrard

"Liverpool, at their best, resounded with youthful enthusiasm. Houllier was quick to identify the

John Arne Riise becomes an instant derby hero. And we wanna know how he scored that goal

average age of his side was 23, and in the 40-minute period in which they seized control of the game, his optimism didn't seem misplaced." **Martin Samuel** Sunday Express

Man of the match Steven Gerrard **Atmosphere** Seemed to be getting going at last, but if you can't at Goodison, where can you? Hey Dude was aired for our new goalie and there was a top YNWA at the end **League position** 10th

---

Wednesday 19 September 2001   **Champions League**

Borussia Dortmund 0   Liverpool 0

Kick-off 7.45pm Westfalenstadion **Att** 50,000 **Referee** V Ivanov (Russia)
BORUSSIA DORTMUND Lehmann, Kohler, Reuter, Wörns, Evanilson, Stevic, Dede, Rosicky, Sorensen (Bobic 87), Koller, Amoroso (Ricken 87) SUBS Metzelder, Madouini, Oliseh, Herrlich, Laux BOOKED Stevic
LIVERPOOL Dudek, Carragher, Henchoz, Hyypia, Vignal, Murphy, Hamann, Gerrard, Riise, (McAllister 74), Owen, Heskey SUBS Wright, Biscan, Barmby, Smicer, Fowler, Arphexad BOOKED Henchoz

Two teams in similarly lowly positions in their domestic leagues fought out a dour goalless draw that was low on incident, goalmouth action and excitement. Dortmund had clearly heeded the warnings about the pace of Liverpool's attack and paid the Reds the compliment of shuffling their formation in order to contain the architects of their national team's recent downfall, Owen and Heskey. Houllier's side nevertheless demonstrated maturity and composure beyond their years and could have taken the lead twice in the first half when Amoroso cleared Hyypia's header off the line and then the referee missed a clear tug on Owen as he wriggled free in the box. Dortmund were denied by the woodwork in the second half when Henchoz headed against his own post after a Vignal mix-up and Rosicky saw his 25-yard volley beat Dudek but not the upright on 68 minutes. Liverpool's last real chance came when an Owen appeal for a penalty was turned down after he was barged over by Kohler.

Vital stats
1 Reds shot on target in 90 minutes | 18 clearances, blocks and interceptions from Sami Hyypia | This was Liverpool's 15th draw in 79 Champions Cup matches

Quote unquote
"Maybe we could've done better on the break. But taking into account the conditions, we did okay. It's an open group and we're still in it." **Gérard Houllier**

"We defended solidly, worked very hard and were well disciplined with Sami Hyypia back to his best, marshalling the defence and putting in some fantastic tackles." **Phil Thompson**

"The cost of keeping Owen quiet was the entertainment value of a match in which Dortmund devoted all their energies to denying the forward the slightest opportunity to emulate the heroics he produced for England." **Oliver Kay** The Times

"The fact Borussia Dortmund changed their usual way of playing to deny us space was an indication of the respect our side now commands on the Continent." **Gérard Houllier**

Man of the match Sami Hyypia **Atmosphere** Travelling Kop makes itself heard, but as both sides cancel each other out there's not much inspiration from the pitch.

Saturday 22 September 2001	Premiership

Liverpool 1   Tottenham Hotspur 0

Litmanen 57

Kick-off 3pm Anfield **Att** 44,116 **Referee** D Gallagher
LIVERPOOL Dudek, Vignal, Henchoz, Hyypia, Carragher, Biscan, Barmby, Hamann, Riise, Litmanen (Owen 68), McAllister 84), Fowler (Heskey 59) SUBS Kirkland, Wright BOOKED Vignal
TOTTENHAM HOTSPUR Sullivan, Taricco, King, Perry, Ziege, Anderton, Freund, Poyet, Davies (Rebrov 73), Sheringham, Ferdinand SUBS Keller, Leonhardsen, Etherington, Thelwell BOOKED Freund

A much changed line-up, featuring rare starts for Igor Biscan, Nick Barmby and Jari Litmanen, traded blows with a confident Spurs outfit that could have gone ahead as early as the second minute if Barmby had not been in the right place to clear Ferdinand's effort off the line. The ever-willing Vignal hit the bar after a neat interchange with Riise and then Litmanen saw a shot from range flash wide on 31 minutes. As the game wore on it was clear the two playmakers, Litmanen and Teddy Sheringham, held the key to the points and just before the hour it was the mercurial Finn who broke free and crashed an unstoppable shot in off Sullivan's post from 25 yards. Jari, who was at the heart of all Liverpool's best moments, got a great ovation when he was replaced by Owen on 68 minutes. But disaster struck for Owen four minutes from time when he raced away from Ledley King and stretched for a through ball before shooting. When he failed to rise from the turf it was clear one of his troublesome hamstrings had again betrayed him. Three points but a dark cloud on the horizon.

Tottenham defender Chris Perry denies John Arne Riise possession on this occasion

Vital stats

Spurs enjoyed 53% possession | Only 5 of Liverpool's 18 shots were on target | Reds were 6/1 to win the game 1-0

Quote unquote

"These things can happen to players with explosive pace." **Gérard Houllier**

"The sudden lift came courtesy of Litmanen, who wowed the crowd with an outstanding pirouetting flick. Just as Tottenham grew in confidence, they were stung. Litmanen let rip. It was at once delightful and deadly." **Amy Lawrence** The Observer

"Litmanen's goal on 57 minutes was the first from open play he had ever scored for Liverpool and the way he ran to celebrate with the Kop, kissing the Liver crest, was somehow fitting." **Tim Rich** The Independent

Man of the match Sami Hyypia **Atmosphere** Still a bit sluggish despite a full rendition of Scouser Tommy. Could have done better with a chorus of Jari, Oh Jari, Jari… after his wonder goal **League position** 5th

Wednesday 26 September 2001	Champions League

Liverpool 1   Dynamo Kiev 0

Litmanen 23

Kick-off 7.45pm Anfield **Att** 33,513 **Referee** P Collina (Italy)

LIVERPOOL Dudek, Carragher, Hyypia, Henchoz, Vignal, Barmby (Murphy 61), Hamann, Gerrard, Riise (McAllister 79), Heskey, Litmanen (Fowler 64) SUBS Kirkland, Smicer, Redknapp, Biscan

DYNAMO KIEV Filimonov, Nesmachnyi, Holovko, Vaschuk, Fedorov, Belkevich (Serebrennikov 81), Gavrancic, Cernat (Peev 69), Ghioane, Melashchenko, Idahor SUBS Reva, Yashkin, Moroz, Bodnar

Liverpool came into this vital Champions League game without the injured Michael Owen and without a win in three previous encounters with former Soviet sides. Houllier's boys, boosted by Owen putting pen to paper on a new five-year contract before the game, started the match in bright fashion and could have been 3-0 up at the break. They had to settle for a single and ultimately decisive goal from Champions League specialist Jari Litmanen. He had already had a goal disallowed and a header cleared off the line when he reacted quickest to Gerrard's shot rebounding off the post. In a flash, the mulleted Finn had crashed the ball in off the Kiev bar to put the Reds in front. Litmanen was again in the thick of it in the second half, releasing Barmby who should have done better. Heskey shot wide when clean through and Barmby hit a post, leav-

28

ing Houllier to settle for one goal and a valuable first three points in the Champions League.

Vital stats

Did Hamann made passes 51, more than any other player | Liverpool had 19 shots on goal | This was Kiev's 46th game in the Champions League

Quote unquote

"Liverpool, echoing in some small way the great teams of the past, have been economical with the risks taken." **Martin Samuel** Daily Express

"Jari's on a good run right now, through he looked tired when I took him off. I thought it was an excellent team performance. We are a young team but we are learning in this competition. I think we are on the fast track now." **Gérard Houllier**

"It was disappointing not to win by a bigger margin, but the stakes were high and this victory could prove imperative for us. The group is delicately balanced but we're confident of progressing through to the next group stage now." **Phil Thompson**

Man of the match Didi Hamann **Atmosphere** Good effort though not yet up to normal European night standards.

Champions League specialist Jari Litmanen celebrates an early strike against Kiev

Newcastle United 0 | Liverpool 2

Riise 3, Murphy 86

Kick-off 2pm St James' Park **Att** 52,095 **Referee** G Barber
NEWCASTLE UNITED Given, Griffin, O'Brien, Dabizas, Elliott, Solano (Ameobi 73), Lee, Acuna (Speed 57), Robert, Shearer, Bellamy SUBS Harper, Lua-Lua, Distin BOOKED Bellamy
LIVERPOOL Dudek, Vignal, Hyypia, Henchoz, Carragher, Biscan, McAllister, Murphy, Riise, Heskey, Fowler SUBS Redknapp, Barmby, Kirkland, Wright, Litmanen BOOKED Carragher, Henchoz, Fowler, Murphy.

A thoroughly professional performance against high-flying Newcastle secured three points and a place in the hearts of all Liverpool fans for John Arne Riise. If his goal against Everton had taken centre stage, another thunderous strike in the third minute at St James's threatened to take the roof off the towering new stand housing Liverpool's large and vocal contingent. Newcastle huffed and puffed and created the odd half chance but the Reds looked far more dangerous when they had the ball. The recalled Robbie Fowler looked particularly sharp and would have made it two were it not for the sharp reflexes of Shay Given. An offside flag then cancelled out an exquisite piece of Fowler finishing on 47 minutes but the Toxteth terror was not to be denied a piece of the action. In the 86th minute, Murphy broke out of defence and played a wonderful one-two with Fowler sprinting on and planting a deft shot past Given. Game, set and match.

Vital stats

Danny Murphy 14/1 to score the last goal | Newcastle enjoyed 58% possession | Liverpool scored 2 goals from 3 shots on target

Quote unquote

"It was a terrific result for us off the back of the Champions League win. This is not an easy place to come and we knew Newcastle would be tough. But we controlled the game." **Gérard Houllier**

"Danny Murphy's goal was top drawer and he has to be my star man. He teamed up well with Jamie Carragher to take care of Laurent Robert. He was very creative and his crossing was excellent. It was a good day for Danny all round as he was later named in the England squad." **Phil Thompson**

"Liverpool's defence is so mean, like four bloody oak trees. They have played and won on a very difficult stage without Owen, Gerrard and Hamann. They've got such good discipline, they just didn't give us a sniff." **Bobby Robson** Newcastle United manager

Man of the match Danny Murphy **Atmosphere** John Arne Riise song was aired all afternoon and pretty good it sounded too. The fledgling Hey Dude was drowned out by We've Got A Big Pole In Our Goal **League position** 6th

OCTOBER 2001

Liverpool 1   Grimsby Town 2
McAllister 101 pen   Broomes 113, Jevons 120

Kick-off 8pm Anfield **Att** 32,672 **Referee** E Wolstenhome
LIVERPOOL Kirkland, Vignal (Kippe 21), Carragher, Hyypia, Wright, Murphy, Hamann (Heskey
62) McAllister, Barmby, Smicer, Litmanen (Redknapp 76) SUBS Dudek, Berger BOOKED Hyypia
GRIMSBY TOWN Coyne, Gallimore, Broomes, Pouton, Campbell, Groves, Butterfield,
Chapman (Allen 104), Beharall Rowan (Boulding 81), Jevons SUBS Coldicott, Ford, Ermes

The Mariners found their sea legs to withstand wave upon wave of
Liverpool pressure in the most one-sided game seen at Anfield in years.
But fortune obviously favoured the brave because try as it might, a
Liverpool line-up packed with internationals could not break down
Lennie Lawrence's courageous battlers. Danny Coyne was a colossus
between the sticks and urged on by a vociferous following of 5,000
Grimsby drew strength from their tireless resistance. Barmby, Litmanen,

31

Gary Mac strokes home an extra-time penalty against Grimsby but it's just not enough

Smicer and Frode Kippe all saw decent chances squandered before the game moved into extra time. When Beharall handled inside the area allowing McAllister to stroke home the spot-kick it looked like a formality but Grimsby didn't buckle and Broomes hammered past debutant Kirkland for the equaliser before former Everton player and Liverpool fan Phil Jevons scored the goal of a lifetime with just seconds remaining on

Nick Barmby threatens the Mariners defence on a night to forget for the cup holders

the clock. His 30-yard volley, reminiscent of the Graeme Sharp effort that infamously dipped over Bruce Grobbelaar at the Anfield Road end, was a goal fit to win any game. The visitors deserved their standing ovation.

Vital stats

This was the first time Grimsby had beaten the Reds in 6 cup matches | Michael Owen scored a hat-trick against the Mariners in the 1997 League Cup | It was the 1st time Liverpool had lost at home to a team from a lower division in League Cup competition

Quote unquote

"My family have been kissing me all over." **Phil Jevons** Grimsby Town

"Despite the intense disappointment, I had no need to reproach the players for their performance, because in spite of injuries and maybe some tiredness their workrate was tremendous and they gave their all to try to get through to the next round." **Gérard Houllier**

"The shock on a grim night at Anfield wasn't just that Liverpool lost but they didn't win 10-2. Houllier's team will never dominate so much again and lose." **Chris Bascombe** Liverpool Echo

Man of the match Vladimir Smicer **Atmosphere** Pretty good with a large and impressively loud following from Grimsby. Reduced ticket prices on the night make for a jovial atmosphere and, at the end, a sporting round of applause for the victors.

Saturday 13 October 2001	Premiership

Liverpool 1   Leeds United 1
Murphy 69   Kewell 27

Kick-off 12 noon, Anfield **Att** 44,352. **Referee** A Wiley

LIVERPOOL Dudek, Carragher, Henchoz, Hyypia, Riise, Murphy (Barmby 90), McAllister (Redknapp 75), Gerrard, Smicer, Fowler, Heskey (Litmanen 45) SUBS Kirkland, Wright BOOKED Hyypia, Murphy, Gerrard

LEEDS UNITED Martyn, Mills, Matteo, Ferdinand, Harte, Bakke, Dacourt, Bowyer, Kewell, Keane (Batty 88), Viduka SUBS Kelly, Woodgate, Robinson, Smith BOOKED Mills, Bakke

Liverpool came close to becoming the first team to beat Leeds in the Premiership but the match was overshadowed by the news that Gérard Houllier had been rushed to hospital after complaining of chest pains at half time. Top of the table Leeds bossed the first half as a disappointing Liverpool struggled to find their rhythm, but changes after the break saw the tide turn and Liverpool cancelled out Harry Kewell's deflected opener. A Riise piledriver flashed by a minute after the restart, Martyn saved well from Litmanen five minutes later and it looked like only a matter of time before the Reds were level. Hyypia fed Gerrard who found Fowler on the edge of the box. His turn and deft chip left Martyn stranded and when the ball rebounded back off the bar Danny Murphy was the first to react. Hyypia then forced a great save from the Leeds keeper before late on, Bowyer was left to rue a chance to take all three points after a rare second-half Leeds attack.

Vital stats
53% possession | 2/1 on the match to finish 1-1 | 2nd goal of season for Danny Murphy

Quote unquote
"The game means nothing. Everything else pales into insignificance." **Gary McAllister**

"I didn't tell the players about his condition, but it was playing on my mind throughout the second half." **Phil Thompson**

"When I had the England job the other managers were great, but Gérard was one above the rest in co-operating. I've tried to leave a message on his answerphone, but it's full. That isn't surprising." **Kevin Keegan**

Man of the match Danny Murphy **Atmosphere** The visitors made themselves heard pretty much from the off but once the Reds went 1-0 down the crowd rallied to get behind them. Tense near the end as news of Houllier's illness filtered through **League position** 7th

Tuesday 16 October 2001	Champions League

Dynamo Kiev 1   Liverpool 2
Ghioane 59   Murphy 43, Gerrard 67

Kick-off 7.45pm Olympic Stadium **Att** 55,000 **Referee** C Colombo (france)
DYNAMO KIEV Reva, Bodnar (Husin 56), Holovko, Vaschuk, Nesmachnyi, Cernat, Ghioane, Gavrancic, Melashchenko (Idahor 80), Belkevich, Khatskevich SUBS Filimonov, Peev, Fedorov, Venhlinskyy, Serebrennikov
LIVERPOOL Dudek, Carragher, Henchoz, Hyypia, Riise, Barmby (Berger 62), Gerrard, McAllister, Murphy, Smicer (Redknapp 80), Heskey SUBS Kirkland, Fowler, Partridge, Wright, Litmanen BOOKED Heskey

An historic first ever away win by a British team in Kiev had its origins in the pre-heart emergency meeting between Gérard Houllier and his coaching staff. Days before being rushed to hospital, le Boss met with his lieutenants in their Melwood Bunker to reveal the blueprint for a victory that would put Liverpool top of their Champions League group. A five-man midfield, with Smicer playing at the apex of the diamond behind sole strike Heskey, swamped Kiev's efforts to break forward with pace and it was the Reds who went in front on 43 minutes. A wonderful turn and first-time pass from Gerrard picked out Murphy ghosting between two defenders and the finish was all first touch and finesse. The defence, with Dudek outstanding, soaked up the pressure and despite an equaliser on the hour from Ghioane, Liverpool demonstrated their mettle by snatching a winner through Steven Gerrard. 'Back in the USSR' proclaimed the banner heralding Liverpool's homegrown fab four, and back to Merseyside with three invaluable points they went.

Vital stats

54% possession | Liverpool had 11 attempts on goal compared to Kiev's 19 | Jerzy Dudek made 4 superb saves

Quote unquote

"The days leading up to this one were very difficult in light of Gérard's illness, but the players are professionals and they knew the best way to respond to the upset was to play well and give a good performance for the boss. That's exactly what they did." **Phil Thompson**

"We were really solid and Danny Murphy and Steven Gerrard got two brilliant goals. That was a difficult match and the fact we're the first British team to have won over there proves that." **Jamie Carragher**

"Liverpool is one of the top European teams. They had just two half chances and managed to score two goals." **Valeri Lobanovskyi** Dynamo Kiev coach

Man of the match Jerzy Dudek **Atmosphere** Those intrepid enough to have made the journey made themselves heard and our victory silenced the home crowd. A 'Back in the USSR' banner featuring our very own Fab Four (Fowler, Owen, Gerrard and Carragher) took centre stage.

Saturday 20 October 2001	Premiership

Leicester City 1   Liverpool 4

Wise 58   Fowler 5, 43, 90 Hyypia 10

Kick-off 3pm Filbert Street **Att** 21,886 **Referee** M Halsey

LEICESTER CITY Walker, Marshall, Sinclair, Elliott, Davidson, Savage, Wise, Jones (Piper 72), Benjamin, Sturridge (Impey 56), Akinbiyi SUBS Royce, Lewis, Heath BOOKED Sinclair

LIVERPOOL Dudek, Wright, Carragher, Hyypia, Riise, Gerrard (Berger 45), McAllister, Redknapp (Smicer 79), Murphy, Fowler, Heskey (Litmanen 83) SUBS Kirkland, Barmby BOOKED Redknapp, Heskey

Phil Thompson selected his first side as stand-in Liverpool manager and prayed he wouldn't be the victim of one of football's banana-skin fixtures. The Foxes were rock bottom after an appalling start to the season but with new boss Dave Bassett in charge, Thommo's pre-match team talk centred on the need to be professional. A rare injury to Stephane Henchoz and an even rarer start for Jamie Redknapp made for a reshuffled Reds line-up but with Robbie Fowler determined to end a 400-minute goal drought in the Premiership, the result was never in doubt. Liverpool's favourite son opened the scoring on five minutes, Sami Hyypia made it two with a header on 10 minutes and Fowler put the game to bed with a second just before the break. At the other end Ade Akinbiyi looked like a 3.5million man, but only in Turkish lira, as ball after ball sailed over Filbert Street's odd-shaped stands. Dennis Wise pulled one back in the second half before Fowler completed his hat-trick, a 10th for the club, with a sublime right-foot volley from Smicer's cross. Little did we know at the time, it would be the last goal he scored for his beloved Reds.

Vital stats
Leicester had 10 shots off target | 33/1 on the Reds to win 4-1 | Fowler's 3rd goal was his 171st and last for the club

The skipper congratulates Robbie on his treble, but both would soon be leaving Anfield

Quote unquote

"Sometimes when you go three up it can take the edge off and you can get sloppy. That happened slightly in the second half, which was disappointing. But we passed the ball very well at times." **Phil Thompson**

"I think the game was lost in those first 10 minutes. We were nervous and apprehensive and had people who went to sleep. They knew what they were doing. We didn't." **Dave Bassett** Leicester City manager

"It was another great result for Gérard Houllier, who was moved out of intensive care (on Saturday). He might even have permitted himself a wry smile at the news of a hat-trick for Robbie Fowler, the player who most frustrates him." **Ian Ridley** The Observer

Man of the match Robbie Fowler **Atmosphere** Great day out on our last ever trip to Filbert Street though a little tense for a while in the second half **League position** 4th

Wednesday 24 October 2001	Champions League

Boavista 1   Liverpool 1

Silva 60   Murphy 17

Kick-off 7.45pm Estadio Do Bessa **Att** 6,000 **Referee** K Nilsson (Denmark)
BOAVISTA Ricardo, Rui Oscar (Martelinho 26), Turra, Pedro Emanuel, Erivan, Frechaut, Petit, Goulart (Marcio Santos 57), Sanchez, Duda (Bosingwa 57), Silva SUBS William, Pedrosa, Loja, Glauber
LIVERPOOL Dudek, Carragher, Henchoz, Hyypia (Wright 6), Riise, Murphy, McAllister (Berger 76), Hamann, Smicer, Fowler, Heskey SUBS Kirkland, Redknapp, Biscan, Partridge, Litmanen
BOOKED Hamann

The outlook looked bleak when Sami Hyypia limped off with a hamstring injury after only six minutes but Danny Murphy's fourth goal in six games underlined Liverpool's superiority in the opening exchanges. Gary McAllister had already had a goal ruled out for offside when Murphy curled a trademark deadball special around the Boavista wall on 17 minutes. Elpidio Silva rattled Dudek's bar before half time but the Reds thoroughly deserved their interval lead. The Portuguese champions came out strong in the second half but Heskey could have settled the tie when he latched on to Fowler's superb pass only to see his blistering shot beaten out by Ricardo. Silva headed an equaliser after 60 minutes but with Liverpool's defence in typically resolute mood, the home side were restricted to a Marcio Santos shot that flashed inches wide with the last kick of the game.

Vital stats

Boavista had 20 attempts on goal compared to Liverpool's 7 | Jamie Carragher made 18 blocks and clearances | Liverpool were caught offside 9 times

Quote unquote

"We controlled the first half and even though they came at us in the second, we didn't feel too threatened as we were creating all the best chances." **Phil Thompson**

"This performance, which embodied the spirit Houllier has done so much to instill, will have done much to cheer him." **Oliver Kay** The Times

"No one did more to offset the absence of the injured Steven Gerrard than Murphy, who is blossoming with every game and fast developing into the sort of player Sven Goran Eriksson could do worse than place his faith in." **Paul Joyce** Daily Express

Man of the match Jamie Carragher **Atmosphere** Allez Allez, Allez Allez, Gérard Houllier… the night the new chant for the boss took off and never stopped for the whole of the second half. A few home fans waited outside to applaud Liverpool's vocal support.

Saturday 27 October 2001	Premiership

Charlton Athletic 0   Liverpool 2

Redknapp 12, Owen 42

Kick-off 3pm The Valley **Att** 22,887 **Referee** P Jones
CHARLTON ATHLETIC Kiely, Young, Fish, Brown, Powell, Robinson, Jensen (Parker 86), Kinsella, Konchesky (Bartlett 60), Johansson, Euell SUBS Roberts, Peacock, Fortune.
LIVERPOOL Dudek, Wright, Henchoz, Carragher, Riise, Gerrard, Redknapp (Berger 71), Hamann, Murphy, Owen (Fowler 62), Litmanen (Heskey 82) SUBS Kirkland, Smicer BOOKED Wright SENT OFF Wright

Gérard Houllier had Phil Thompson's mobile number on constant redial before Liverpool's trip to The Valley but three more points will have had the gaffer plumping up his pillows in delight. In front of the biggest crowd at The Valley for 25 years, Carragher filled in for the injured Hyypia and Jamie Redknapp started his second consecutive Premiership match and looked extremely sharp. Indeed, it was the skipper who opened the scoring after latching on to Steve Gerrard's flick. Jensen and Johansson then threatened for the home team before Michael Owen celebrated his return after seven games out through injury with a sublime goal in the 42nd minute. A Hamann through ball split the defence and Owen ran through before chipping expertly over Kiely for his 14th goal in 14 games for club and country. The second half was a big disappoint-

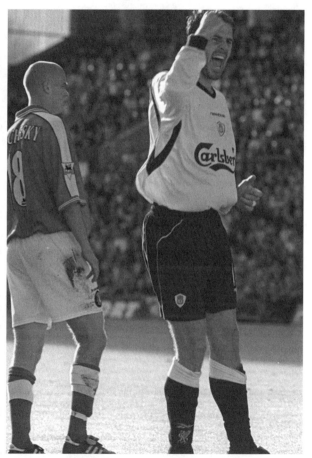

I'm back roars Jamie Redknapp after getting on the Liverpool scoresheet at The Valley

ment as Liverpool failed to muster a shot and Charlton came back into the game. Young Stephen Wright was also sent off four minutes from time after picking up a second booking. Still, victory made it four games unbeaten for the new man at the helm.

Vital stats

Charlton had 13 attempts off target compared to Liverpool's 2 | 7/1 on Liverpool to win 2-0 | 54% possession

Quote unquote

"Hopefully I'll stay fit for a long time to come. It was a big result for us because some teams would suffer after a tough trip to Portugal but we showed a lot of character." **Jamie Redknapp**

"It was caviar and cabbage stuff but the defenders did the job in the second half." **Phil Thompson**

"Liverpool allowed us to come back into the match but when we had the chance to play, we gave the ball away." **Alan Curbishley** Charlton Athletic manager

Man of the match Jamie Carragher **Atmosphere** Big cheers for Jamie Redknapp when he scored. A few old classics were aired but it all got a bit tense in the second half as the south Londoners made themselves heard **League position** 4th

| Tuesday 30 October 2001 | Champions League |

Liverpool 2   Borussia Dortmund 0

Smicer 15, Wright 81

Kick-off 7.45pm Anfield **Att** 41,507 **Referee** K Milton Nielsen (Denmark)

LIVERPOOL Dudek, Wright, Henchoz, Carragher, Riise, Murphy, Hamann, Gerrard (Redknapp 84), Smicer (Berger 64), Owen (Fowler 75), Heskey SUBS Kirkland, Litmanen, Biscan, McAllister BOOKED Hamann

BORUSSIA DORTMUND Lehmann, Wörns, Evanilson, Reuter, Koller, Rosicky, Oliseh (Bobic 67), Dede, Ricken, Metzelder, Sorensen SUBS Laux, Stevic, Demel, Madouini, Bugri, Thorwart BOOKED Metzelder, Dede

At stake was a place in the next phase of the Champions League and in the first match at Anfield since Gérard Houllier was taken ill, a packed crowd attempted to lift the roof off the stadium. After both sets of fans joined together for an impeccable version of You'll Never Walk Alone (also a Borussia anthem), the name of the manager rang round the ground. And how his players responded to the clarion call. Captained by Jamie Carragher, Liverpool tore into Dortmund with both Hamann and

Murphy going close before Smicer settled the nerves with a finely executed volley from the edge of the box. Dortmund commanded the lion's share of possession but Carragher and Henchoz stood firm in the face of a physical battering from 6ft 8in Jan Koller. A sloppy period before the break was followed by Liverpool stepping up the pace. And when substitute Berger's swerving cross was met by Stephen Wright's flying header in the 81st minute, we knew we were through. It was the local lad's first goal for the club and ensured Liverpool topped the group.

Vital stats

100% success rate in tackling for Didi Hamann | Liverpool had 6 shots on target compared to Dortmund's 2 | The visitors are the best-supported side in Germany

Quote unquote

"Playing with Europe's elite means more than anything to Gérard, so the players were really psyched up for it." **Phil Thompson**

"This was a victory rooted in collective endeavour, in the leadership of Jamie Carragher, the good preparation of Phil Thompson and the foundations laid by Gérard Houllier, whose name was chanted constantly." **Henry Winter** The Daily Telegraph

"Liverpool on their present form will be hard to beat because as Dortmund and others have already found out, they are hard to break down." **David Lacey** The Guardian

Man of the match Didi Hamann **Atmosphere** Packed house. Pouring rain. Both fans singing YNWA. Songs all night. This was how it should be. This was Anfield in Europe.

Danny, Vlad and John Arne celebrate the Czech's strike as Thommo whistles in delight

NOVEMBER 2001

Liverpool 3   Manchester United 1

Owen 32, 51, Riise 39   Beckham 50

Kick-off 11.30am Anfield **Att** 44,361 **Ref** G Poll
LIVERPOOL Dudek, Carragher, Henchoz, Hyypia, Riise, Murphy, Gerrard, Hamann, Smicer (Berger 68), Heskey, Owen (Fowler 68) SUBS Kirkland, Redknapp, Wright
MANCHESTER UNITED Barthez, G Neville, Brown, Silvestre, Irwin (O'Shea 84), Beckham (Scholes 76), Butt, Veron, Fortune, Van Nistelrooy, Solksjaer (Yorke 51) SUBS P Neville, Carroll

A giant mosaic featuring the initials 'GH' at the centre of a French tricolor provided the backdrop on the Kop as the players ran out for a morning kick-off in the most keenly anticipated game of the season. Liverpool's play matched the passion of the fans and after an early Van Nistelrooy scare, the Reds began to dominate. Owen had a half chance before a fine move involving Hamann, Smicer and Heskey culminated in England's top striker bending a delicious rising drive past the hapless Barthez. Eight minutes later and the Kop's favourite new song was in full voice as John Arne Riise hammered a 65.8mph shot between the angle of crossbar and post to make it two. Beckham hit back just after half time and with United beginning to dominate the ball, nerves began to fray. But Liverpool's gameplan worked a treat and with enormous performances from the likes of Heskey, Hamann and Murphy, a third goal was always on the cards. It came when Heskey flicked on a cross and Owen outjumped Silvestre to score his second of the game. 'One Jaap Stam' roared the Kop before belting out a massive You'll Never Walk Alone. Four wins on the bounce against United and top spot in the viewfinder. Nice.

Vital stats

18/1 on Liverpool winning 3-1 | Emile Heskey made 9 successful tackles, more than any other Red | United enjoyed 58% possession

Quote unquote

"I think you could see how happy I was to score against United. I hit it and it just went bang. It goes down as one of my best goals but also one of the most important. Thinking about it gives me a fantastic feeling and it was great to hear the fans sing my name." **John Arne Riise**
"It's lovely to beat United but to do it in such convincing style is even better. People are talking about us winning the title and it's fair enough." **Danny Murphy**

That masked man John Arne Riise celebrates his spectacular strike against Man United

"Liverpool worked harder than us, showed greater hunger and desire. They are where we were four years ago." **Sir Alex Ferguson** Manchester United manager

Man of the match Emile Heskey **Atmosphere** GH mosaic at the start, followed by YNWA and Gérard Houllier. The Kop was on its best form of the season to date **League position** 2nd

43

Blackburn Rovers 1   Liverpool 1

Jansen 51   Owen 29

Kick-off 12noon Ewood Park **Att** 28,859 **Ref** M Riley.

BLACKBURN ROVERS Friedel, Curtis, Berg, Short, Bjornebye, Gillespie, Flitcroft (Hignett 65), Tugay, Dunn, Duff (Bent 78), Jansen SUBS Hughes, Taylor, Kelly BOOKED Flitcroft, Bent

LIVERPOOL Dudek, Carragher, Hyypia, Henchoz, Riise, McAllister, Gerrard, Hamann, Berger (Murphy 62), Fowler, Owen (Heskey 72) SUBS Smicer, Redknapp, Kirkland.

Before this game, much had been made of the reunion between bitter enemies and former team-mates Phil Thompson and Graeme Souness, the man who crushed Thommo by sacking him when he was Liverpool boss. A brief, frosty handshake before kick-off got the formalities out of the way for two proud servants of the club who agree to disagree on why their relationship turned sour. Thommo looked like having the last laugh when in the 29th minute Michael Owen outjumped Henning Berg to power home Steven Gerrard's diagonal cross. A chance to establish a foothold at the top of the table, however, went begging in the second half as Matt Jansen fired home the equaliser following a period of sustained Rovers pressure. Both teams had good penalty shouts turned down in the latter stages before Danny Murphy squandered a chance to secure all three points by scooping wide of the goal when one on one with Brad Friedel. Top of the League but nothing like top form from the Reds.

Vital stats

Liverpool had just 2 shots on target | 11/2 on the match finishing 1-1 | Michael Owen scored his 4th goal in 4 games

Quote unquote

"It was a difficult game because of the tactics Blackburn employed. They weren't going all out to try to win, and put a lot of men behind the ball, hoping we'd react and pile forward, but we're too experienced to fall for this ploy." **Phil Thompson**

"I back Liverpool to win the League. They're very difficult to play against and they work so hard when they haven't got the ball. Owen is the key, he had no right to win the header for his goal." **Henning Berg** Blackburn Rovers

"I am not going to be critical of Liverpool. How a team plays football is their business. I know they have had their critics but I am not one of them and never would be for obvious reasons." **Graeme Souness** Blackburn manager

Man of the match Jerzy Dudek **Atmosphere** The team's performance on the pitch was echoed in the stands. Bland **League position** 1st

Liverpool 1   Barcelona 3

Owen 26   Kluivert 40, Rochemback 65, Overmars 84

Kick-off 7.45pm Anfield **Att** 41,521 **Ref** H Krug
LIVERPOOL Dudek, Carragher, Henchoz, Hyypia, Riise, Gerrard, Murphy, McAllister (Berger 69), Smicer (Litmanen 80), Owen, Heskey (Fowler 65) SUBS Kirkland, Diomede, Biscan, Wright
BARCELONA Bonano, Christanval, Andersson, de Boer, Coco, Luis Enrique (Overmars 17), Gabri (Rochemback 57), Xavi, Cocu, Rivaldo, Kluivert (Reiziger 89) SUBS Reina, Saviola, Gerard, Geovanni BOOKED Luis Enrique, Gabri, de Boer

After being dumped out of the previous season's Uefa Cup at the semi-final stage, Barcelona's squad of underachieving superstars certainly cranked up the war of words in the build-up to this first match in the second phase of the Champions League. Kitted out in unfamiliar gold shirts, the Catalan giants must have got an awful sense of déjà-vu when Liverpool, minus the suspended Hamann, tore out of the blocks and could have already been two to the good when Michael Owen broke free from the cover of the defence and chipped Bonano on 26 minutes. It was his 18th goal in as many games. Heskey squandered a good chance to double the advantage and instantly rued his miss when Kluivert latched on to Rivaldo's flick to volley the equaliser five minutes before half time. The game hung in the balance as both sides probed for the second and when Owen miskicked in front of an open goal on 62 minutes, Barça perhaps sensed the pendulum had swung. Rochemback exchanged a one-two with Kluivert and smashed a 20-yarder past Dudek before Carles Rexach's team turned on the style in the final 10 minutes. Nearly three minutes of constant possession, embroidered by some 60 unanswered passes, culminated in Overmars scoring a decisive and deserved third. At the final whistle, the stylish victors were applauded off the pitch from all sides of the ground.

Vital stats
Barcelona commanded 60% possession | Michael Owen was on target with 94% of his passes | The home defeat was Liverpool's heaviest in European competition

Quote unquote
"I feel the result fully vindicated our approach to the game compared to Liverpool's negative approach. We tried to play football and got our reward for trying to be constructive while Liverpool continued to be preoccupied with keeping men behind the ball and paid the price."
Frank De Boer Barcelona

"What the younger players, especially, will have realised is possession of the ball is king. What matters now is to take on board the lesson from that defeat and not panic." **Gary McAllister**

"They are very astute at keeping the ball and in the second half outclassed us because we simply couldn't get a grip of it. But they are one of the best teams in Europe, and proved it." **Phil Thompson**

Man of the match Michael Owen **Atmosphere** Started out loud and raucous, silenced by the skill, passing and goals of the visitors who were applauded off the pitch at the end.

46

Barcelona's Gabri tracks Vladimir Smicer during the Champions League encounter at Anfield

Sunday 25 November 2001 Premiership

Liverpool 1 Sunderland 0

Heskey 22

Kick-off 2pm Anfield **Att** 43,537 **Ref** S Bennett

LIVERPOOL Dudek, Carragher, Henchoz, Hyypia, Riise, Murphy (Berger 68), Hamann, Gerrard, Smicer (Wright 76), Heskey, Fowler (McAllister 45) SUBS Kirkland, Litmanen BOOKED Gerrard SENT OFF Hamann

SUNDERLAND Sorensen, Haas, Williams (McCartney 72), Thome, Gray, McAteer, McCann, Thirlwell (Laslandes 76), Arca (Butler 58), Quinn, Phillips SUBS Schwarz, Macho BOOKED Haas, Thome, McAteer

Fresh from being named manager of the month, super stand-in Phil Thompson asked for a response from the players after the midweek defeat to Barcelona and got it. Top of the League, and with the Premiership's player of the month Danny Murphy partnering Didi Hamann in the centre, Liverpool gave Robbie Fowler what turned out to be his last start for the club. The frustrated striker saw two chances go close in the first 16 minutes before Murphy curled over a free-kick that Heskey powered into Sorensen's net. It was his first goal in 20 games for club and country. In the minutes before half time Jerzy Dudek saved brilliantly from Kevin Phillips and Hamann was sent off for a two-footed challenge on Bernt Haas. Fowler was sacrificed as the Reds were down to 10 men and replaced by McAllister for the second half. The veteran Scot should have doubled the advantage on 66 minutes when Vladimir Smicer cut the ball back from the byline. Unfortunately, his shot from 10 yards flew high over the bar into the Kop. Liverpool survived a hairy final 10 minutes thanks to some typically strong defending from Hyypia and Henchoz before a dose of argy-bargy in the tunnel saw two Scousers, Thompson and Sunderland boss Peter Reid, trading insults. Two points clear at the top with a game in hand.

Vital stats

William Hill made Liverpool 7/4 favourites to win the title after this victory | It was Liverpool's 6th win in 9 games under Thompson | Sunderland had 18 shots on goal compared to Liverpool's 11

Quote unquote

"I was delighted for Emile today. I thought he was fantastic. When he came into the dressing room at the end the players all stood to applaud him. That's the type of unity Gérard has built here." **Phil Thompson**

"If this was Fowler's last appearance for Liverpool – Leeds United, Blackburn Rovers and Lazio

lead the £15million chase for his signature – it was no way for his time here to end."
Matt Lawton The Daily Telegraph

"Liverpool maintained themselves at the top of the Premiership in largely the way they got there. They had resilience, blanket defence and a midfield-stifling operation that reduced Sunderland to the most optimistic of long-range sniper fire." **James Lawton** The Independent

Man of the match Emile Heskey **Atmosphere** A quiet Kop after the previous two games, though there was a good rendition of YNWA before kick-off. After Didi Hamann is sent off, the Kop rallied round to become 11th man **League position** 1st

DECEMBER 2001

Derby County 0   · Liverpool 1

Owen 6

Kick-off 3pm Pride Park **Att** 33,289 **Ref** G Barber
DERBY COUNTY Poom, Grenet, Mawene, Riggott, Higginbotham, Zavagno, Ducrocq,
Carbone, Powell, Christie, Ravanelli SUBS Oakes, Burton, Kinkladze, Murray, Boertien BOOKED
Higginbotham
LIVERPOOL Dudek, Carragher, Henchoz, Hyypia, Riise, Murphy, Hamann, Gerrard, Berger
(McAllister 75), Owen (Litmanen 82), Heskey SUBS Kirkland, Smicer, Wright BOOKED Owen,
Heskey

A sad week for the city of Liverpool – the death of George Harrison and
the sale of Robbie Fowler to Leeds – ended on a high note as a 10th consecutive unbeaten game extended the Reds' lead at the top of the
Premiership. Michael Owen returned from his latest hamstring scare to
continue his rich vein of scoring form: a Patrik Berger special proved too
hot for Poom to handle and Owen was on hand to bury the rebound after
six minutes. Two minutes later Poom denied Berger with his feet before
an unmarked Riise headed straight at the busier of the two keepers from
the resulting corner. But rather than fold, as their lowly league position
suggested might happen, Derby hit back through an inspired Fabrizio
Ravanelli. Powell volleyed over and Dudek foiled Christie before half
time. Liverpool continued to invite Derby forward in the second half and
Carbone, Christie and Powell all wasted good opportunities as Dudek
excelled between the sticks. There were four minutes left on the clock
when referee Barber penalised Heskey for handball. Ravanelli stepped up,
Dudek plunged to his left and for the second week in a row the Italian had
missed a spot-kick and Liverpool had ground out a useful 1-0 victory.

Vital stats
7/2 on Michael Owen to score the first goal | 5 shots on target for both sides | 6/1 on the
Reds winning 1-0

Quote unquote
"People may say we were lucky because they missed a penalty but I don't go along with that.

Jerzy is the goalkeeper and is there to make the saves. He did it really well and has been an outstanding, calming influence on the club." **Phil Thompson**

"It's the first time in my career I've missed successive penalties. I missed last week, I missed this, my

head is very confused. It hurts me very much, I'm very upset." **Fabrizio Ravanelli** Derby County

"Derby deserved to get something out of the game. They had us on the back foot for a long time. Jerzy's save earned us two points but we are getting used to that now because he has been brilliant for us all season. We know we can't dominate teams for 90 minutes every week, but these are the three points that win you titles." **Steven Gerrard**

Man of the match Jerzy Dudek **Atmosphere** First post-Fowler game, the travelling Reds were pretty loud throughout, clapping Derby's efforts at goading us about Robbie's departure. Filed out to the strains of 'Big Pole In Our Goal' thanks to Jerzy's penalty save **League position** 1st

Wednesday 6 December 2001	Champions League

Roma 0   Liverpool 0

Kick-off 7.45pm Olympic Stadium **Att** 57,819 **Ref** D Jol (Holland)
LIVERPOOL Dudek, Carragher, Henchoz, Hyypia, Riise, Murphy (Berger 61), Gerrard (Biscan 84), Hamann, Smicer (McAllister 63), Heskey, Owen SUBS Kirkland, Diomede, Wright, Litmanen
ROMA Antonioli, Zebina, Aldair, Samuel, Guigou (Assuncao 45), Candela, Emerson, Lima, Tommasi (Fuser 79), Batistuta, Totti SUBS Cejas, Zago, Cufre, Cassano, Delvecchio BOOKED Tommasi

A match that had been billed as a duel between two of the world's great strikers, Michael Owen and Gabriel Batistuta, developed into a tactical stalemate as Liverpool ground out a satisfying draw at a ground that has become something of a lucky charm over the years. The result left the Reds at the bottom of the group but meant that when the campaign resumed in the new year, hopes would be alive of progressing to the quarter-finals. Liverpool were clearly the better side in the first half and could have been 2-0 up had Vladimir Smicer's volley not been directed straight at the keeper after 14 minutes and Emile Heskey not shot wide from 12 yards on 31 minutes. As Roma became more frustrated, their players hit the deck with theatrical predictability but Thompson's charges were in the professional frame of mind that had made for a long unbeaten run away from home. The hosts came out stronger in the second half but a combination of excellent goalkeeping, solid defending and no-frills efficiency from Didi

Danny Murphy gets a timely foot in to deny Francesco Totti during the goalless draw in Rome

Hamann meant Liverpool never looked in danger of coming away empty-handed. At the end, We Never Lose In Rome rang out from the 2,000 Liverpool fans in one corner of their home from home.

Vital stats
Liverpool had 1 shot on target in the 90 minutes | Roma enjoyed 60% of the possession | Barcelona drew 2-2 with Galatasary to stay top on 4 points

Quote unquote
"A lot of nonsense has been said about negative, boring Liverpool recently. Even though this game ended in a draw, I think we dispelled that myth with our first-half performance."
Phil Thompson

"I think we've seen how hard this side is to overcome. At home we just can't manage to beat them. It was so hard to break through their defence." **Francesco Totti** Roma

"Liverpool are one of the best teams in Europe right now. They are one of the teams who can win the Champions League. They kept us to long shots because they are so strong defensively." **Fabio Capello** Roma coach

Man of the match Didi Hamann **Atmosphere** On a cold night, all the flags were in evidence and the travelling Reds did their best to be heard, including the 90 minutes we're kept in after the whistle. The home fans started loud with cheers, but ended in jeers as Roma failed to score.

Saturday 8 December 2001   Premiership

Liverpool 2   Middlesbrough 0
Owen 25, Berger 45

Kick-off 3pm Anfield **Att** 43,674 **Ref** D Gallacher
LIVERPOOL Dudek, Henchoz, Hyypia, Carragher, Riise, Murphy, Berger, Hamann, McAllister, Owen (Heskey 77), Litmanen SUBS Gerrard, Kirkland, Biscan, Wright
MIDDLESBROUGH Crossley (Beresford 18), Southgate, Ehiogu, Cooper, Queudrue, Mustoe, Greening, Ince, Johnston (Wilson 45), Boksic, Nemeth (Ricard 45) SUBS Okon, Gavin BOOKED Queudrue, Cooper

Liverpool's best performance of the season to date was embroidered by two goals from the very top drawer. The Reds started very brightly with Murphy forcing a good save before Mark Crossley in the Boro goal was stretchered off following an accidental collision with Gary McAllister. Patrik Berger, playing his first game since his comeback from serious injury, looked outstanding on the left flank and it was his pass that set up Michael Owen's opening goal, a wicked curler from 25 yards. It was Owen's 99th goal for Liverpool. The Czech international then got the reward his work deserved when he made space on the edge of the box and rifled in a trademark thunderbolt on the stroke of half time. Alen Boksic forced a good save out of Jerzy Dudek just after the break but the Reds were always in control, with Berger again going close on 59 minutes. Boro did enjoy a period of sustained pressure near the end but with the rocks at the heart of Liverpool's defence standing firm, five successive corners were repelled without incident. Top of the League by six points and positive signs of the form we had come to expect.

Vital stats
Liverpool had 18 attempts on goal to Boro's 5 | 3/1 on Michael Owen opening the scoring | 55% of possession for the home side

Quote unquote
"We played some brilliant football and Patrik's goal was no less than our dominance deserved. It was a classic Berger strike, he made himself space before driving it home, and it's good to see him on form." **Phil Thompson**

"When those thousands of misty eyes on Merseyside lamenting the loss of Robbie Fowler finally clear, the pleasing vision that awaits is of a Liverpool side six points clear at the top of the Premiership. And who more fitting to wipe away the tears than the remarkable Michael Owen?" **Joe Melling** The Mail On Sunday

"Nothing Michael Owen does surprises me. He can score goals out of nothing. He scores goals with his head, with his right foot, with his left foot and today he showed he can score goals from 30 yards out too." **Steve McClaren** Middlesbrough manager

Man of the match Didi Hamann **Atmosphere** A fairly quiet crowd throughout although there were audible strains of the Dalglish and Fowler chants for Owen just after he scored. Will it take off? **League position** 1st

---

Wednesday 12 December 2001 — Premiership

Liverpool 0 — Fulham 0

Kick-off 8pm Anfield **Att** 37,153 **Ref** J Winter
LIVERPOOL Dudek, Carragher, Henchoz, Hyypia, Riise, Murphy (Biscan 81), Gerrard, McAllister, Berger (Litmanen 66), Heskey, Owen SUBS Kirkland, Diomede, Wright
FULHAM Van der Sar, Finnan, Melville, Goma, Brevett, Boa Morte, Davis (Legwinski 59), Malbranque, Collins, Saha, Hayles SUBS Clark, Taylor, Knight, Stolcers

Liverpool set out to extend their lead at the top of the Premiership to six points but with Edwin van der Sar in inspired form for Fulham and the ball not bouncing kindly for the home team, this goalless draw was ultimately viewed as an opportunity missed. Tigana's boys had established a reputation for neat, attractive football and from the outset they frustrated Liverpool and restricted the number of attempts on goal. Gerrard's header clipped a post on 41 minutes, the keeper denied Owen on 43 and then Gerrard's deft chip narrowly failed to clear the stretch of the giant Dutchman. The pattern was similar in the second half but as the breakthrough goal continued to elude Liverpool, the quality of final ball began to deteriorate. Danny Murphy's 16-yarder, tipped over by Van der Sar just past the hour, represented the best of the Reds' second-half endeavours. The only consolation was that if Boa Morte had made better contact on Brevett's 86th minute cross, things could have been much worse.

Vital stats

Liverpool had 17 shots on goal compared to Fulham's 11 | 52% possession | Steven Gerrard made more passes and tackles than any other player

Quote unquote

"We started out being aware of their counter attacks, but we got more confident as the game went on. We are happy with the point." **Jean Tigana** Fulham manager

"The most pleasing aspect for the management was that once again the players worked very, very hard. I felt they got a little bit anxious at times, trying to get forward, but it was a good performance." **Phil Thompson**

"Owen saw enough chances come his way to reach the milestone of 100 goals for Liverpool, but neither he nor his team-mates had reckoned with the heroics of Edwin van der Sar."
Paul Joyce Daily Express

Man of the match Steven Gerrard **Atmosphere** Didn't really happen as Anfield had all the atmosphere of a library **League position** 1st

---

Sunday 16 December 2001	Premiership

Chelsea 4   Liverpool 0

Le Saux 3, Hasselbaink 28, Dalla Bona 71, Gudjohnsen 90

Kick-off 4pm Stamford Bridge **Att** 41,174 **Ref** M Halsey

CHELSEA Cudicini, Melchiot, Terry, Gallas, Babayaro, Le Saux (Zenden 90), Dalla Bona, Stanic (Jokanovic 67), Lampard, Hasselbaink (Zola 88), Gudjohnsen SUBS de Goey, Forssell BOOKED Stanic, Gudjohnsen

LIVERPOOL Dudek, Riise, Hyypia, Henchoz, Carragher, McAllister, Gerrard, Murphy, Biscan (Wright 46), Heskey, Litmanen SUBS Kirkland, Heggem Diomede, Partridge BOOKED Heskey, Wright, Murphy

Liverpool's dismal run of results at Stamford Bridge continued in cataclysmic fashion as the Londoners ran out four-goal winners in a game that in no way reflected the landslide nature of the scoreline. The Reds' customary bad start came earlier than usual when first Owen pulled out with a hamstring injury and then in the third minute Dudek saved well from Hasselbaink only to see the ball rebound conveniently to Graeme Le Saux who scored with ease. Carlo Cudicini made the first in a string of fine saves to deny Gerrard in the 23rd minute and was on hand again to tip Igor Biscan's fierce drive round the post four minutes later. Unfortunately, the Italian's touch was not seen by the referee and from the resulting goalkick Hasselbaink was put through, won a one-on-one with Dudek and made it 2-0. Liverpool's response in the second half was encouraging and when Melchiot brought down the tireless John Arne Riise five minutes after the restart it appeared Liverpool would get back in the game. Sadly for all travelling Reds, Cudicini was again on hand to smother McAllister's weakly struck spot-kick. More Liverpool pressure came to nothing and the result was put beyond doubt when first Dalla Bona fired home from six yards before Gudjohnsen rubbed salt in the wounds in the final minute by pouncing on Dudek's parry to make it four. It was Liverpool's first Premiership defeat since September and their heaviest in nine years.

Vital stats
66/1 on Chelsea winning 4-0 | 28/1 on Graeme Le Saux being 1st scorer | Chelsea only had 46% possession

Quote unquote
"If you lose 4-0 and the opposition keeper wins man of the match above the attacking players, that says a lot. Cudicini was brilliant and when Gary McAllister's penalty was saved, I think our fans realised it was not going to be our day." **Phil Thompson**

"The combination of Hasselbaink's vision and touch and Gudjohnsen's ability to hold the ball under pressure, drawing opponents on to him, frequently disturbed Liverpool's composure, finding space where normally little exists." **David Lacey** The Guardian

"A phenomenal host of curious circumstances combined to inflict this defeat upon the League leaders. But the main reason for the embarrassment was that Owen was missing."
Alyson Rudd The Times

Man of the match John Arne Riise **Atmosphere** Began in good voice, quieter after four minutes and dumbstruck by the end. One day we will win here **League position** 1st

Liverpool 1   Arsenal 2

Litmanen 55   Henry 45pen, Ljungberg 53

Kick-off 4pm Anfield **Att** 44,297 **Ref** P Durkin
LIVERPOOL Dudek, Carragher, Henchoz, Hyypia, Riise, Berger, McAllister (Smicer 45), Gerrard, Murphy, Heskey (Litmanen 45), Owen SUBS Kirkland, Wright, Heggem BOOKED Henchoz
ARSENAL Taylor, Lauren, Keown, Campbell, Cole, Ljungberg, Parlour, Van Bronckhorst, Pires (Upson 84), Kanu (Luzhny 88), Henry (Wiltord 90) SUBS Wright, Edu BOOKED Lauren, Van Bronckhorst, Ljungberg SENT OFF Van Bronckhorst

A first home defeat to a London side in eight years, and a first reversal at Anfield against Arsenal in nine, turned the tide in the title race in Highbury's favour. Arsène Wenger pinpointed this victory, achieved with 10 men once Van Bronckhorst had been dismissed for a second bookable offence, as the one that infused his players with the belief they could go all the way. It could have been so different had Michael Owen, recently crowned European footballer of the year and in search of his 100th goal for the club, seen his 24th-minute effort evade Ashley Cole's outstretched leg and cross the line. Liverpool needed to match Arsenal's spirit, but with loan signing Nicolas Anelka watching from the stands, they found the

Patrik Berger duels with Arsenal's Ray Parlour on a successful afternoon for the Gooners

Frenchman's former team-mates in determined, resolute and resourceful mood. Henry put the visitors in front from the spot on the stroke of half time after Dudek felled Ljungberg in the box. A switch in personnel at half time couldn't prevent Pires crossing for Ljungberg to make it 2-0 on 53 minutes. Litmanen pulled one back, heading home after Owen had miscued his shot, but with Kanu and Parlour having inspirational games in midfield, and Berger leaving his shooting boots at home, the Reds could ultimately have little complaint with the result.

Vital stats

Liverpool's goal was only their 7th in 9 games | Liverpool enjoyed a massive 63% possession | The home side had 20 attempts on goal to Arsenal's 14

Quote unquote

"There was a lack of quality in our passing at vital times. We showed our immaturity. Steven Gerrard's passes from deep were occasionally too wayward and were picked off by alert Arsenal counter attackers." **Phil Thompson**

"It was one of those matches that turned into a mighty drama. The injustice of the sending-off was followed by a double injustice in which the referee failed to send off a Liverpool player for a sending-off offence and yet Arsenal contrived to take the lead, go 2-0 up, suffer a frightful onslaught, concede a goal and still hang on for the victory." **Simon Barnes** The Times

"I know Nicolas (Anelka). And I know he wants to play in the World Cup. I examined his desire and his motivation and I don't think I've deceived myself. He knows he's been given a good card to play." **Gérard Houllier**

Man of the match John Arne Riise **Atmosphere** Encouraging and supportive for most of the match, trying to lift players who weren't on their game. Got louder after Jari's goal but there was a fair bit of moaning too **League position** 3rd

---

Wednesday 26 December 2001   Premiership

Aston Villa 1   Liverpool 2

Hendrie 18   Litmanen 8, Smicer 72

Kick-off 3pm Villa Park **Att** 42,602 **Ref** A D'Urso

ASTON VILLA Schmeichel, Samuel (Stone 81), Staunton, Mellberg, Wright, Boateng, Merson, Hendrie (Taylor 47), Kachloul, Vassell, Angel SUBS Enckleman, Dublin, Barry BOOKED Boateng.

LIVERPOOL Dudek, Carragher, Hyypia, Henchoz, Riise, Hamann, Gerrard (Murphy 77), Smicer (McAllister 85), Berger, Litmanen (Anelka 68), Owen SUBS Kirkland, Wright

Liverpool began the game with an attacking attitude that was anathema to those who insisted on labelling the Reds as 'boring'. Litmanen headed wide in the third minute before capitalising on Schemichel's poor throw out, which hit the ref on the back, to pass the ball into an empty net from 35 yards for the opener. Villa equalised 10 minutes later when Hendrie lashed home following Angel's blocked shot, but constant pressure brought its rewards when Gerrard was fouled in the box by Boateng for a penalty. Unfortunately, Jari's spot-kick hit the foot of the post – a let-off that did not stop John Gregory from blowing his top and being dismissed from the dugout. Villa bit back in the second half and Kachloul, Taylor and Merson all missed good chances before Berger fed Smicer who chested down and beat Schmeichel to put Liverpool in front. Czech mate indeed. Anelka came on for his debut with 22 minutes remaining and was within a whisker of setting up Owen's long-awaited 100th Liverpool goal. Sadly, on this occasion Schmeichel was equal to the task.

Vital stats

Smicer's goal was his 1st Premiership strike of the season | Both teams committed 11 fouls | Liverpool enjoyed 53% possession

Quote unquote

"This was a demonstration of the talent and commitment of our players. It was an important week after those setbacks but we came to a difficult place like Villa Park and dominated the game in a manner that did my players credit." **Phil Thompson**

"I thought the referee showed a bit of flair and even shouted to Jari 'stick that one in'. But I think it was a bit strong when he ran to the Kop to celebrate." **John Gregory** Aston Villa manager

"There are a number of teams around the country who will fancy their chances of the title and we're just one of those. We have to set out sights high – whether we get there or not remains to be seen, but we'll give it our best shot." **Sami Hyypia**

Man of the match Dietmar Hamann **Atmosphere** A traditionally loud post-Christmas game was a bit on the quiet side, until a superb rendition of YNWA near the end saved the day. **League position** 3rd

Saturday 29 December 2001	Premiership

West Ham United 1   Liverpool 1

Sinclair 38   Owen 88

Kick-off 3pm Upton Park **Att** 35,103 **Ref** R Styles

WEST HAM UNITED James, Repka, Schemmel, Dailly, Winterburn, Carrick, Cole, Hutchison, Sinclair, Defoe, Kanouté SUBS Courtois, Foxe, Hislop, Moncur, Todorov

LIVERPOOL Dudek, Carragher, Henchoz, Hyypia, Riise, Smicer (Litmanen 74), Murphy (Owen 58), McAllister (Gerrard 46), Berger, Anelka, Heskey SUBS Kirkland, Wright

Michael Owen's annus mirabilis ended in fine style when he jumped from the bench to notch his 100th goal for the club and rescue a valuable point just as it appeared West Ham had driven a dagger into Liverpool's title hopes. In truth, a buoyant West Ham side dominated much of the game

Michael Owen completes his scoring century at Upton Park. Bring on the *next* 100...

and could have been further in front when Owen struck the equaliser in the 88th minute. The Reds had an inspired Jerzy Dudek to thank for still being in the hunt as the Pole made a string of superb first-half stops. Missing Gerrard, who was on the bench, and Hamann, who was taken ill before the game, Smicer and McAllister had their work cut out in containing the youthful exuberance of Joe Cole and Michael Carrick. Defoe should have put the home team ahead in the 18th minute and twice Henchoz blocked Kanouté, but on 39 minutes Sinclair shot through Carragher's legs to give the Hammers the lead. Anelka, starting his first match for Liverpool, had a double chance in the first half but was foiled by James. Liverpool were a different proposition in the second half however, and pinned West Ham back. The goal, when it came, merely emphasised Owen's class – shooting high into the net from Litmanen's left-wing cross.

Vital stats

Michael Owen became the 15th member of Liverpool's 100 club | Owen scored his 1st 100 at an average of 0.54 goals per game | Since the start of 1998/99 Owen scored with 24% of his shots

Quote unquote

"It's been an incredible year for me. It's the stuff dreams are made of. Now I have made my name alongside some of the other Liverpool strikers who have scored 100 goals. It's a great honour and something I'm very proud of." **Michael Owen**

"He's not only a top class player, he's a top-class person." **Glenn Roeder** West Ham United manager on Michael Owen

"The one thing I didn't want to do was let Michael score his 100th goal and the bastard did it!" **David James** West Ham United

Man of the match Jerzy Dudek **Atmosphere** Loud. Very loud when Michael scored although trying to make ourselves heard over the racket in the Bobby Moore Stand was a tall order **League position** 4th

JANUARY 2002

Liverpool 1   Bolton Wanderers 1

Gerrard 50   Nolan 78

Kick-off 3pm Anfield Att 43,710 Ref C Wilkes
LIVERPOOL Dudek, Wright, Henchoz, Hyypia, Riise, Smicer (Anelka 67), Hamann, Gerrard, Berger (Litmanen 85), Owen, Heskey SUBS McAllister, Kirkland, Carragher BOOKED Hyypia
BOLTON WANDERERS Jaaskelainen, Diawara, Hendry (Farrelly 32), N'Gotty, Charlton, Southall, Warhurst, Frandsen, Nolan, Ricketts, Holdsworth (Pedersen 72) SUBS Poole, Barness, Johnson BOOKED Southall, Hendry, Frandsen, Nolan

Kevin Nolan, a 19-year-old who spent six years as a Liverpool schoolboy, was given the captain's armband for the day and returned to Anfield to put another dent in his old club's championship aspirations. Liverpool would have returned to the top of the table had they been able to hold on to the lead supplied by Steven Gerrard's opportunistic opener on 50 minutes. The home side created little in a disappointing first half and Bolton would have gone into the dressing rooms leading at half time were it not for the alert reflexes of the ever-dependable Jerzy Dudek. An off-colour Michael Owen also missed two golden opportunities either side of Gerrard's well-taken goal as Jaaskelainen excelled in the Bolton goal. Liverpool's profligacy was finally punished 14 minutes from time when they failed to clear their lines and an unmarked Nolan was allowed to sweep home Pedersen's low cross. Two points dropped and the collective feeling of disappointment at the final whistle was tangible.

Vital stats
Gerrard's goal was Liverpool's 150th against Bolton | This was Liverpool's 6th point from the last 6 matches | Liverpool conceded 17 fouls to Bolton's 9

Quote unquote
"One was never going to be enough with Bolton's fighting qualities. We seemed to fall under a spell after we'd grabbed the goal we had worked so hard to score. The effort's there but there's a lack of conviction in the final pass." **Phil Thompson**

"It was like a dream come true for me." **Kevin Nolan** Bolton Wanderers

Man of the match Steven Gerrard **Atmosphere** Non-existent. Hungover **League position** 4th

Saturday 5 January 2002	FA Cup 3rd round

Liverpool 3   Birmingham City 0

Owen 17, 25, Anelka 86

Kick-off 3pm Anfield **Att** 40,875 **Ref** M Halsey
LIVERPOOL Dudek, Carragher, Henchoz, Hyypia, Riise, Murphy, Hamann, Gerrard, Smicer
(Berger 82), Owen (Heskey 77), Anelka SUBS Kirkland, Wright, Litmanen
BIRMINGHAM CITY Bennett, Gill, Purse, Vickers, Burrows, Andrew Johnson, O'Connor
(Hughes 80), Woodhouse (Marcelo 66), Bak, Mooney, Horsfield SUBS Eaden, Michael Johnson,
Vaesen BOOKED Woodhouse, Andrew Johnson, Bak

Backed by a massive travelling support, City came to Anfield to avenge
defeat in the previous season's Worthington Cup final. But faced with a
Liverpool side playing the crisp, confident passing game that had taken
them to the top of the League, there was little hope for Steve Bruce's
men. Michael Owen and Nicolas Anelka caused problems all afternoon
and when Murphy fed a 22nd minute pass into the channel, Owen was
on to it in a flash before hammering a rising drive past Bennett into the
top corner. Midway through the second half, Anelka demonstrated his
commitment to the cause by tracking back, winning the ball and playing a slide-rule pass for Owen to beat Bennett again, this time with his
left foot. The Frenchman almost broke his duck for the club on 37 minutes but Bennett saved after two of his defenders had been turned inside
out. Owen saw a hat-trick effort crash back off the bar on 65 minutes
before Anelka got the goal his efforts deserved four minutes from

Celebrating the first of what we hoped would be many from Nico, against Birmingham City

time. A trademark low skimmer from the angle of the box looked so much easier than it was. And Anelka's reward? A visit to Highbury in the next round.

Vital stats

7/1 on the Reds winning 3-0 | Nicolas Anelka's goal was his 1st for the club | Liverpool enjoyed 57% possession

Quote unquote

"It was nice for him (Anelka) that it (his debut goal) was in front of the Kop. They appreciated everything he did today. I thought, you deserve it, son, you deserve that." **Phil Thompson**

"There was an element of fear about us. At times in the first half it was like a testimonial pace for them. That upset me a bit." **Steve Bruce** Birmingham City manager

"The portents for a famous giant-killing act evaporated from the opening minutes once Birmingham had mounted a retreat so deep they might well have finished defending half a mile away at Goodison Park." **Peter Gardner** The Daily Telegraph

Man of the match Michael Owen **Atmosphere** Outsung visitors for most of game, which isn't always the case at cup matches like this, but kept it going to end. Not a great repertoire but better than Birmingham's one-song afternoon.

Wednesday 9 January 2002	Premiership

Southampton 2   Liverpool 0

Beattie 62 pen, Riise o.g 70

Kick-off 7.45pm St Mary's Stadium **Att** 31,527 **Ref** G Poll
SOUTHAMPTON Jones, Dodd, Lundekvam, Williams, Bridge, Telfer, Delap (Oakley 35), Svensson, Marsden, Beattie, Pahars (Ormerod 76) SUBS Moss, Monk, Fernandes
LIVERPOOL Dudek, Wright (Riise 69), Hyypia, Henchoz, Carragher, Murphy (Berger 77), Hamann, Gerrard, Smicer (Heskey 57), Anelka, Litmanen SUBS Kirkland, McAllister BOOKED Carragher

Less said about this one the better, as arguably the worst performance of the season saw Liverpool start poorly and get worse in a dismal second half. Minus an injured Michael Owen, Thommo was determined to halt the run of poor results and get Liverpool's challenge back on track. But after Litmanen had given Anelka a sniff of goal with a wonderful pass and Paul Jones had saved smartly from the French striker's first-half snapshot, Liverpool came apart at the seams in the second period. On 63 minutes an unusually rash challenge from Sami Hyypia led to a penalty that was comfortably dispatched by James Beattie. The in-form Saints then went further ahead through a freak own goal. John Arne Riise had only been on the pitch a matter of seconds when he attempted to deflect Pahars' cross into touch but only succeeded in looping it over Dudek and into the net. Defeat meant Liverpool had collected six points from a possible 21, plunging them to fifth, three points behind leaders Leeds.

Vital stats
Liverpool had 1 shot on target | 16/1 on Southampton winning 2-0 | 50% of possession enjoyed by both teams

Quote unquote
"You look at Manchester United. People were saying disrespectful things about them. We knew they were capable of putting a run together and that's what this team is capable of."
Phil Thompson

"For as long as their French manager remains away from the office, the mediocrity that is threatening to drag Liverpool down the Premiership table appears likely to continue."
Matt Lawton Daily Mail

"Victory would have taken Liverpool level at the top but they were undone by Southampton's rousing second-half display and two self-inflicted wounds." **Jon Brodkin** The Guardian

Man of the match Nicolas Anelka **Atmosphere** It was a long, long way from home but that's no excuse. Perhaps the worst game of the season and no better on the terraces **League position** 5th

---

Sunday 13 January 2002	Premiership

Arsenal 1   Liverpool 1

Ljungberg 62   Riise 68

Kick-off 4pm Highbury **Att** 38,132 **Ref** S Dunn.
ARSENAL Taylor, Luzhny (Dixon 85), Campbell, Keown, Upson, Pires (Wiltord 78), Vieira, Grimandi, Ljungberg, Henry, Kanu (Bergkamp 55) SUBS Edu, Wright BOOKED Vieira
LIVERPOOL Dudek, Murphy (Heskey 66), Hyypia, Henchoz, Riise, Hamann, Gerrard, Berger, Carragher, Anelka (McAllister 85), Owen SUBS Kirkland, Wright, Litmanen BOOKED Hamann

Neither side could afford to lose after seeing Manchester United claim top spot for the first time and it was Arsenal who looked more progressive in the first half. Scourge of Anfield, Freddie Ljungberg, could, and should, have put the Gunners one up in the 21st minute after being put clean through on Dudek from an expertly-weighted Pires pass. The Frenchman was the main threat throughout and he fashioned himself a chance in the 40th minute but volleyed straight at Dudek. In the second half, Murphy headed agonisingly over from a Riise cross two minutes before substitute Dennis Bergkamp unlocked the Liverpool defence for the goal Arsenal had been threatening. The Dutchman's trickery gave Pires space down the flank and his cross was met, predictably, by the in-rushing Ljungberg. Steven Gerrard rediscovered his passing touch six minutes later with an inspired ball bent from the outside of his right foot into the path of a rampaging Riise. The Norwegian, who started the move on the edge of his own box, raced a full 70 yards and finished coolly with a low shot inside Taylor's near post. A late Bergkamp scare aside, Liverpool were in the ascendancy for the remainder of the game and deserved their hard-won point. 'Boring, boring Scousers,' squawked the cockneys, who had given the returning Nic Anelka a predictably sour reception. Whatever.

Vital stats
20/1 on Riise scoring the last goal | Liverpool had 1 shot on target all game | Liverpool had a 49% share of possession

Quote unquote
"It wasn't the greatest game ever but it was extremely important for our confidence to get a point. We had an extremely good spell when we rocketed from fifth to top of the table but we knew it would be difficult to keep that momentum." **Phil Thompson**

"The important thing is we showed character and unity to fight back." **John Arne Riise**

"Liverpool are very good defensively because they fight for each other and make sure there is no space. They frustrated us." **Freddie Ljungberg** Arsenal

Man of the match Steven Gerrard **Atmosphere** Most seem up for it but it was one of those days when a song never gets to the end. New continental Liverpool chant got its first airing **League position** 5th

| Saturday 19 January | Premiership |

Liverpool 1
Owen 8

Southampton 1
Davies 46

Kick-off 3pm Anfield **Att** 43, 710 **Ref** N Barry
LIVERPOOL Dudek, Carragher, Henchoz, Hyypia, Riise, Murphy (McAllister 72), Hamann, Gerrard (Smicer 33), Anelka 59), Berger, Owen, Heskey SUBS Heggem, Arphexad
SOUTHAMPTON Jones, Dodd, Lundekvam, Williams, Bridge, Svensson, Marsden, Telfer, Fernandes (Tessem 75), Davies, Pahars (Le Tissier 90) SUBS Moss, Monk, Delgado
BOOKED Davies

The Reds went into this rematch with Southampton on the back of a run that had seen them grab just one win in eight games but a breathless start promised sweet revenge for the mauling at St Mary's. Paddy Berger launched an exocet free-kick in the second minute that was miraculously saved by Jones and then Sami Hyypia's header from a Danny Murphy free-kick rebounded to safety off the Welshman's legs. Owen finally put Liverpool ahead on eight minutes after Jones failed to hold Hamann's shot. Kevin Davies equalised soon after half time after Chris Marsden was allowed to make 40 yards through Liverpool's midfield, and when Gerrard retired midway through the second half with a tight hamstring, the Reds inexplicably began to sit back, inviting Southampton to build a momentum that was almost rewarded with all three points. In the final 10 minutes Dudek clawed out a Marsden header, Svensson hit the inside of a post and Davies somehow put the rebound wide. All Liverpool had to show was an Owen shot that flew wide and a McAllister volley. Seven weeks after missing an opportunity to move 14 points clear of United, the Reds trailed the champions by five. Boos rang round Anfield at the end, though those who barracked the departing Murphy would be left red-faced a few days later.

Vital stats
Liverpool 16 attempts on goal | The Reds enjoyed 55% of possession | Previously, Michael Owen had scored his 50th goal in all competitions, and his 50th league goal, against the Saints

Quote unquote
"We started really well but then just stopped playing. Their goal was a bit unlucky from our point of view but it could've been stopped." **Stephane Henchoz**

"The second half was truly poor and very disappointing. There weren't too many positives to take out of this half, they got the goal too quickly and we didn't respond." **Phil Thompson**

"This was a good time to be playing Liverpool. We beat them 10 days ago and their fans started getting on their backs in the second half. I can only see Manchester United winning the title." **Kevin Davies** Southampton

Man of the match Emile Heskey **Atmosphere** Another bad day when we did very little to lift spirits or the team. More whining than singing. As for the 'Who the effing hell are you?' crew – we're better than that **League position** 5th

Tuesday 22 January 2002	Premiership

Manchester United 0

Liverpool 1
Murphy 84

Kick-off 8pm Old Trafford **Att** 67,599 **Ref** G Barber
MANCHESTER UNITED Barthez, Phil Neville, Gary Neville, Blanc, Silvestre, Beckham (Solskjaer 87), Keane, Scholes, Veron, van Nistelrooy, Giggs SUBS Carroll, Wallwork, O'Shea, Butt

BOOKED Veron
LIVERPOOL Dudek, Wright, Henchoz, Hyypia, Carragher, Murphy (Berger 88), Hamann, Gerrard, Riise, Heskey, Owen (Anelka 77) SUBS Arphexad, McAllister, Biscan BOOKED Gerrard, Carragher

Cometh the hour and all that. Just days after being booed off the pitch against Southampton, Danny Murphy, boosted by a phone call from Gérard Houllier in Corsica, returned to his own personal theatre of dreams and came up trumps once again. It was a massive and timely victory that opened up the title race, proving beyond doubt that Liverpool were not yet a spent force. United were on the crest of a winning wave and widely tipped to brush a spluttering Reds outfit aside, but Liverpool had

67

Stevie and Danny celebrate our second straight win at OT. We're good at things like that...

the sign on their bitter rivals and proved it when Murphy pounced to score the vital goal six minutes from time. The home team enjoyed the early possession but as the match progressed and Steven Gerrard grew in stature in the middle of the park, Liverpool created the better of the chances. After Giggs wasted the best of United's early opportunities, Gerrard, Anelka and Riise all brought the best out of Barthez. Having soaked up all United could offer, Liverpool sprang forward decisively – a sweet Gerrard pass found Murphy in space and his delicate lob over Barthez was enough for a fifth straight win over United, and a second consecutive home and away double. Who put the ball in United's net? Super Danny Murphy.

Vital stats

Liverpool commanded 60% of the possession | United had 2 shots on target compared to Liverpool's 5 | This was Liverpool's 5th straight win over the champions

Quote unquote

"It's a wonderful result. I would be a liar if I said it was just three points. We didn't just battle, there was more quality in our performance. The lads showed a lot of character, showing the qualities that made this club great. The players were absolutely magnificent and I'm particularly thrilled for Danny." **Phil Thompson**

"Liverpool just kicked the ball forward and hoped to get a break. We were desperately unlucky." **Sir Alex 'sour grapes' Ferguson** Manchester United manager

"People tend to forget the positive things you've done for the team when you aren't having a good time. That's a shame, because we want Anfield to be a place where we can intimidate teams, not feel intimidated ourselves. In football you can be the hero one minute and villain the next. Hopefully the fans will have a certain fondness for me now after another winner against United." **Danny Murphy**

Man of the match Steven Gerrard **Atmosphere** Why can't it be like this every game? New continental Liverpool chant really took off **League position** 3rd

---

Sunday 27 January 2002   FA Cup 4th round

Arsenal 1   Liverpool 0

Bergkamp 28

Kick-off 1pm Highbury **Att** 38,092 **Ref** M Riley

ARSENAL Wright, Luzhny, Keown, Campbell, Cole, Pires (Parlour 20), Vieira, van Bronckhorst (Grimandi 84), Wiltord (Upson 68), Bergkamp, Henry SUBS Dixon, Stack BOOKED Cole SENT OFF Keown, Bergkamp.

LIVERPOOL Dudek, Riise, Hyypia, Henchoz, Wright (Murphy 80), Carragher, Hamann, Gerrard, Heskey, Anelka (Litmanen 45), Owen SUBS Berger, Arphexad, McAllister BOOKED Heskey, Wright, Gerrard, Henchoz SENT OFF Carragher

An old-school cup-tie with an old-school atmosphere ended in controversy and defeat for the holders. 'One-nil down, two-one up, Michael Owen won the Cup' sang the Liverpool fans in the Clock End, in a neat twist on a Gunners favourite that harked back to the League Cup final of 1987. But despite the warm memories of our sun-kissed May afternoon in Cardiff, there was to be no repeat showing once Bergkamp gave Arsenal the lead with a fine header following a neat interchange with Henry. On another day, Owen might have helped himself to a hat-trick but a combination of poor shooting and resolute Arsenal defending meant the hero of the Millennium Stadium left a wet North London empty-handed. Anelka hit the frame of the goal with a snapshot before the game exploded into a blizzard of cards in the second half. Keown was dismissed for holding back Owen, then Bergkamp went in for a spiteful stamp on Carragher. Liverpool's two-man advantage lasted all of 20 seconds before Carragher had a rush of blood and threw a coin that had been aimed at him back into the crowd. Mike Riley reached for his pocket once again and it was 10 against 11. In the final minutes Gerrard headed over and Richard Wright got his fingers to a final effort from the constantly thwarted Owen, but there was to be no return trip to Cardiff.

Vital stats
6/1 on the result being 1-0 to the Arsenal | 18 fouls conceded by both sides | Liverpool had 4 shots on target compared to Arsenal's 3

Quote unquote

"It was a fantastic Cup tie apart from certain incidents and we're very, very disappointed to go out. It was two teams believing that if they could get through this round, their team could go all the way." **Phil Thompson**

"It was a real cup tie. Both teams were up for it. If I was a neutral supporter, I'd like to pay to see a game like we saw today." **Arsène Wenger** Arsenal manager

"If Carragher's behaviour was inexcusable, it might nevertheless have done football a favour by putting a worrying phenomenon firmly into the spotlight. For several weeks players have been required to dodge all kinds of objects while venturing near the touchline in matches carrying a high-emotional tariff." **Richard Williams** The Guardian

Man of the match Didi Hamann **Atmosphere** A good afternoon apart, of course, from the result. Plenty of taunts about Adams going to lift the FA Cup and it not being there plus, 'One-nil down, two-nil up Michael Owen won the Cup, with a pinpoint Paddy pass setting up the goal…'

Liverpool 1   Leicester City 0

Heskey 57

Kick-off 8pm Anfield **Att** 42,305 **Ref** B Knight.
LIVERPOOL Dudek, Wright, Henchoz, Hyypia, Carragher, Smicer, Hamann, McAllister (Murphy 74), Berger (Riise 86), Heskey, Anelka SUBS Arphexad, Owen, Litmanen BOOKED Smicer
LEICESTER CITY Walker, Laursen, Elliott, Davidson, Impey, Izzet, Jones (Marshall 61), Oakes (Benjamin 85), Stewart (Rogers 16), Piper, Scowcroft SUBS Flowers, Lewis BOOKED Stewart, Scowcroft

Injury-hit and rooted to the bottom of the Premiership, Leicester City nevertheless proved a tough nut to crack. Patience, as Thommo had said in his pre-match team talk, was the key and no one had shown more of it than Emile Heskey who scored his first goal since late November. Liverpool dominated from the outset, even without Gerrard and Owen, who was left on the bench. Hamann thudded a free-kick over Walker's bar on five minutes, Anelka almost capitalised on Berger's fine work on eight and then Hamann and Anelka again let fly from long range. Stephen Wright created the home team's best chance of the opening period when

Patience proves a virtue for Emile Heskey as he nets a second-half winner against his old club

he wriggled free but couldn't decide whether to shoot or centre. Twelve minutes after the restart Hamann broke up a Leicester attack and fed Heskey who sprinted from the halfway line, drew Walker and finished with an adroit chip. It was a goal that all his hard work over previous months deserved and justified the faith Houllier and Thompson had shown in him. The former Leicester favourite then should have doubled his tally on 66 minutes but he headed weakly from Berger's cross. Abel Xavier, recently signed from Everton and watching from the directors box, resolved to ensure the big striker got plenty of the same service in the games to come.

Vital stats

Liverpool had 56% possession | This was Liverpool's 23rd home win over Leicester in 43 games | It was the 2nd consecutive 1-0 home win over the Foxes with Heskey as the only scorer

Quote unquote

"Emile's goal was tremendous and capped a magnificent all-round, 90-minute performance from him. He showed his power, pace and a subtle finish and everyone was delighted to see him on the scoresheet." **Phil Thompson**

"That's the way it goes with us at the moment. Matthew Jones gives the ball away in the middle of the field and Emile, who hasn't scored for a long time, gets his goal against his old club. Typical." **Dave Bassett** Leicester City manager

"Emile Heskey took the role of big, bad wolf, to finally blow former club Leicester's house of straw down, after Liverpool had huffed and puffed for much of a drab contest." **David Maddock**
The Mirror

Man of the match Emile Heskey **Atmosphere** Back to where we were at the previous home game more or less. A few try with the Allez, Allez chant but it was one of those nights where we just couldn't seem to lift ourselves **League position** 4th

FEBRUARY 2002

Leeds United 0   Liverpool 4

Ferdinand 15 (og), Heskey 61, 63, Owen 90

Kick-off 12 noon Elland Road **Att** 40,216 **Ref** G Poll
LEEDS UNITED Martyn, Kelly, Ferdinand, Matteo, Harte, Dacourt (Wilcox 57), Bowyer, Batty, Kewell (Keane 74), Fowler, Viduka SUBS Robinson, McPhail, Duberry BOOKED Matteo, Kewell
LIVERPOOL Dudek, Wright, Henchoz, Hyypia, Riise, Hamann, Gerrard (McAllister), Murphy, Heskey, Owen SUBS Arphexad, Xavier, Smicer, Anelka BOOKED Carragher

A sizeable travelling contingent made its way to Elland Road for a noon kick-off, pondering the once unthinkable scenario that Robbie Fowler might score the goal that put paid to Liverpool's season. The former Reds favourite had been on goalscoring form for his new club and both teams came into the game knowing only three points would suffice. Liverpool were a different team to the stuttering outfit seen in previous weeks and hammered into their title rivals from the opening whistle, as epitomised by Steven Gerrard's crunching challenge on Olivier Dacourt. Michael Owen had already had a penalty appeal turned down when a wicked Danny Murphy free-kick was turned into his own net by Rio Ferdinand on 15 minutes. Further first-half chances for Gerrard and Owen went begging before the Reds showed their class in a rampant second half display. A Gerrard pass on the hour found Emile Heskey who took the ball wide of Nigel Martyn before finishing with power from a tight angle. Two minutes later and the big man had his third goal in two games after volleying home John Arne Riise's corner. Fowler had a half chance in a goalmouth scramble but the icing was applied to the cake when Michael Owen showed the spring in his heels by outleaping the Leeds defence to nod home after his initial effort had hit the bar. The travelling Kop treated a fast-emptying Elland Road to the full repertoire, including a rousing 'Boring, boring Scousers', but at least Fowler waited behind at the end to offer a rueful wave to his longtime admirers.

Vital stats

Liverpool bossed an incredible 60% possession | The Reds made 31 tackles compared to 17 for Leeds | 100/1 on Liverpool winning 4-0

Quote unquote

"He (Heskey) was outstanding for us when we went top of the League but people said he wasn't scoring. He never hides. Emile and Michael work well in tandem. Their partnership with Liverpool could tip the balance in their favour for England." **Phil Thompson**

"We've had a lot of stick, saying we're boring, but hopefully the critics will have seen this game and changed their minds." **Steven Gerrard**

"Liverpool began in a huddle, Leeds in a muddle, and nothing much changed. Thompson's men were a team united, every player covering for each other, every player working overtime at closing down or breaking out." **Henry Winter** The Daily Telegraph

Man of the match Steven Gerrard **Atmosphere** This was how it should be every game. Loud and proud for the full 90 minutes and a good repertoire to boot **League position** 3rd

---

Saturday 9 February 2002   **Premiership**

Ipswich Town 0   Liverpool 6

Xavier 16, Heskey 43, 90, Hyypia 52, Owen 62, 71

Kick-off 3pm Portman Road **Att** 25,608 **Ref** S Bennett
IPSWICH TOWN Marshall, Makin, McGreal, Hreidarsson, Venus, Holland, Clapham, Wright (Stewart 38), Peralta, Armstrong (Magilton 71), Bent SUBS Salmon, Counago, Reuser
LIVERPOOL Dudek (Arphexad 55), Wright, Henchoz, Hyypia, Xavier, Murphy, Hamann, Gerrard (McAllister 81), Riise (Anelka 73), Heskey, Owen SUBS Smicer, Litmanen

Ipswich had won seven of their previous eight games when Liverpool came to town but as the famous banner said, 'Form is temporary, class is permanent.' Liverpool showed they had both in abundance on an afternoon when every player performed at his peak and the finishing was nothing short of deadly. Abel Xavier set the ball rolling with a goal on his full debut after 16 minutes before Heskey, flying after his recent strikes, slotted a second with his left foot from Gerrard's perfectly weighted pass. If the first half was good the second half was sublime as the Reds put in a performance that ranked alongside Forest in 88 and Palace in 89. Hyypia made it three with a header seven minutes into the second half, Owen made it four after a stunning passing move, the no10 then scored his 23rd of the season after being released by Heskey before Anelka picked out Heskey to complete the rout. 'Boring, boring Liverpool' had scored 10 goals in the last two Premiership games and were now back on top of the table. Had it not been for an inspired Andy Marshall in the Ipswich goal, that tally could have been significantly more.

Riise celebrates as the Reds rout Ipswich Town. And Andy Marshall actually had a *good* game...

Vital stats

Liverpool had 14 shots on target | 50/1 on Abel Xavier scoring the 1st goal | 100/1 on Liverpool winning 6-0

Quote unquote

"It was a fantastic all-round team performance. Today was one of those games when the players can truly pat themselves on the back. That's as good a win as anything I've seen at Liverpool." **Phil Thompson**

"It tells you something that our goalkeeper was our best player. We were lucky only to have six goals put past him." **George Burley** Ipswich Town manager

"It's the biggest pasting of my life. Watching Owen and Heskey run at me was one of the most awesome sights I have seen. People talk about Heskey not scoring enough but he showed his quality today." **Andy Marshall** Ipswich Town

Man of the match Emile Heskey **Atmosphere** Another good afternoon with the best rendition yet of The Fields Of Anfield Road **League position** 1st

Wednesday 20 February 2002	Champions League

Liverpool 0   Galatasaray 0

Kick-off 7.45pm **Att** 41,605 **Ref** M Pereira (Portugal)
LIVERPOOL Kirkland, Xavier, Henchoz, Hyypia, Carragher (Smicer 67), Murphy, Hamann, Gerrard (McAllister 72), Riise, Owen, Heskey SUBS Arphexad, Baros, Biscan, Wright, Litmanen
GALATASARAY Mondragon, Perez, Asik, Bulent Korkmaz, Victoria, Fleurquin, Bulent, Penbe, Sas (Sozkesen 80, Niculescu 90), Goktan, Karan SUBS Inan, Inceefe, Erdem, Suat, Aykut
BOOKED Asik, Fleurquin, Karan, Bulent

'Welcome to Heaven' proclaimed the banner on the Kop as Galatasaray ran out to stifle Liverpool's Champions League ambitions in a game the hosts needed to win in order to move off the bottom of the group. But despite exerting an enormous amount of pressure on the Turkish side, the Reds found themselves up against a keeper in inspired form. Faryd Mondragon single (and sometimes double) handedly kept his team in the game, producing a string of unlikely and spectacular saves. Hamann curled a free-kick just wide of the target after seven minutes and went on to test the goalkeeper twice more in the first half with typical long-range efforts. In between, Riise let fly from a free-kick and Hyypia's header struck the post and bounced away. Murphy was next to try his luck from distance but his 47th-minute screamer flew wide. With 25 minutes left on the clock it was Murphy again who went closest to breaking the deadlock, weaving between Gala defenders before screwing a low shot fractionally wide of the post. A minute later Heskey hit the bar with a free header from six yards. Worryingly, Gerrard was stretchered off after 72 minutes but with time running out, his replacement Gary McAllister combined with Hamann to release Owen. Inevitably, his shot was beaten away by a keeper who just refused to be beaten on the night. Chris Kirkland, making his European bow in the absence of the injured Dudek, could only watch from afar and admire.

Vital stats
70% pass completion rate for both sides | Liverpool produced 18 attempts on goal to Gala's 8 | 9/1 on the match finishing 0-0

Quote unquote

"It isn't going to be easy for us now. We're left with two points from three games and the fact
is we're going to need to get at least eight to qualify. We are still confident of going through.
We showed last season anything is possible and we'll go for it." **Didi Hamann**

"Without doubt it was two points dropped, bearing in mind the number of chances we had.
There will not be any fear from us as we go into the next two games. They have seen how
strong we are and they will know that we have a strong away record both in Europe and the
Premiership." **Phil Thompson**

"Hell has never been the place to make amends for past mistakes, but Liverpool now face just
such a mission. By failing to win last night's Champions League encounter at Anfield, Phil
Thompson's side left themselves with the most daunting of tasks." **Matt Lawton** Daily Mail

Man of the match Didi Hamann **Atmosphere** First European night of the year and the Kop was in
good voice, as it should have been but frustration crept in as chances went begging.

Saturday 23 February 2002   Premiership

Liverpool 1   Everton 1
Anelka 72   Radzinzki 52

Kick-off 3pm Anfield **Att** 44,371 **Ref** D Elleray
LIVERPOOL Kirkland, Xavier, Henchoz, Hyypia, Wright (Heskey 55), Murphy, Hamann,
McAllister (Smicer 66), Riise, Owen, Anelka SUBS Arphexad, Biscan, Litmanen
EVERTON Simonsen, Clarke, Weir, Stubbs, Pistone, Gemmill, Carsley, Linderoth (Gravesen 45),
Naysmith, Campbell, Ginola (Radzinski 45) SUBS Gerrard, Unsworth, Pombridge BOOKED
Clarke, Gravesen.

Liverpool dominated possession in the 166th derby, a typically frenetic
and scrappy encounter that saw both teams in search of three equally
vital points at opposite ends of the table. The home side enjoyed the best
of a fairly dire first half with Anelka showing glimpses of the pace and
touch that made him a regular for France. In the seventh minute he
streaked away from the Blues defence but shot wide of Steve Simonsen's
near post. Kirkland then saved well from Carsley before Anelka was
denied twice more by the Everton keeper. The predictable booing of
Xavier by the Evertonians in the Anfield Road end provided the soundtrack for the first half but the introduction of substitutes for both sides
changed the tune in the second period. First, Tomasz Radzinski, on for
David Ginola, struck with a mishit shot that bobbled past Kirkland following a neat one-two between Naysmith and Pistone. Thompson

responded by releasing Smicer and Heskey from the bench and the immediate impact was two chances created for, and missed by, Owen. As Liverpool found the width they had been lacking, the cracks appeared and Anelka was on hand to capitalise. Murphy and Owen exchanged passes, Heskey dummied and Anelka beat Simonsen with a precise flick from six yards. Hamann and Riise then tried their luck before Simonsen again rescued with an arching tip over from Murphy's 85th-minute header. Honours even.

Vital stats
73% pass completion for the Reds | 19 fouls conceded by Everton compared to Liverpool's 10 | 5/1 on Anelka scoring the last goal

Quote unquote
"We deserved to win but it wasn't to be. It's been the story of our home games. I feel sorry for the fans because we are not turning our superiority into goals at home." **Phil Thompson**
"If ever a match needed a spark of genius, it was this one. It was marred by a series of ill-directed passes, clumsy tackles and poor finishing that not even the swirling wind could be blamed for." **Kevin Mitchell** The Observer
"Even if his latest marriage of convenience is dissolved in the summer, when he could be offered unlikely solace in the love he left behind, Nicolas Anelka has assured himself a lasting place in Liverpudlian hearts." **Oliver Kay** The Times

Man of the match Nicolas Anelka **Atmosphere** If you can't make a noise when the Blues are visiting, when can you? Normal derby day vitriol plus the new Liverpool chant. Volume increased when we went behind **League position** 3rd

---

Tuesday 26 February 2002	Champions League

Galatasaray 1   Liverpool 1
Niculescu 71   Heskey 79

Kick-off 7.45pm Ali Sami Yen Stadium **Att** 22,105 **Ref** U Meier (Germany)
GALATASARAY Mondragon, Korkmaz, Erdem, Goktan, Sas, Victoria, Perez, Akman, Fleurquin, Niculescu (Aykut 79), Penbe SUBS Inan, Inceefe, Suat, Sabri, Sedat, Jersson BOOKED Victoria, Korkmaz
LIVERPOOL Kirkland, Xavier, Henchoz, Hyypia, Carragher, Smicer (Litmanen 74), Murphy, Hamann, Riise, Owen, Heskey SUBS Arphexad, Baros, Barmby, McAllister, Biscan, Wright BOOKED Hamann, Heskey

Liverpool were again left to lament a string of missed chances and the form of a goalkeeper Franz Beckenbauer rates as the best in Europe.

Defeat would have been a bitter pill to swallow after a performance that dampened the ardour of Gala's famous fans, but only a late equaliser kept Liverpool's Champions League flame flickering faintly. Colombian keeper Mondragon was at it again from the start, saving brilliantly from Riise in the 16th minute before young Chris Kirkland responded in kind with a wonderful stop at the other end from Arif Erdem. Hyypia then cleared a header off the line and Kirkland was on hand to deny Goktan Berkant's follow-up. Gradually, however, Liverpool began creating space for the front two and just after half time Mondragon saved with his legs from Owen before again thwarting Riise with ease. When the first goal came it was against the run of play. A cross from Victoria found Niculescu stealing in to head past Kirkland. Liverpool wasted a golden opportunity to hit back within a minute when Smicer skewed wide after Riise had played him clean through. Staring elimination in the face, the white shirts of Liverpool swarmed forward and reward came when Litmanen, on for Smicer, shielded the ball expertly before teeing up Heskey to hammer home from close range.

Vital stats
7/1 on Emile Heskey to score the last goal | Liverpool had 15 attempts on goal to Gala's 18 |

Gala enjoyed 54% of the possession

Quote unquote
"We should have won both matches with Galatasaray. People say I'm starting to sound like Arsène Wenger and Alex Ferguson, but I'll take that as a compliment." **Phil Thompson**

"We blocked all the things that they do best, like free-kicks. Liverpool have problems when they force the attack but they are very dangerous when they counter attack." **Mircea Lucescu** Galatasaray coach

"While the stand-in boss can be justifiably proud of the manner in which his players survived a seething cauldron of hate, he will lament the wastefulness that continues to be their undoing." **Paul Joyce** Daily Express

Man of the match Danny Murphy **Atmosphere** Valiant effort from those who made the trip. If we didn't always make ourselves heard, the Grafton banner made sure we were seen.

MARCH 2002

Fulham 0   Liverpool 2

Anelka 13, Litmanen 89

Kick-off 3pm Craven Cottage **Att** 21,103 **Ref** A Wiley
FULHAM Van der Sar, Finnan, Goma, Ouaddou, Brevett, Legwinski, Malbranque, Davis (Clark 25, Collins 76), Saha, Marlet, Boa Morte (Hayles 66) SUBS Taylor, Melville BOOKED Legwinski, Brevett, Boa Morte
LIVERPOOL Dudek, Xavier, Hyypia, Henchoz, Wright, Smicer (Barmby 71), Hamann, Murphy, Riise, Anelka (Litmanen 80), Heskey SUBS Kirkland, McAllister, Owen BOOKED Wright, Hyypia

A last chance to visit Craven Cottage before it was redeveloped into a modern, all-seater stadium represented a step back in time. In addition to being able to support the team from old-fashioned terracing, Liverpool's travelling fans were also treated to the spectacle of their side not playing well but taking all three points with relative ease. Fulham, as had been their problem all season, enjoyed the majority of possession but despite their pretty passing patterns, rarely threatened to puncture Liverpool's rearguard. That was due in no small part to the tenacious spirit of Stephane Henchoz who demonstrated with one block his incalculable value to the team. Anelka had put the Reds in front on 13 minutes after his first attempt had been blocked, and Louis Saha had hit the bar for the home team, when French international striker Steve Marlet burst into the box and pulled back his right foot to score what seemed like a certain goal. Then, in a blur of red shirt and blond hair, Henchoz was there to take the ball off his boot and clear to safety. Defensive colleagues Jerzy Dudek and Sami Hyypia were similarly miserly and kept Fulham at bay long enough for Jari Litmanen to come on as a late substitute and make the game safe with a typical piece of quick-thinking invention. Van der Sar rushed out of his box to clear a long ball from Xavier, Litmanen headed over his former Ajax team-mate and rolled the ball into the net from a tight angle. A 10th away win of the season, and Thompson's 15th win from 31 games in charge, was safely in the bag.

Vital stats
Liverpool had 46% possession | 11/2 on Jari Litmanen scoring the last goal | Stephane Henchoz made 22 blocks, tackles and clearances

Quote unquote

"People talk about the best goals, the best saves. But I'm in the centre-back union and I think it's nice to have a few saving tackles as well. Stephane deserves to be in the union. He needed stitches after that tackle." **Phil Thompson** on Stephane Henchoz

"I think we were unlucky and Liverpool were lucky. We played well, the players gave their maximum and we deserved to get at least a point." **Christian Damiano** Fulham coach

"This victory, following the triumphs at Ipswich, Leeds and Old Trafford, meant they had succeeded in four consecutive Premiership trips. Indeed, for all the perception that this Liverpool are more dour than daring, a 13-0 aggregate suggests they could scarcely have been more swashbuckling were their French manager Alexander Dumas."

John Aizlewood The Sunday Times

Man of the match Stephane Henchoz **Atmosphere** With half of us standing it was fantastic from start to finish. Fields Of Anfield Road, Liverbird Upon My Chest, Red And White Kop and a great YNWA at the end. Plus a rousing Jari, Oh Jari, Jari after the great man's wonder goal **League position** 3rd

Wednesday 6 March 2002 — Premiership

Liverpool 3 — Newcastle United 0

Murphy 32, 53, Hamann 75

Kick-off 8pm Anfield **Att** 44,204 **Ref** J Winter
LIVERPOOL Dudek, Xavier, Henchoz, Hyypia, Riise, Smicer (Barmby 81), Murphy, Hamann, Heskey, Owen (Litmanen 71), Anelka SUBS Kirkland, McAllister, Wright
NEWCASTLE UNITED Given, Hughes, O'Brien, Dabizas, Distin, Solano, Jenas, Speed (Acuna 37), Robert, Shearer, Cort (Bernard 76) SUBS Harper, Elliott, Ameobi

An attacking Liverpool line-up that featured the pace of Owen, Anelka, Heskey and Smicer, put the distraction of a floodlight failure behind them to illuminate Anfield on a night that consigned Newcastle's faint championship hopes to the dustbin. All the pre-match talk had centred on Michael Owen's phenomenal goalscoring record against the Toon but it was Nicolas Anelka, aided by two goals from Danny Murphy, who really shone on the night. Twice inside the first 20 minutes the Frenchman forced acrobatic saves out of Shay Given and it was Anelka who set up Murphy's opener on 32 minutes, when his cutback evaded Owen but found the midfielder on hand to score his sixth of the season. Murphy's seventh was better still as he danced through the Newcastle defence to net eight minutes after half time. Carl Cort had a goal disallowed for handball just before the hour but Liverpool were rampant and on 75 minutes Didi Hamann settled the matter with a fine goal against his old club. Smicer drew three defenders to him before slipping it to the German who passed the ball inside Given's left-hand post from 22 yards. Gérard Houllier, who had returned to Merseyside in the days before the game, would have been rubbing his hands with glee.

Vital stats

Liverpool had 21 attempts on goal | 14/1 on Danny Murphy scoring the first goal | 22/1 on Didi Hamann scoring the last goal

Quote unquote

"We came out of the blocks very quickly. It was a high-powered performance, with pace, precision passing and discipline." **Phil Thompson**

"Take nothing away from Liverpool, they beat us fair and square. We were second best all night. They have pace and always threatened to get in behind us and they did. We were all at sea and looked overawed tonight." **Bobby Robson** Newcastle United manager

"Anelka shone on a night when Liverpool had numerous beacons, lighting the blue touch paper on a Premiership challenge gathering pace at just the right time. This was world class." **Chris Bascombe** Liverpool Echo

Man of the match Nicolas Anelka **Man of the match** Great game, great night, great songs with the new Liiiiiiverpool chant firmly established as a favourite **League position** 3rd

---

Wednesday 13 March 2002	Champions League

Barcelona 0   Liverpool 0

Kick-off 7.45pm Nou Camp **Att** 75,362 **Ref** K Vassaras (Greece)
BARCELONA Bonano, Puyol, Christanval, De Boer, Coco, Luis Enrique (Gerard 77), Motta, Rivaldo, Saviola (Geovanni 88), Cocu, Kluivert SUBS Reina, Abelardo, Xavi, Rochemback, Gabri BOOKED Cocu
LIVERPOOL Dudek, Xavier, Henchoz, Hyypia, Carragher, Murphy, Gerrard (Barmby 80), Hamann, Riise, Litmanen (Smicer 70), Heskey (Baros 74) SUBS Kirkland, McAllister, Biscan, Wright BOOKED Murphy, Gerrard, Hamann

The taunts of Patrick Kluivert, Frank De Boer et al were ringing in Liverpool ears as the Reds walked out at a packed Nou Camp in a game many felt they needed to win in order to stand a chance of progressing to the Champions League quarter-finals. The Catalans were still fuming at being dumped out of the previous season's Uefa Cup and tried everything to get one up on the visitors in the build-up. Gérard Houllier had returned to training at Melwood but did not travel, and nor did the injured Michael Owen who aggravated a hamstring against Newcastle. But Steven Gerrard was passed fit and for the second time in a year Liverpool frustrated and contained Barcelona, with Henchoz and Hyypia once again outstanding at the heart of defence. Indeed, Gerrard had the best of Liverpool's chances, miscuing a shot in the second minute and sending a free header wide in the 22nd minute. Rivaldo, nursing a knee injury, was quiet throughout and Barça's best chances fell to Luis Enrique in the first half, Christanval, whose header hit the post after the break, and Saviola. Heskey, who led the line tirelessly all night, had a couple of half chances and Milan Baros, who replaced him, could have sealed the points after an inspired late run on his debut. But as the boos and white handkerchieves came out for Barça at the end, Liverpool trooped off to learn that a 2-0 win over Roma would be enough to take them through

Steven Gerrard goes close with a header during a magnificent performance at the Nou Camp

to the quarter-finals. Unfortunately, Didi Hamann's booking meant he would miss the crunch date at Anfield.

Vital stats

Barça had 16 attempts on goal to Liverpool's 13 | 7/1 on the match ending goalless | Barcelona enjoyed 59% possession

Quote unquote

"It is down to the Barcelona players what they say but it was a motivation to our players. No one likes to be criticised, particularly by players who will be in Disneyland this summer and not Japan." **Phil Thompson**

"Phil Thompson's side made their point to much gnashing of teeth among the home support last night, a 14th successive unbeaten match on their European travels." **Dominic Fifield** The Guardian

"A ripple of grudging applause confirmed they had made their point to the footballing purists of Barcelona last night but, for Liverpool, two points dropped threaten to be of far greater significance." **Oliver Kay** The Times

Man of the match Sami Hyypia **Atmosphere** Once again we were split on the top tiers at both ends of the stadium but still made a noise. Down at the bottom of the cauldron it sounded louder than at the top. Our hosts were fairly quiet till the hankies come out at the end.

Saturday 16 March	Premiership

Middlesbrough 1   Liverpool 2

Southgate 89   Heskey 33, Riise 84

Kick-off 12 noon, Riverside Stadium **Att** 31,253 **Ref** A D'Urso

MIDDLESBROUGH Schwarzer, Stockdale (Marinelli 81), Southgate, Festa, Queudrue, Wilkshire (Nemeth 73), Ince, Mustoe (Gavin 73), Greening, Carbone, Boksic SUBS Windass, Crossley

LIVERPOOL Dudek, Xavier, Henchoz, Hyypia, Carragher, Smicer (Gerrard 70), Hamann, Murphy, Riise, Anelka, Heskey SUBS Arphexad, Barmby, McAllister, Litmanen BOOKED Henchoz, Hamann

Steve McLaren's Boro knew how Liverpool felt before the Barcelona game. Gary Lineker had labelled the Teessiders boring but in front of one of their biggest crowds of the season, Boro proved anything but. The home side dominated for much of a first half in which Liverpool were limited to a few chances but still turned a goal up. Anelka, in fine recent form, streaked away in the 13th minute and forced a fine save out of Schwarzer before turning provider with a cross-cum-shot to Hamann whose shot was parried, allowing Heskey to crash the ball into the net.

83

Murphy almost made it two on the stroke of half time when his 20-yarder curled just over. Boksic and Carbone continued causing plenty of problems for a below-par Liverpool side in the second half and former Red Paul Ince almost got on the scoresheet with a rasping left-foot drive with nine minutes remaining. However, a minute later the points were sealed as John Arne Riise bagged his sixth goal of the season with a fierce drive from the edge of the area following good work by Heskey. Gareth Southgate got a deserved consolation goal for Boro on 88 minutes but it was too little, too late to stop Liverpool securing a 12th league win on the road.

Vital stats
Boro had 18 attempts on goal to Liverpool's 9 | Liverpool had 8 shots on target to Boro's 5 | 16/1 on John Arne Riise scoring the last goal

Quote unquote
"I'm not going to be daft and pretend we played magnificently, but I've been with this group of players long enough to know that, if things are not going right and you have to dig deep to get a result, there's none better in the Premiership." **Phil Thompson**

"I didn't leave Liverpool in the best circumstances but their fans never gave me stick and that's why I'd like them to win the title. I still live in Liverpool and Jamie Redknapp is my best mate and I'd like them to do it." **Paul Ince** Middlesbrough

"Down at Anfield these days they are a touch sensitive to the claim, delivered by many an expert, that they are just a counter-attacking team. It hurts them like a harpoon in the back but, in reality, there is no denying the strategy." **Peter Fitton** The Mail On Sunday

Man of the match Sami Hyypia **Atmosphere** A Barça hangover led to a pretty subdued 90 minutes in what must be one of the most soulless grounds in the country. As for the Boro boys, they did their best to back the team as they went 2-0 down **League position** 2nd

Tuesday 19 March 2002	Champions League

Liverpool 2   Roma 0

Litmanen 6pen, Heskey 63

Kick-off Anfield **Att** 41,794 **Ref** R Pedersen (Norway)
Liverpool Dudek, Xavier, Henchoz, Hyypia, Carragher, Smicer (McAllister 90), Gerrard, Murphy, Riise, Litmanen (Biscan 88), Heskey SUBS Arphexad, Baros, Barmby, Diomede, Wright BOOKED Xavier
Roma Antonioli, Panucci, Samuel, Aldair, Tommasi, Emerson, Assuncao (Cassano 68), Lima (Montella 45), Candela, Totti, Batistuta (Delvecchio 45)
SUBS Pelizzoli, Zago, Zebina, Guigou BOOKED Tommasi, Samuel

One hundred-and-fifty seven days after being rushed from Anfield in an ambulance, Gérard Houllier returned to give the most rousing team talk of his managerial career before taking his seat in the dugout, unbeknown to most of the 41,794 people in the ground. His appearance took Roma boss Fabio Capello by surprise and when the legendary Italian hugged his opposite number, the Kop realised its leader had returned and cranked the noise up to a decibel level rarely reached even in the days when the stadium held 54,000. A mosaic bearing the legend 'Allez' set the tone on a night that ranks alongside the greatest in the club's long and distinguished European history. There was no Owen, no Anelka and no Hamann but belief coursed through Liverpudlian veins and when Jari Litmanen scored nervelessly from the spot following a trip on Murphy, the place exploded. It was all Liverpool in a first half of controlled passion and fury, with Riise going close on a number of occasions and Gerrard quite imperious in the middle of the park. Requiring another goal to make sure of progression, Heskey wrote his name in the Anfield annals alongside that of David Fairclough against St Etienne in 1977, leaping like a salmon to bullet home an unstoppable and decisive second in the 63rd minute. There was no way back for Roma – a sensation they are all too accustomed to when facing Liverpool. Houllier was back, Liverpool were through. Allez indeed.

Vital stats

Liverpool had 16 attempts on goal to Roma's 9 | This was Roma's only away defeat in Europe |

This was Liverpool's 96th European tie at Anfield

Quote unquote

"Roma are a top-class side, but I think even they were taken aback by the atmosphere in the stadium and the way we began the game. The supporters were fantastic and in those sort of situations a team can become unstoppable." **Phil Thompson**

"It is not just about technical and tactical things. Heskey was the key. This was a different Liverpool. I have not seen them play like this before." **Fabio Capello** Roma coach

"It was like a choir, Mozart sung in a cathedral, but it was only as I listened, my eyes welling up, to the Kop on Tuesday night that I realised that the Liverpool fans act as psychologists as well as parishioners." **Alyson Rudd** The Times

Man of the match Emile Heskey **Atmosphere** Inter 65. St Etienne 77. Roma 2002. The best.

Liverpool 1   Chelsea 0

Smicer 90

Kick-off 2pm Anfield **Att** 44,203 **Ref** M Halsey

LIVERPOOL Dudek, Xavier (Owen 57), Henchoz, Hyypia, Carragher, Murphy, Hamann, Gerrard (Smicer 28), Riise, Heskey, Anelka (Litmanen 83) SUBS Arphexad, McAllister BOOKED Carragher

CHELSEA Cudicini, Melchiot, Desailly, Gallas, Babayaro, Stanic, Lampard, Petit, Gronkjaer, Hasselbaink, Gudjohnsen (Zola 82). SUBS de Goey, Dalla Bona, Terry, Forssell BOOKED Babayaro

Liverpool returned to the top of the table in the most dramatic fashion, thanks to an injury-time goal from Vladimir Smicer. The Czech international came on as a 30th-minute replacement for the injured Steven Gerrard and answered his critics after Chelsea had dominated large chunks of the game. Eidur Gudjohnsen miscued on 17 minutes before Jimmy Floyd Hasselbaink somehow scooped high and wide following a wonderful Dudek save from Stanic. After the break, Jesper Gronkjaer screwed a shot wide after being put through by Lampard. Liverpool were restricted to playing hopeful balls towards Heskey and Anelka but with Gallas and Desailly in fine form, the vital goal looked like eluding them. Two minutes from time, Hasselbaink combined well with sub Zola and chipped Dudek from six yards. The ball, which looked like nestling in the back of the net at the Kop end, landed on the roof of the goal and the sigh from the Liverpool supporters massed behind was one of pure relief. The blood pressure hardly had time to return to normal levels when some wonderful Litmanen skill freed Heskey charging down the left. The cross was perfect, the finish was deadly – a rasping 12-yard volley leaving Cudicini helpless and Anfield delirious. Anything was now possible.

Vital stats

Liverpool had 4 shots on target to Chelsea's 1 | Both sides enjoyed an equal share of possession | Chelsea had only won one game at Anfield since the reign of George V

Quote unquote

"As soon as I saw Emile get the ball on the left I knew he would deliver a good cross. Then it was up to me to be in the right place to receive it. I am very happy. It's only my second goal of the season and I missed a similar chance against Galatasaray last month." **Vladimir Smicer**

Man of the match Jamie Carragher **Atmosphere** We got behind the lads, but it was always going to seem a bit flat after Roma – until Vlad's goal went in… **League position** 1st

Liverpool 2   Charlton Athletic 0

Smicer 23, Owen 36

Kick-off 3pm Anfield **Att** 44,094 **Ref** D Gallagher

LIVERPOOL Dudek, Carragher, Henchoz, Hyypia, Riise, Murphy, Hamann, Berger (McAllister 84), Heskey (Smicer 19), Owen (Litmanen 78), Anelka SUBS Arphexad, Wright BOOKED Smicer

CHARLTON Kiely, Young, Costa, Rufus, Powell, Stuart, Bart-Williams, Parker (Kinsella 57), Konchesky (Robinson 69), Svensson (Johansson 75), Euell SUBS Ilic, Fortune BOOKED Bart-Williams, Parker

Charlton arrived at Anfield having only conceded two goals in their last nine matches but Liverpool, starting with Owen, Anelka and Heskey, doubled that tally in an efficient, professional display. The opener almost came from the unlikeliest of sources when Jamie Carragher let fly in the second minute, but the ball flew narrowly over. Smicer continued his recent goalscoring heroics by grabbing the opener with a rare header from a Danny Murphy free-kick in the 23rd minute. It was his first touch of the ball after replacing Heskey. Thirteen minutes later it was two after Henchoz released Anelka who in turn found Smicer. The Czech took two touches, fed Owen with a mishit shot and the finish, his 24th goal of the season, was a formality. Carra saw another good effort go close in the second half after Owen's attempt was cleared off the line by Euell. Dudek made a smart save from the Charlton striker two minutes later before Liverpool again stepped on the gas. Smicer and Riise brought the best out of Dean Kiely but could not ultimately add to Liverpool's tally. A fifth straight Premiership win and a 13th game unbeaten nevertheless put the Reds on top for 24 hours at least.

He's Czech, he's great, he's scored again

Patrik Berger evades Charlton defender Jorge Costa on a victorious afternoon for Liverpool

Vital stats

This was the 46th league encounter between the two clubs | There has only been one goalless draw | Liverpool had 17 attempts on goal to Charlton's 9 | 9/1 on Smicer scoring the first goal

Quote unquote

"Somebody just said to me it was winning ugly but that isn't the fact. I've been working on Smicer coming on to score all week! He's been great. You might think Emile coming off upset the balance but we don't believe that. We have the players to switch things around."
Phil Thompson

"You have to give Liverpool some credit. They worked very hard, they closed us down and didn't give us a chance to play. The form of the sides at the top at the moment is ferocious. I still can't see it being sorted out until the end of the season." **Alan Curbishley** Charlton manager

"One of Liverpool's subtler advantages is that key men have a habit of emerging from all sections of their ranks and Vladimir Smicer has taken his turn of late." **Patrick Barclay** The Sunday Telegraph

88 **Man of the match** Danny Murphy **Atmosphere** Not the best but not the worst and with the three points wrapped up by half time it was never going to be one to remember. Charlton aren't Roma, they're not even Chelsea **League position** 1st

APRIL 2002

Wednesday 3 April 2002   Champions League quarter-final 1st

Liverpool 1   Bayer Leverkusen 0

Hyypia 44

Kick-off 7.45pm Anfield **Att** 42,454 **Ref** A Frisk (Sweden)
LIVERPOOL Dudek, Carragher, Henchoz, Hyypia, Riise, Murphy, Hamann, Gerrard, Smicer (Berger 76), Owen (Litmanen 70), Heskey SUBS Arphexad, Barmby, McAllister, Biscan, Wright BOOKED Carragher, Hyypia
BAYER LEVERKUSEN Butt, Sebescen, Lucio, Ramelow, Placente, Schneider, Ballack, Basturk, Ze Roberto, Neuville (Kirsten 74), Berbato (Zivkovic 66) SUBS Juric, Babic, Dzaka, Burkhardt, Kleine BOOKED Lucio

Manchester United had won 2-0 at Deportivo the night, before meaning that if Liverpool could turn it on at home against the Bundesliga leaders, an all-English Champions League semi-final would be on the cards. It was the first time Liverpool had graced a quarter-final of Europe's premier tournament for some 17 years and Gérard Houllier, normally so careful not to draw misleading comparisons with the past, challenged his players to write a new chapter in the club's European story, insisting his team were 'ten games from greatness'. Unlike the Roma match, there was no Kop-inspired blitzkrieg on the Leverkusen goal and a strangely tense, subdued atmosphere reflected the action on the pitch. Half chances fell to Heskey and Gerrard before Smicer missed the best opportunity of the opening 45 minutes, heading over from Gerrard's pinpoint cross. But just as the half looked like finishing goalless, Michael Owen fashioned a cross from Riise's overhit corner and Sami Hyypia was on hand to prod home from point-blank range. Riise drilled over after the restart, Riise directed a shot straight at Hans-Jorg Butt in the Bayer goal, and Litmanen almost got a scoring touch on a Murphy cross, but the tide turned in the Germans' favour. Leverkusen came out of their shell and prompted by Bernd Schneider in midfield, began to see more of the ball. Ulf Kirsten and Ballack should have both done better before Jamie Carragher's excellent tackle stopped Ze Roberto claiming a vital away goal with four minutes left on the clock. Any extension to an unbeaten away record stretching 15 games in Europe would now be enough for a probable date with United.

89

Vital stats

Bayer Leverkusen bossed 58% of the possession | Liverpool were caught offside 8 times to Bayer's 3 | This was Liverpool's 25th clean sheet of the season

Quote unquote

"Sami is always present when you need him. You need big players to play big when it matters.In the first half we lacked a little composure in the final third but maybe that was down to tension. We had more chances in the second half and could have scored again while Leverkusen had only one chance." **Gérard Houllier**

"One-nil is a dangerous situation for us because we know what Michael Owen, Emile Heskey and Steven Gerrard can do. We think we can go through because we have the players to get the result we need." **Klaus Toppmöller** Bayer Leverkusen coach

"They played like we do when we're away. Leverkusen were superb tactically. But we still had more chances, even in the second half when John Arne Riise was unlucky." **Sami Hyypia**

Man of the match Steven Gerrard **Atmosphere** Another mosaic and another chorus of Just Like A Team… A bit quieter than other European nights but that was inevitable with this being the first leg. Good effort from all around the ground though.

Tuesday 9 April 2002 Champions League quarter-final 2nd leg

Bayer Leverkusen 4   Liverpool 2

Ballack 15, 63, Berbatov 67, Lucio 84   Xavier 41, Litmanen 79

Bayer Leverkusen win 4-3 on aggregate

Kick-off 7.45pm BayArena **Att** 22,500 **Ref** M Pereira

BAYER LEVERKUSEN Butt, Nowotny, Lucio, Placente, Ze Roberto, Basturk, Ballack, Schneider, Sebescen (Neuville 46), Kirsten (Berbatov 46), Brdaric (Zivkovic 70) SUBS Juric, Babic, Vranjes, Kleine BOOKED Nowotny, Ze Roberto

LIVERPOOL Dudek, Xavier (Berger 75), Hyypia, Henchoz, Murphy, Riise, Hamann (Smicer 61), Gerrard, Carragher, Heskey (Litmanen 41), Owen SUBS Kirkland, Barmby, McAllister, Biscan BOOKED Riise, Henchoz, Xavier

On a breathless night of high drama, Liverpool collapsed to their first away defeat in Europe in 16 games, and crashed out of the Champions League in the most painful, unexpected fashion. Jerzy Dudek had not conceded a goal in 377 minutes when Michael Ballack, a supreme performer on the night, dropped a shoulder, sent Steven Gerrard the wrong way and crashed an unstoppable shot into the net after 15 minutes. It was a strike that set the tone on a evening when Leverkusen established an attacking platform from which they controlled the tempo of the game.

Liverpool came back when Danny Murphy swung over a corner, Xavier connected with his head and put Liverpool ahead on aggregate at the break. The smart money would have been on Liverpool's famed backline keeping things tight in the second half and had Owen capitalised on two excellent chances after the restart, the tie would have surely been put beyond reach. Unfortunately, 13 minutes after Owen struck a post, and two minutes after Hamann had surprisingly been withdrawn, Bayer were in front, thanks once again to that man Ballack. This lead was then extended on 67 minutes when Dimitar Berbatov made it 3-1 after Henchoz had cleared off the line. Liverpool were now chasing the game and Litmanen, on for Heskey, danced inside two defenders before spearing a right-footed shot into the corner. Eleven minutes remained but only five had elapsed when Brazilian centre back Lucio scored the decisive fourth goal, powering a low shot through Dudek's legs. It was no less than Leverkusen deserved, a fact acknowledged by the generous applause from Liverpool's travelling fans. The stadium emptied to the strains of You'll Never Walk Alone. Sadly, it was being sung in a German accent.

Pile on! Somewhere, under that lot, is Jari Litmanen. Sadly his wonder goal at Bayer was all in vain

Vital stats

Leverkusen had 11 shots on target compared to Liverpool's 3 | Liverpool conceded 20 fouls to Leverkusen's 9 | 50/1 on Bayer winning 4-2

Quote unquote

"Leverkusen put on a great performance and you have to acknowledge that Ballack was decisive in the game. We need to work harder on some situations like our build-up play and perhaps at some stage we will need a couple of players who will bring a bit more to the team." **Gérard Houllier**

"As a defence we have taken a lot of credit but I think we have to look at ourselves today. The lads are devastated. We were all very upset in the dressing room after the game. It feels like we've lost a cup final, that's how sick we all are." **Jamie Carragher**

"There are two aspects of Liverpool's game that tend to be reliable: the finishing of Michael Owen and the steadiness of their back line. Last night, on an evening of extraordinary drama, both deserted them when they were most required." **Jon Brodkin** The Guardian

Man of the match Jamie Carragher **Atmosphere** Fantastic. Vocal support for the lads throughout was topped when Jari turned despair to delirium and 1-3 to 2-3. It all ended in tears but we'd done ourselves proud.

Saturday 13 April 2002	Premiership

Sunderland 0

Liverpool 1

Owen 55

Kick-off 5.35pm Stadium of Light **Att** 48,335 **Ref** D Gallagher

SUNDERLAND Sorensen, McCartney, Craddock (Kyle 80), Bjorklund, Williams, Kilbane, McCann, Reyna, McAteer, Phillips, Quinn SUBS Thirlwell, Butler, Haas, Macho BOOKED Reyna SENT OFF Reyna

LIVERPOOL Dudek, Carragher, Hyypia, Henchoz, Xavier, Gerrard, Hamann, Riise, Litmanen (Murphy 58), Anelka, Owen (Berger 90) SUBS Smicer, McAllister, Kirkland BOOKED Gerrard, Xavier.

Liverpool bounced back from the disappointment of Leverkusen with a victory that kept them firmly in the championship hunt. A slide-rule pass from Steven Gerrard and an exquisite lob on the run from Michael Owen was the decisive combination that separated the two sides. It was the perfect riposte from two players who had come in for some unfair criticism following the Champions League exit. That it was Owen's only chance in a game that rarely threatened to reach the excitement levels of midweek merely demonstrated that his predatory instincts had not, as widely held, deserted him. The second half was altogether more lively with Quinn going close for Sunderland before Owen broke the deadlock. Dudek denied the tall Irishman again on 66 minutes with an acrobatic save before Anelka almost got the goal his all-round play deserved. Some nifty foot-work bamboozled two defenders and only the width of a post denied the Frenchman a goal to equal Owen's opener. Dudek came to the rescue one final time when he made a great stop from Kevin Phillips. A sixth succes-sive Premiership win showed the character within the squad and secured the club a top-four place and Champions League football in 2002/03.

Vital stats
73% pass completion rate for Steven Gerrard | Liverpool enjoyed 51% of the possession | 6/1 on Liverpool winning 1-0

Quote unquote
"I said to the players before the game we were starting our next European campaign today. I always think a good team is one that has the capacity to bounce back after a bad result and I thought the players showed a lot of courage to do that today." **Gérard Houllier**

"You have just got to take your hat off to Owen and applaud that top-quality finish. Owen is a truly great player. With that sort of finishing touch, his pace and his goals record, he has got it all." **Joachim Bjorklund** Sunderland

Man of the match Steven Gerrard **Atmosphere** It could have been oh so different after Europe but from start to finish the travelling Kop was absolutely superb. Pushed Elland Road as best away day of year **League position** 2nd

---

Saturday 20 April 2002	Premiership

Liverpool 2   Derby County 0

Owen 16, 90

Kick-off 3pm Anfield **Att** 43,510 **Ref** M Riley
LIVERPOOL Dudek, Carragher, Henchoz, Hyypia, Riise, Gerrard, Hamann, Murphy (Litmanen 89), Smicer (Berger 82), Anelka (Heskey 65), Owen SUBS Xavier, Kirkland
DERBY COUNTY Oakes, Barton, Riggott, Higginbotham, Jackson, Kinkladze, Lee, Boertien, Morris, Christie, Strupar SUBS Zavagno, Elliott, Foletti, Evatt, Bolder BOOKED Boertien, Morris, Kinkladze

Arsenal held the advantage in the championship race, Manchester United were temporarily top after winning that morning but, as le Boss, the skip-per and anyone else within the club kept reminding the critics, Liverpool had demonstrated during the historic treble campaign their ability to string together do-or-die winning sequences. Two goals conceded in the last 990 minutes of Premiership football suggested the much-vaunted foundations underpinning Liverpool's 13-match unbeaten streak were

93

still in rude health. Michael Owen, who had captained England in mid-week, received the Ballon d'Or before the game and duly went on to notch the 25th and 26th goals of his most prolific season to date. They were strikes that maintained the pressure on Arsenal and also consigned Derby to relegation to the Nationwide League. Houllier started with a diamond formation in midfield with Vladimir Smicer operating at the apex, tucked in behind Anelka and Owen. And it almost paid immediate dividends as Smicer played Anelka in after less than a minute, but Andy Oakes made the first in a series of fine saves. Riise went close from a corner as Liverpool cranked up the pressure, before Owen opened his account with a fine individual effort following Smicer's pass. Anelka, who had a header blocked by Riggott before half time, must have thought the gods were conspiring against him when three second-half chances went begging through a mixture of profligacy and last-ditch defending. Murphy then sent a free-kick just over on 68 minutes before Owen eased his manager's stress levels with a goal in the 90th minute. Taking a long pass in his stride, Europe's best footballer rounded Andy Oakes in the Rams goal and slotted home from a tight angle. Liverpool went back to the top of the Premiership, for the time being at least.

Vital stats
Liverpool had 18 attempts on goal compared to Derby's 6 | The Reds made 28 tackles to Derby's 17 | 7/1 on Liverpool winning 2-0

Quote unquote
"We still feel we can win the title and that has got to be the next target. Arsenal are in with the best chance because they have the games in hand, but if they slip up then we are there waiting,and they know that. That brings pressures of its own." **Michael Owen**

"In big games Michael is always there. I was not disappointed by his game at Leverkusen andnor was he. He is mentally strong and has this confidence about himself and he is very sharp. Itis very unfair to have a go at him over missed chances." **Gérard Houllier**

"Time and time again, Liverpool knocked balls behind Derby, aware the pace of their strikers would get them in. With the number of situations they had they should have won by about seven." **Ron Atkinson** The Guardian

Man of the match Michael Owen **Atmosphere** Applause for Michael receiving his European footballer of the year award and a minute's silence for the 96 was magnificently observed by home and away fans. Then it all went quiet. Derby were relegated and applauded by both sets of supporters at the end **League position** 1st

The boy can't help it. Europe's player of the year has scored once more, against Derby County

Tottenham Hotspur 1   Liverpool 0

Poyet 41

Kick-off 12 noon White Hart Lane **Att** 36,017 **Ref** P Jones
TOTTENHAM HOTSPUR Keller, Taricco, Perry, Gardner, Thatcher, Anderton, Poyet, Clemence, Davies, Sheringham, Iversen SUBS Sullivan, Doherty, Leonhardsen, Etherington, Jackson
LIVERPOOL Dudek, Xavier (Berger 68), Henchoz, Hyypia, Carragher, Smicer, Murphy (Litmanen 82), Hamann, Riise, Owen, Heskey (Anelka 64) SUBS Kirkland, Wright BOOKED Riise

A game we should have won signalled the end of the title road. Jamie Redknapp was paraded on the pitch to the Spurs fans before the game and Liverpool could have done with his experience on a day when poor defending and an inability to turn pressure into goals saw the Reds troop off 1-0 down at half time. In truth, they had created enough chances in the first half an hour to have made the game safe. In the absence of the injured Gerrard, Smicer kept his place in the centre of the park, but a lacklustre performance expressed little about Liverpool's season – a porous backline, toothless attack and shortage of ideas in midfield betrayed the consistency that had seen the Reds go 14 games unbeaten in the League. Spurs were first to show and Sheringham spurned two good chances before Hyypia, Heskey and Riise all went agonisingly close. Having weathered the storm, Spurs managed to get a foothold which was quickly translated into a goal. Poyet ghosted into the box to capitalise on a fortunate ricochet and score from eight yards. After the break, Owen had two great chances in the space of a minute but they both went begging and when Hyypia failed to connect when the Spurs goal was begging, and Hamann drove an 89th-minute free-kick into the wall, all hopes of flying the champions flag outside Anfield evaporated. Ironically, Spurs had unwittingly done their North London rivals the biggest favour of all.

Vital stats
11/1 on Poyet scoring the first goal | Both teams had 5 shots on target

Quote unquote
"I think we could have done better. Especially in the second half, the effort was there but perhapswe lacked a bit of sparkle. Maybe there was a bit of nerves out there too." **Gérard Houllier**
"The most fight Liverpool showed was on the touchline, where Phil Thompson took on the massed ranks of the Tottenham bench as his frustrations boiled over." **Mark Fleming** Sunday Express

Man of the match Jamie Carragher **Atmosphere** We tried in the first half but it was half-hearted. They roused themselves for 10 minutes in the second half but that was about it **League position** 3rd

MAY 2002

Liverpool 4   Blackburn Rovers 3

Murphy 23, Anelka 39, Hyypia 52, Heskey 84   Duff 28, Cole 49, Jansen 80

Kick-off 8pm Anfield **Att** 40,663 **Ref** A Wiley

LIVERPOOL Dudek, Carragher, Henchoz, Hyypia, Riise, Murphy, Gerrard, Hamann (Xavier 81), Heskey, Anelka, Owen (Smicer 90) SUBS Arphexad, Barmby, McAllister BOOKED Gerrard.

BLACKBURN ROVERS Kelly, Curtis (Gillespie 60), Berg (Hughes 90), Short, Neill, Dunn, Tugay, Johansson, Duff, Cole, Jansen SUBS Yordi, Unsal, Miller BOOKED Duff

As Arsenal put the finishing touches to the League and Cup Double with a win at Old Trafford, Liverpool moved above United into second place with a dramatic victory over gallant Blackburn Rovers. Three times the Reds led and three times Rovers pegged them back before Emile Heskey grabbed the winner in the 84th minute, leaving Liverpool one game from their highest ever Premiership finish and, more importantly, automatic qualification to the Champions League. Steven Gerrard returned to the side, allowing Houllier to select Owen and Anelka upfront and pick Heskey on the left of midfield, a position from where he would be encouraged to join the front two. Danny Murphy impressed the watching England manager with the opening goal on 23 minutes before Damian Duff equalised following a slick interchange of passes with Matt Jansen and Henning Berg. On 39 minutes, Anelka strengthened his claim for a permanent move with a fine solo goal to restore Liverpool's lead. Andy Cole headed Rovers level on 49 minutes before the pendulum swung yet again, this time thanks to Hyypia's thumping header from a Murphy free-kick. With 10 minutes remaining substitute Keith Gillespie set up Matt Jansen for Blackburn's third equaliser and it appeared the chance to finish above United had gone. But with time running out, Heskey set off on a surging run, twisted away from his marker on the edge of the box and drilled a sweet low shot into the corner of Kelly's goal. The Kop sang One-nil To The Arsenal – small consolation for not being able to sing Champions at the end of a long, emotional season.

Vital stats

100/1 on Liverpool winning 4-3 | Liverpool had 17 attempts on goal | The Reds enjoyed 55% of the possession

Quote unquote

"We have our own cup final again on Saturday. It is a mark of our progress. I knew the score at Old Trafford with about 15 minutes to go. Now it will be a very exciting final at Anfield. We deserve it. You can't do any more, it's wonderful." **Gérard Houllier**

"You feel hard done by when you score three goals at Anfield and don't get a point. It's the story of our season. We scored good goals but conceded poor ones." **Graeme Souness** Blackburn Rovers manager

"Having conceded three goals, two of which were sloppy, you have to be disappointed, but we were tremendously attacking. We went for it with three strikers and we got our just rewards in the end." **Phil Thompson**

Man of the match Danny Murphy **Atmosphere** We ran the gamut of emotions for most of the evening but were treated to a great ending with noise to match. Plus a nod to what's going on down the road with a chorus of One-nil To The Arsenal..." **League position** 2nd

Saturday 11 May 2002   Premiership

Liverpool 5   Ipswich Town 0

Riise 13, 36, Owen 46, Smicer 57, Anelka 88

Kick-off 3pm Anfield **Att** 44,088 **Ref** S Dunn
LIVERPOOL Dudek, Xavier (Anelka 84), Henchoz, Hyypia, Carragher, Murphy (McAllister 82), Gerrard (Smicer 33), Hamann, Riise, Heskey, Owen SUBS Arphexad, Vignal
IPSWICH TOWN Marshall, Bramble, McGreal (Wilnis 39), Hreidarsson, Venus, Reuser, Holland, Miller, Clapham, D Bent (Stewart69), M Bent (Armstrong 82) SUBS Sereni, Peralta

An exciting, traumatic and ultimately successful season finished with the biggest home win of the season against a dispirited, disorganised and ultimately demoted Ipswich Town. In bright sunshine the Kop bade farewell to Gary McAllister, who was cheered every time he came out of the dugout to warm up, and celebrated another year of progress in some of the most trying circumstances imaginable. Ipswich needed to win to stand any chance of staying up and despite the backing of their vocal army of supporters, the game was up for them by half time. A superb double from John Arne Riise, capping a fine first season in the Premiership, illuminated an otherwise scrappy encounter. Any faint Ipswich hopes had were then snuffed out seconds after the restart when Michael Owen pounced on Titus Bramble's mistake to lob Marshall for the third. Substitute Smicer, who came on in the first half for the injured Gerrard, danced through some flimsy tackles to make it 4-0 before the hour and after Liverpool wasted a series of decent chances to go nap, Anelka did his chances of a big-money contract no harm with an excellent fifth two minutes from time. The biggest cheer of the afternoon was reserved for Gary Mac, who came on with nine minutes left, almost scored and was chaired off at the end. Second in the League, a points total high enough to have won the title almost any other year, automatic qualification for the Champions League, consigning United to their worst finish in the Premiership, and a fourth significant year-on-year improvement: these were all valid reasons to applaud the players and staff on their well-deserved lap of honour. Here's to going one better in 2002/03.

Vital stats

Liverpool had 17 attempts on goal to Ipswich's 11 | Liverpool conceded 12 fouls to Ipswich's 3 | This was Liverpool's 28th clean sheet of the season

Quote unquote

"Although Liverpool hold the Charity Shield and the Super Cup, those are events in football's social calendar rather than its true fixture list. Houllier cannot be at peace until the club secures the FA Barclaycard Premiership title and the main pleasure to be had on Saturday lay in anticipation of the season to come." **Kevin McCarra** The Times

"I can see a big push coming from here next season. When a team accumulates 80 points and people still say they haven't played well, you have to wonder what they might achieve if they do play well. The sort of ovation I got is usually reserved for proper Liverpool legends. Maybe I've had more of an impact than I thought." **Gary McAllister**

"When you take into account the trials and tribulations that we have been through as a club this season – losing Markus Babbel, my illness, Nicky Barmby being injured, Patrik Berger being injured too often for my taste – I can't find words to describe how remarkable their performance has been." **Gérard Houllier**

Man of the match John Arne Riise **Atmosphere** Final mosaic of the season and a party atmosphere as we scored five and secured second place. Gary McAllister was given his own show and it was smiles and songs all round during the lap of honour. Credit to the visitors for joining in **Final league position** 2nd

STATISTICS 2001/02
Opta Index's top-five players

Tackling

	Tackles	won
Dietmar Hamann	186	69.4%
Jamie Carragher	121	75.2%
Danny Murphy	106	73.6%
Sami Hyypia	105	69.5%
John Arne Riise	102	73.5%

Dribbling

	dribbles	success
John Arne Riise	174	70.3%
Danny Murphy	122	67.2%
Michael Owen	105	42.9%
Steven Gerrard	90	64.4%
Vladimir Smicer	85	71.8%

Passing

	passes	pass%
Dietmar Hamann	1,803	84.3%
Sami Hyypia	1,539	77.3%
Steven Gerrard	1,408	73.5%
Danny Murphy	1,382	74.2%
Jamie Carragher	1,380	75.7%

Crossing

	crosses	crosses
John Arne Riise	154	18.2%
Gary McAllister	103	26.2%
Danny Murphy	95	23.2%
Steven Gerrard	93	21.5%
Vladimir Smicer	61	29.5%

Shooting

	SHOTS	GOALS	GOALS TO SHOTS %	SHOOTING ACC %
Owen	63	19	30.2	60.3
Riise	48	7	14.6	54.2
Murphy	43	6	14.0	46.5
Heskey	42	9	21.4	45.2
Anelka	37	4	10.8	59.5

Disciplinary

	FOULS	YELLOW	REDS	POINTS
Heskey	66	3	0	75
Hamann	51	2	1	63
Carragher	32	7	0	53
Gerrard	31	5	1	52
Henchoz	28	4	0	40

Foul = 1pt, Yellow = 3pts, Red = 6pts

FA Barclaycard Premiership 2001/02

	P	W	D	L	F	A	GD	Pts
Arsenal	38	26	9	3	79	36	43	87
Liverpool	38	24	8	6	67	30	37	80
Manchester United	38	24	5	9	87	45	42	77
Newcastle United	38	21	8	9	74	52	22	71
Leeds United	38	18	12	8	53	37	16	66
Chelsea	38	17	13	8	66	38	28	64
West Ham United	38	15	8	15	48	57	-9	53
Aston Villa	38	12	14	12	46	47	-1	50
Tottenham Hotspur	38	14	8	16	49	53	-4	50
Blackburn Rovers	38	12	10	16	55	51	4	46
Southampton	38	12	9	17	46	54	-8	45
Middlesbrough	38	12	9	17	35	47	-12	45
Fulham	38	10	14	14	36	44	-8	44
Charlton Athletic	38	10	14	14	38	49	-11	44
Everton	38	11	10	17	45	57	-12	43
Bolton Wanderers	38	9	13	16	44	62	-18	40
Sunderland	38	10	10	18	29	51	-22	40
Ipswich Town	38	9	9	20	41	64	-23	36
Derby County	38	8	6	24	33	63	-30	30
Leicester City	38	5	13	20	30	64	-34	28

League Record 2000/01

POINTS 69

	W	D	L	F	A
Home	13	4	2	40	14
Away	7	5	7	31	25

League Record 2001/02

POINTS 80

	W	D	L	F	A
Home	12	5	2	33	14
Away	12	3	4	34	16

Liverpool scorers 2001/02

	Premiership	FA Cup	Worthington Cup	Champions League	Total
Michael Owen	19	2	0	5	26
Emile Heskey	9	0	0	4	13
Danny Murphy	6	0	0	2	8
John Arne Rise	7	0	0	0	7
Jari Litmanen	4	0	0	3	7
Nicolas Anelka	4	1	0	0	5
Sami Hyypia	3	0	0	2	5
Vladimir Smicer	4	0	0	1	5
Robbie Fowler	3	0	0	1	4
Steven Gerrard	3	0	0	1	4
Abel Xavier	1	0	0	1	2
Jamie Redknapp	1	0	0	1	2
Gary McAllister	0	0	1	0	1
Patrik Berger	1	0	0	0	1
Dietmar Hamann	1	0	0	0	1
Stephen Wright	0	0	0	1	1

Michael Owen scored one in the Charity Shield and one in the Uefa Super Cup. Gary McAllister scored one in the Charity Shield. John Arne Riise and Emile Heskey scored one each in the Uefa Super Cup

Liverpool crowds 2001/02

All Competitions	59 games	
Total 2,343,432	Average 39, 719	
Highest 75,362	Barcelona (a)	
Lowest 6,000	Boavista (a)	
Premiership	36 games	
Total 1, 508, 829	Average 41,912	
Total Home 824, 385	Average 45, 799	
Total Away 684, 444	Average 38, 025	
Highest Home 44,371	Everton	
Lowest Home 37,153	Fulham	
Highest Away 67,599	Man United	
Lowest Away 21,103	Fulham	
Champions League	16 games	
Total 561, 195	Average 35, 075	
Total Home 272, 409	Average 34, 051	
Total Away 288, 786	Average 30, 098	
Highest Home 42,454	Bayer Leverkusen	
Lowest Home 30,015	Boavista	
Highest Away 75,362	Barcelona	
Lowest Away 6,000	Boavista	

In and out of the box

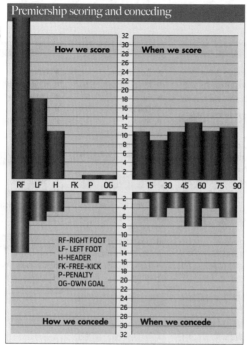

Premiership scoring and conceding

How we score

When we score

How we concede

When we concede

RF-RIGHT FOOT
LF- LEFT FOOT
H-HEADER
FK-FREE-KICK
P-PENALTY
OG-OWN GOAL

RF LF H FK P OG

15 30 45 60 75 90

Month by month

August

H	West Ham United	2-1
A	Bolton Wanderers	1-2
Monthly form ranking		**12th**

September

H	Aston Villa	1-3
A	Everton	3-1
H	Tottenham Hotspur	1-0
A	Newcastle United	2-0
Monthly form ranking		**4th**

October

H	Leeds United	1-1
A	Leicester City	4-1
A	Charlton Athletic	2-0
Monthly form ranking		**4th**

November

H	Manchester United	3-1
A	Blackburn Rovers	1-1
H	Sunderland	1-0
Monthly form ranking		**2nd**

December

A	Derby County	1-0
H	Middlesbrough	2-0
H	Fulham	0-0
A	Chelsea	0-4
H	Arsenal	1-2
A	Aston Villa	2-1
A	West Ham United	1-1
Monthly form ranking		**7th**

January

H	Bolton Wanderers	1-1
A	Southampton	0-2
A	Arsenal	1-1
H	Southampton	1-1
A	Manchester United	1-0
H	Leicester City	1-0
Monthly form ranking		**4th**

February

A	Leeds United	4-0
A	Ipswich Town	6-0
H	Everton	1-1
Monthly form ranking		**3rd**

March

A	Fulham	2-0
H	Newcastle United	3-0
A	Middlesbrough	2-1
H	Chelsea	1-0
H	Charlton Athletic	2-0
Monthly form ranking		**1st**

April

A	Sunderland	1-0
H	Derby County	2-0
A	Tottenham Hotspur	0-1
Monthly form ranking		**11th**

May

H	Blackburn Rovers	4-3
H	Ipswich Town	5-0
Monthly form ranking		**1st**

Premiership form 2001/02

	Points won	H	A
Ipswich Town	■ ■ ■ ■ ■ ■ ■	5-0	6-0
Newcastle United	■ ■ ■ ■ ■ ■	3-0	2-0
Leicester City	■ ■ ■ ■ ■ ■ ■	1-0	4-1
Charlton Athletic	■ ■ ■ ■ ■ ■	2-0	2-0
Manchester United	■ ■ ■ ■ ■ ■ ■	3-1	1-0
Middlesbrough	■ ■ ■ ■ ■ ■ ■	2-0	2-1
Derby County	■ ■ ■ ■ ■ ■ ■	2-0	1-0
Sunderland	■ ■ ■ ■ ■ ■	1-0	1-0
Leeds United	■ ■ ■ ■	1-1	4-0
Everton	■ ■ ■ ■	1-1	3-1
Fulham	■ ■ ■ ■	0-0	2-0
Blackburn Rovers	■ ■ ■ ■	4-3	1-1
West Ham United	■ ■ ■ ■	2-1	1-1
Tottenham Hotspur	■ ■ ■	1-0	0-1
Aston Villa	■ ■ ■	1-3	2-1
Chelsea	■ ■ ■	1-0	0-4
Arsenal	■	1-2	1-1
Bolton Wanderers	■	1-1	1-2
Southampton	■	1-1	0-2

Goals in Premiership fixtures 1992-2002

	Points	Goals	Average
Newcastle United	18	61	3.39
Southampton	20	66	3.30
Manchester City	10	31	3.10
Tottenham Hotspur	20	60	3.00
Bolton Wanderers	6	18	3.00
Charlton Athletic	6	18	3.00
Norwich City	6	18	3.00
Aston Villa	20	58	2.90
Leeds United	20	58	2.90
Nottingham Forest	10	29	2.90
Ipswich Town	8	23	2.88
Blackburn Rovers	14	39	2.79
Middlesbrough	14	39	2.79
Chelsea	20	55	2.75
Manchester United	20	55	2.75
Sheffield Wednesday	16	43	2.69
Derby County	12	30	2.50
QPR	8	20	2.50
Crystal Palace	6	15	2.50
Coventry City	18	44	2.44
Wimbledon	16	39	2.44
Everton	19	43	2.26
Leicester City	14	30	2.14
West Ham United	20	40	2.00
Arsenal	20	36	1.80
Sunderland	8	13	1.63

Does not include less than five Premiership games (Barnsley, Bradford City, Oldham Athletic, Swindon Town, Sheffield United and Watford)

THE CAST

THE CAST

First team squad | Reserves | Coaching staff | Academy

In less than four years in sole charge at Anfield, Gérard Houllier has systematically refreshed almost the entire squad from front to back. The departure of Jamie Redknapp towards the end of the 2001/2002 season symbolically spelt the end for the so-called Spice Boys, with Houllier having already dispensed with the likes of Fowler and McManaman. In their stead has come a steady stream of new faces, many of them unknowns in the Premiership and many from abroad. With finds of the calibre of Hyypia and Riise, Houllier has struck gold, although other pricey imports such as Djimi Traore and Bernard Diomede have yet to impress. And of course, the likes of Gerrard and Wright have graduated from the Academy during GH's tenure. Here, we run the rule over the entire Liverpool first team squad...

The goalkeepers

Jerzy Dudek

Born Rybaik, Poland 23.3.73
Height 6ft 1in **Weight** 12st 7lb
Previous clubs Sokol Tychy, Feyenoord (£4.85m, 31.8.01)
Debut 8.9.01 vs Aston Villa, Anfield PL 1-3
Appearances 49 **Goals** 0

109

Many people's choice as player of the season, Dudek arrived at Anfield on the same day as understudy Chris Kirkland, signalling the end of Sander

110

The big Pole in our goal, Jerzy Dudek, enjoyed a hugely successful first season at Liverpool

Westerveld's reign as Liverpool's number one. A Reds supporter since watching fellow countryman Zbiginew Boniek play for Juventus against Liverpool in the 1985 European Cup final, Dudek is the first Polish player to sign for the club.

"This is a wonderful club to be at," says Dudek, "and I always knew it was the right decision to come. In life you have to strive for higher things and I knew I couldn't turn down the opportunity. When the deal was done I was very happy." Less happy, but no less supportive of the new arrival, was Westerveld, who in a strange twist was on the same flight as the Pole when he came over to finalise the deal. Jerzy did not enjoy the best of starts, conceding three goals to Villa on his debut, but it was not long before his bravery, sure handling and quiet authority began to win over Kopites and further bolster the meanest defence in the land. His consistency makes it difficult to single out individual performances but decisive contributions away to West Ham, Barcelona and Fulham, and at home to Chelsea, were perhaps the pick of an outstanding first season at Anfield.

The son of a miner, Dudek was strongly linked with a move to Arsenal after impressing scouts across the Continent during the four years he spent at Feyenoord. Twice voted best keeper in Holland and congratulated by fellow celebrated custodian of the onion bag Pope John Paul II for winning Dutch player of the year, he was described as "the best goalkeeper I have seen in 30 years" by legendary Dutch coach Leo Beenhakker. His 26 clean sheets make it hard to argue, and suggest 'the big Pole in our goal' is on course to become the best Liverpool keeper since Ray Clemence.

Last season Appearances 49 **Goals** 0

Chris Kirkland

Born Leicester 2.5.81
Height 6ft 6in **Weight** 11st 7lb
Previous clubs Coventry City (£6m, 31.8.01)
Debut 9.10.01 vs Grimsby Town, Anfield WC 1-2
Appearances 4 **Goals** 0

Widely considered to be the future England number one, Chris Kirkland has impressed in the handful of first-team appearances he has made since joining Liverpool from Coventry City in August 2001. Like Dudek, he is a fan – he used to travel by coach from Hinckley to watch the Reds in action – and like the man ahead of him in the Anfield goalkeeping queue he did not enjoy the best of debuts, conceding two goals as Liverpool lost at home to Grimsby in the Worthington Cup.

"Even though Grimsby Town put us out I was so pleased to make my debut," says the England under-21 international. "It'd been a dream to play for Liverpool at Anfield and to run out in the shirt in front of the fans was a great moment." It was another four months before Kirkland got his next chance but when Dudek picked up a rare injury, the blond giant showed his maturity with solid showings home and away against Galatasaray in the Champions League and at home to Everton in the Premiership. "It's going to be hard to get into the side," admits Chris, "but I've signed a six-year contract so this is a long-term thing. Gérard Houllier has said he will make sure I am looked after. That means a lot." Gary McAllister, who first saw the youngster break through at Highfield Road, says "he could play for the club for the next 10 years." Our future, it seems, is in very safe, very large, hands.

Last season Appearances 4 Goals 0

Pegguy Arphexad

Born Guadeloupe 18.5.73
Height 6ft 2in **Weight** 14st 2lb
Previous clubs Racing Club Lens, Leicester City (free, 1.7.00)
Debut 1.11.00 vs Chelsea, Anfield WC 2-1
Appearances 6 Goals 0

After appearing in three of Liverpool's first four games last season, Arphexad was released on a month's loan to Portsmouth at the beginning of September. Unfortunately, injury limited his opportunities at Fratton Park and he returned north without having had the chance to impress.

Originally signed as cover for Sander Westerveld, the first player in the club's history to hail from Guadeloupe caught Gérard Houllier's eye with some penalty-saving heroics in Leicester's 1999/2000 Worthington Cup run, and again when he played a blinder in the Foxes' 2-0 win at Anfield in May that same season – a performance that contributed to Liverpool's failure to qualify for the Champions League. However, the signing of Dudek and Kirkland has relegated Arphexad to third in the pecking order at Anfield. Of his decision to take the plunge as a goalkeeper, Pegguy explains, "It was because of one our goalkeepers in Guadeloupe that I finally decided to try and make it as a keeper. His name was Gervais Geoeier, but we all just called him 'Piff'. He was very good and he used to wear bright and beautiful jerseys when he played. He became my idol and I simply wanted to be like him." So there you have it.

Last season Appearances 4 **Goals** 0

113

Pegguy became our first player from Guadeloupe. It's in the Caribbean, before you ask

The defence

Markus Babbel

Born Munich, Germany 8.9.72
Height 6ft 1in **Weight** 12st 13lb
Previous clubs Bayern Munich, SV Hamburg (on loan), Bayern Munich (free, 1.6.00)
Debut 19.8.00 vs Bradford City, Anfield PL 1-0
Appearances 66 **Goals** 6

After complaining of influenza-like symptoms during the away defeat to Bolton Wanderers in late August, Markus Babbel did not appear again for the first team all season. Indeed, it was not until December that Liverpool's Mr Consistency was diagnosed with Guillain Barre Syndrome, a disease that attacks the nervous system. Babbel lost his strength and 22lbs in weight and returned to Germany to begin a long, brave fightback against this rare, debilitating condition.

Fight back he did and after watching Liverpool's Champions League defeat in Leverkusen from the stands, Babbel made a welcome return to Melwood and training in April 2002 and even played 10 minutes of Thomas Helmer's testimonial against Bayern Munich in Germany at the start of May.

He made the right-back spot his own during the Treble-winning season and chipped in with some vital goals, not least against Everton at Goodison Park and in Dortmund against Alavés.

"It's great to be back at the best club in the world," says the former German international who won a host of domestic and European honours with his hometown club Bayern Munich before signing on a Bosman free transfer. "Now I want to breathe the special air at Anfield again. It's the best stadium in the world and we have the best fans in the world." Indeed, so committed is Babbel to the club that he turned his back on a huge pay rise at Munich to sign for the Reds and quit international football in order to concentrate on Liverpool.

There is no doubt that a player who starred for Germany in their victorious Euro 96 campaign would have added considerably to his 51 caps by now had he not decided to call time on his international career. German national coach Rudi Völler will be hoping Babbel might one day change his mind while Gérard Houllier is delighted to have the popular German all to himself. We look forward to his return this season.

Last season Appearances 6 **Goals** 0

Jamie Carragher

Born Bootle 28.1.78
Height 6ft 1in **Weight** 12st 10lb
Previous clubs Trainee
Debut 8.1.97 vs Middlesbrough, Riverside Stadium LC 1-2
Appearances 221 **Goals** 2

A member of Liverpool's 1996 FA Youth Cup-winning team, Jamie Carragher has emerged as a durable, highly prized player from Steve Heighway's conveyor belt of homegrown talent. Able to play across the back four or in midfield, the former England under-21 captain has proved versatility need not be a curse having forced himself into Sven Goran Erikson's full international set-up as a defender of some distinction.

After scoring on his full first-team debut at Anfield against Aston Villa in early 1997, Carragher made 20 starts during the 1998/99 campaign before establishing himself as a regular a season later. He has now made more first-team appearances than any other player at the club.

Though naturally right-sided, Carragher was first-choice left back during the Treble-winning season, scoring his only goal from the penalty spot in the Worthington Cup final shootout at Cardiff. His willingness to step forward when the heat was on and the aplomb with which he dispatched the kick, speaks volumes for a player who is Liverpool through and through. As he himself says, "There may be more skilful players in the squad, but no one can ever say I don't give 100 per cent."

Another consistently solid season pushed the player to the brink of a place in the World Cup squad, although he eventually missed due to a knee operation. But as Tord Grip said after Carragher won his second full England cap against Italy in November 2000, "Every game Jamie has played, even at left back with no left foot, he's good. He can play central defender, right or left back, or holding midfielder. He's a very useful player." Messrs Houllier and Thompson would certainly concur.

Last season Appearances 53 **Goals** 0

Vegard Heggem

Born Trondheim, Norway 13.7.75
Height 5ft 11in **Weight** 12st 2lb
Previous clubs Rennebu, Orkdal, Rosenborg (£3.5m, 21.7.98)
Debut 16.8.98 vs Southampton, The Dell PL 2-1
Appearances 65 **Goals** 3

Persistent hamstring problems have hampered the Norwegian international's progress since he became the first signing for the joint management team of Gérard Houllier and Roy Evans – he has played just four games in the last two years after impressing Anfield regulars with his effervescent, attacking displays in his first two seasons at the club.

A second operation on the troublesome hamstring in April 2002 left Heggem cautiously optimistic about being able to rejoin the first-team squad for pre-season training but after so many recent setbacks he is taking nothing for granted. At home at right back or right midfield, the nimble-footed Heggem is still fondly remembered for providing the cross for Michael Owen to score against Man United and for his wonderful display in a 4-1 win at St James' Park. He also scored on his international debut against world champions France.

Last season Appearances 0 **Goals** 0

Stephane Henchoz

Born Billens, Switzerland 7.9.74
Height 6ft 2in **Weight** 12st 8lb
Previous clubs Stade Payern, Bulle, Xamax Neuchatel, SV Hamburg, Blackburn Rovers (£3.5m, 3.6.99)
Debut 14.9.99 vs Hull City, Boothferry Park LC 5-1
Appearances 142 **Goals** 0

A regular leader in end-of-season 'unsung hero' polls, Stephane Henchoz is Liverpool's very own Swiss brick wall. Signed from Blackburn at the end of season 1998/99, after being voted the fans' player of the season, such is his contribution to the Reds defence that a rare absence through injury provokes collective anxiety among Kopites.

116

His partnership with Sami Hyypia bears comparison with any defensive pairing in the club's history. "We clicked very quickly," says Stephane. "You never know how a new pairing is going to develop until you try it and we were pleased with how we settled down together." While Hyypia is comfortable taking the ball into opposition territory, the ruddy-cheeked Henchoz is invariably the last line of defence. As the song lyrics state, 'When they attack, he's always back…'

There are few better athletes at the club and while he might sometimes look like he's blowing hard, his powers of recovery are excellent, unlike his goal-scoring record at Anfield – he has yet to open his account, hardly surprising given he rarely ventures into the opposition's half. But who cares when he makes comments like, "I'd do anything to stop the ball crossing the line?"

As Phil Thompson says, "If there is a block to be made in the area and you see a red shirt flying in to prevent a goal, you can be fairly sure it will have a no2 on the back of it. Head, foot, whatever it takes to prevent a goal." Just ask Thierry Henry. Henchoz twice foiled Arsenal with goalline clearances in the 2001 FA Cup final – and neither interception involved head or foot.

Now approaching 150 games for the Reds, Henchoz has played under Roy Hodgson three times during his career (Neuchatel, Switzerland and Blackburn) and gave up a business studies course to become a full-time professional. He has won more than 50 caps for Switzerland.

Last season Appearances 56 **Goals** 0

Sami Hyypia

Born Porvoo, Finland 7.10.73
Height 6ft 4in **Weight** 14st
Previous clubs MyPa-47, Willem II (£3m, 18.5.99)
Debut 7.8.99 vs Sheffield Wednesday, Hillsborough PL 2-1
Appearances 157 **Goals** 10

"Sami who?" enquired most Reds when the tall centre half was unveiled following his transfer from Willem II in May 1999. But just a few short weeks into what promises to be a legendary Anfield career, Kopites were drooling over the arrival of a long-awaited successor to Jocky Hansen's throne. As for Hansen, he puts him in the same class as Phil Thompson and Mark Lawrenson, "two of the greatest centre backs of all time."

The signing of the tall Finn was undoubtedly one of Gérard Houllier's shrewdest business deals, even if it did mean Hyypia putting his Champions League ambitions on hold for a couple of seasons. "I could have played in [the Champions League] a lot earlier had I stayed with my old club rather than joining the Reds," says Hyypia. "When I came to Liverpool we weren't even in the Uefa Cup so there was no European football at all. It was a sacrifice I made, but I did it because I knew when I signed that this club was going places and I wanted to be a part of that."

Hyypia's partnership with Stephane Henchoz now threatens to eclipse the memories of Hansen and Lawrenson and is the cornerstone on which the modern Liverpool side is built. Comfortable on the ball, powerful in the air and blessed with an almost intuitive ability to read the game, Hyypia is now widely regarded as one of Europe's top defenders. Remarkably, he played the entire Treble-winning season without picking up a single booking.

The Reds' most consistent performer in his first season at the club, he was made stand-in captain of the side in the absence of Jamie Redknapp and Robbie Fowler. The armband has proved something of a lucky charm with the imposing Finn leading out Liverpool for the victorious FA and Uefa Cup finals, Charity Shield and Super Cup – it is his aim to become Anfield's first foreign captain to lift the League title.

The natural choice as club captain following Jamie Redknapp's departure, the Finnish international has been tipped by assistant manager Phil Thompson to become one of the club's greatest leaders. And the plaudits continue – Hyypia was named in World Soccer magazine's 'best team in the world', and was voted the Liverpool Matchday Magazine's player of the year last term. Sami who? Sami Hyypia, that's who.

Oh Sami, Sami Hyypia, the mighty Finn

Last season Appearances 57 **Goals** 5

Djimi Traore

Born Laval, France 1.3.80
Height 6ft 3in **Weight** 12st 8lb
Previous clubs Laval (£500,000, 17.02.99)
Debut 14.9.99 vs Hull City, Boothferry Park LC 5-1
Appearances 15 **Goals** 0

Hailed as one of Europe's brightest prospects and coveted by the likes of Milan, PSG and Lazio when he signed for Liverpool, Djimi Traore spent last season furthering his football education on a year's loan at Lens, teaming up with former Treble-winning coach Patrice Bergues.

Houllier had such faith in Traore, a product of the French academy system, that he sanctioned the sale of Dominic Matteo to Leeds and turned down hefty bids from Blackburn Rovers and Fulham. Joe Corrigan made the French under-21 international captain of the reserve team and was rewarded with the FA Premier Reserve Championship North title trophy at the end of the player's first year.

Traore made his first-team debut in 1999/00 going on to earn 13 starts a season later, during which time the tall, ball-playing defender faced Lilian Thuram in a pre-season friendly against Parma and Patrick Vieira and Thierry Henry in the Premiership. All three sought him out for a post-match chat, which suggests they expect Djimi to fulfil his enormous promise by eventually joining them in the French national side.

Last season Appearances 1 **Goals** 0

Grégory Vignal

Born Montpellier, France 19.7.81
Height 5ft 11in **Weight** 12st 3lb
Previous clubs Montpellier (£500,000, 23.9.00)
Debut 6.1.01 vs Rotherham United, Anfield FAC 3-0
Appearances 16 **Goals** 0

The young French defender caught the eye when he came off the bench 119
at Goodison Park in 2001 and set off on a surging run before being brought down just inside the Everton half. From the resulting free-kick

Gary McAllister conjured up his unforgettable 44-yard winner and Liverpool's season was back on course for glory. It was a brief cameo appearance but vital nonetheless.

Signed from Montpellier where he had been converted from midfielder to combative defender, Vignal figured in tandem with John Arne Riise at the beginning of last season but a broken toe halted him in his tracks and he has struggled to get back into the first-team picture since.

An under-18 European Championship winner with France in 2000, he represented his country in the under-20 World Cup in Argentina a year later and has also been capped at under-21 level and played in the Toulon tournament. A dynamic performer who admits to getting a thrill each time he touches the This Is Anfield sign, Vignal is definitely one for the future.

Last season Appearances 9 **Goals** 0

Stephen Wright

Born Liverpool 8.12.80
Height 6ft **Weight** 12st 8lb
Previous clubs Trainee
Debut 29.11.00 vs Stoke City, Britannia Stadium LC 8-0
Appearances 21 **Goals** 1

In November 1998 Gérard Houllier took one look at Stephen Wright and Steven Gerrard and promoted them both to first-team training at Melwood. Within days, the Academy graduates were on a plane to Spain for the Uefa Cup tie with Celta Vigo. Wright went on loan to Crewe soon afterwards but a snapped ankle ligament saw him back at Anfield before he returned to Gresty Road to complete an impressive spell at left back.

Originally a midfielder, Wright was transformed by Steve Heighway's staff into a centre half and then a full back and it is here that he has played the majority of games for the first team. Fast, strong in the tackle and ever willing to join in when the team goes forward, Wright has all the makings of an Anfield cult hero, in the mould of a Joey Jones or Alan Kennedy. Certainly, his performances against the likes of Robert Pires, Ryan Giggs and Harry Kewell suggest he's unfazed by the prospect.

The former Evertonian played in the Fifa World Youth Championship in 1999 and was voted Liverpool's young player of the season in 2000/01.

Stephen Wright has graduated with honours from the Academy to the Champions League

Now, with England under-21 caps and Champions League experience, including a memorable goal against Borussia Dortmund at Anfield, under his belt, he will be pushing Markus Babbel and Jamie Carragher hard this season. "I've had a taste and I want more," he says. "I feel I've shown people what I can do now and I certainly don't feel I've let anyone down." The local lad, whose dad is a member of the physio staff at Melwood, is made of the Wright stuff indeed.

121

Last season Appearances 17 **Goals** 1

Abel Xavier

Born Nampula, Mozambique 30.11.72
Height 6ft 2in **Weight** 13st 6lb
Previous clubs Estrela Amadora, Benfica, Bari, Real Oviedo, PSV Eindhoven, Everton
(£800,000, 31.1.02)
Debut 9.2.02 vs Ipswich Town, Portman Road PL 6-0
Appearances 15 **Goals** 2

Undoubtedly the most bizarre creation ever to pull on the red of Liverpool, Abel Xavier clearly has little respect for convention. An approach to grooming that makes him resemble King Neptune crossed with a frost-bitten Santa Claus is merely the outward manifestation of Xavier's eccentric streak. A fine plus nine-month Uefa ban for manhandling an assistant referee in the 2000 European Championship semi-final against France, coupled with his willingness to run the gauntlet by jumping ship from Everton to join Liverpool, further underline the fact our Portuguese full back is nothing if not a one-off.

Xavier can play across the back four and has shown glimpses of the form that makes him a regular starter alongside Figo, Gomez and Rui Costa for the Portuguese national team. His desire to play European football and displeasure at only being offered a pay-as-you-play contract at Goodison enabled Houllier to land his man for a cut-price fee. He became only the second player after Nick Barmby to make the switch since 1958. A goal on his debut in the 6-0 win at Ipswich, plus his strike in the Champions League quarter-final at Bayer Leverkusen suggest he will add an attacking dimension to Liverpool's backline.

Last season Appearances 15 **Goals** 2

The midfield

Nick Barmby

Born Hull 11.2.74
Height 5ft 6in **Weight** 11st 4lb
Previous clubs Tottenham Hotspur, Middlesbrough, Everton (£6m, 18.07.00)
Debut 19.8.00 vs Bradford City, Anfield PL 1-0
Appearances 58 **Goals** 8

'He's red, he's white, he scored against the…' you know the rest. Barmby grew up supporting Liverpool but caused a storm of protest when he left Everton to make the short journey across Stanley Park in the close season of 2000. He then further sullied his reputation with our neighbours by scoring his first Liverpool goal against the Blues at Anfield.

"I was brought up watching some of the best footballers around and it's amazing to think I'm following in their footsteps," said Barmby at the end of a first season that also saw him become England's first choice on the left flank. Unfortunately, injury kept Barmby out of the FA Cup and Uefa Cup finals and he continued to suffer last season, having to undergo two ankle operations and deny rumours he was on his way out of the club after just a handful of appearances.

Fully fit and on top of his game, Barmby adds a different dimension to Liverpool's midfield with his elusive running and ability to link up with the front players. Eight goals in that first season showed the sort of promise that had seen the diminutive Barmby once hailed as the natural successor to Peter Beardsley.

Last season is one he will want to forget, meaning the boyhood Red now faces a battle to win back his place for both club and country.

Last season Appearances 12 **Goals** 0

Barmby is still to show his full promise

Patrik Berger

Born Prague, Czech Republic 10.11.73
Height 6ft 1in **Weight** 12st 8lb
Previous clubs Sparta Prague, Slavia Prague, Borussia Dortmund (£3.2m, 1.9.96)
Debut 7.9.96 vs Southampton, Anfield PL 2-1
Appearances 192 **Goals** 34

An Anfield favourite after bursting on to the scene with some swashbuckling displays in his first season at the club, Patrik Berger has suffered more than most with injuries in recent years. A knee problem sustained in the opening game of the 2000/01 season kept Paddy out for two months and his comeback was then cut short when the injury flared up again, depriving Liverpool of the midfielder for another five, frustrating months.

Signed soon after starring for the Czech Republic in their run to the final of Euro 96, Berger did return to figure in the glorious Treble run-in. First, he showed his class with a superb long ball to set up Michael Owen's winner against Arsenal in the FA Cup final and days later he came off the bench to help turn the tide in Dortmund. We all hoped it would be the start of a prolonged run in the side and a return to the form that made him such an instant hit.

Unfortunately, injury struck again and another operation ensured last season did not get going for Paddy until mid October 2001. Used mainly from the bench, he has struggled to recapture the dynamic thrust that characterised his first years at Anfield.

"He's a class player who scores vital, unique goals," says Phil Thompson of the man with the sweet left foot. His one goal last term was a typical thunderbolt from outside the box against Middlesbrough. Sadly, another injury that kept him out for nearly the whole of February and March, prevented him from adding to that tally.

Last season Appearances 31 **Goals** 1

Igor Biscan

Born Zagreb, Croatia 4.5.78
Height 6ft 3in **Weight** 12st 8lb
Previous clubs Samobor, Dinamo Zagreb (£5.5m, 7.12.00)
Debut 10.12.00 vs Ipswich Town, Anfield PL 0-1
Appearances 31 **Goals** 1

Pitched into his first game just three days after signing from Dinamo Zagreb, the rangy Igor Biscan impressed in an otherwise disappointing home defeat to Ipswich in December 2000. A week later, he looked equally assured in a famous win at Old Trafford and it appeared the gaffer's European scouting network had come up trumps again.

Hailed as one of Europe's finest youngsters, Igor was already a Croatia international and captain of Zagreb at just 22 years of age when the Reds saw off competition from Barcelona, Juventus and Milan for his signature. But as Igor soon found, reputations count for little at Anfield.

The depth of midfield talent coupled with the restriction on non-EU players in the squad has not helped the midfielder establish himself in the first team. But time is on his side and like many of the promising youngsters at Anfield, he knows Houllier always has an eye on the future.

Next season Igor will be looking to add to the single goal to his credit so far, a superb solo run and strike against Crystal Palace in the Worthington Cup semi-final second-leg victory at Anfield in 2001. "As far as I'm concerned my career here is just starting," he insists. "The fans definitely haven't seen the best of me yet – I just hope they will soon."

Last season Appearances 10 **Goals** 0

Croat Igor Biscan has time on his side

125

Bruno Cheyrou

Born Paris, France 10.5.78
Height 6ft **Weight** 12st 7lb
Previous clubs Racing Club Paris, Racing Club Lens, Lille (£3.7m, 16.5.02)
Debut n/a
Appearances 0 **Goals** 0

The left-sided midfielder was the first of Houllier's summer signings, joining from Lille where he'd enjoyed a fine season, including a stand-out equalizer at Old Trafford in the Champions League. He netted three goals in seven European fixtures, and 11 in the League, helping Lille to fifth place.

Bruno and his brother Benoit were introduced to the game by their grandfather, Jack Buzier. A football man through and through, Buzier spent seven years as president of Racing Club Paris and has compiled scrapbooks charting the boys' progress – and he will have been proud that Bruno was voted Lille's player of the season last year by the fans. Houllier visited Lille to run the rule over the attack-minded player, tipped for international honours, in a 1-0 win over PSG towards the end of last season. He wasted no time in finalising the deal once the French transfer window opened, beating a number of top European clubs to Cheyrou's signature, including French champions Lyon.
Last season Appearances 0 **Goals** 0

Salif Diao

Born Senegal 10.2.77
Height 6ft **Weight** 11st 6lb
Previous clubs Monaco, Sedan (£4.3m, 7.02)
Debut n/a
Appearances 0 **Goals** 0

The value of Houllier's scouting network was underlined by the performances of Salif Diao in the World Cup. The midfielder agreed terms with the club before travelling to the Far East, where his massive performance in Senegal's shock victory over holders France in the opening match, and an incident-packed display against Denmark – giving away a penalty, scoring a memorable goal and earning a red card – suggested his £4.3million transfer fee would have been higher after the finals.

Diao went to France at the age of 15 after graduating from Monaco's academy in Senegal. His progress was hampered by injury but since moving to Sedan, he has caught the eye of clubs across Europe. The defensive midfielder starred at the 2002 African Cup of Nations, and also helped steer Sedan to safety in France's le Championnat. "I used to say that even if a second division club in England came in for me I would go without thinking," he says. "The fact it is Liverpool is just magic." Diao, who signed on a five-year contract, played in France for six seasons and was known for his tough tackling, if not his goals, having never scored for any of his previous clubs. We look forward to that changing at Anfield.

Bernard Diomede

Born Saint-Doulchard, France 23.1.74
Height 5ft 6in **Weight** 11st
Previous clubs Auxerre (£3m, 8.6.00)
Debut 14.9.00 vs Rapid Bucharest, Stadionul Giulesti UC 1-0
Appearances 5 **Goals** 0

Having made an impressive Reds debut in the 1-0 Uefa Cup win over Rapid Bucharest in September 2000, Bernard Diomede has become one of Anfield's forgotten men. Injuries hampered his first season and he has not managed to force his way back into the first-team reckoning. He made a rare start in the club's Champions League qualifier against Haka last August but was anonymous thereafter.

Diomede plays wide and is capable of taunting defenders with the pace and close control that earned him a place in the 1998 French World Cup squad, yet he has struggled to impose himself after being reunited with his old national coach, Gérard Houllier. He scored freely for the reserves in his first season and appeared willing to remain patient for an opportunity of a run in the first team. "There's a grand plan in place at Anfield and I want to be part of it," he said. How long that is the case remains to be seen. 127
Last season Appearances 1 **Goals** 0

Steven Gerrard

Born Liverpool 30.5.80
Height 6ft 1in **Weight** 12st 6lb
Previous clubs Trainee
Debut 29.8.98 vs Blackburn Rovers, Anfield PL 2-0
Appearances 139 **Goals** 15

It's hard to know where to start when talking about a footballer who seems destined to rank alongside Duncan Edwards, Graeme Souness, Patrick Vieira and Roy Keane in the pantheon of great midfield generals. Stevie G possesses the qualities needed to become a Red legend. Speed, strength, vision, bravery and an eye for goal are just a few of the attributes the Huyton-raised battler has brought to bear on opponents since being spotted by Gérard Houllier as a precocious youngster bossing an under-19 game. The gaffer liked what he saw so much he instantly promoted Gerrard to the first-team squad.

Gerrard has not looked back. Crowned Liverpool's player of the season in 2000/01, an insatiable appetite for the game and unquenchable will to win were the catalysts in a campaign that saw Liverpool win three cups.

England recognition followed and expectations were duly raised but the mark of the man is that Gerrard rarely disappoints. He scores stunning goals – witness the long-range effort against Manchester United at Anfield or the sweetest of half volleys against Germany in Munich – he tackles like a beast and can run all day. Add to that his ability to pick out Michael Owen with laser accurate, long-range passes, a knack honed as the two came through the Anfield ranks together, and you can see why Houllier, Erikson and all Liverpool fans value him so highly.

So how good can he become? "Footballers can always get better," he says, "and very rarely can you say someone is the finished article. You can never say to yourself you've reached the peak of your game and I know for sure I'm a long, long way off anything like that yet."

If that's bad news for opponents, there's good news for Liverpool supporters. "I used to be a Liverpool fan watching the open-top parades and now I'm a part of that success," says Steven. "It means the world to me to play for this club. I would sign for the rest of my career if Liverpool want me to." Get that contract drawn up quickly.

Last season Appearances 45 **Goals** 4

Steven Gerrard looks set to boss the Liverpool midfield for years to come. Pure class

Dietmar Hamann

Born Waldsasson, Germany 27.8.73
Height 6ft 2in **Weight** 12st 9lb
Previous clubs Bayern Munich, Newcastle United (£8m, 27.7.99)
Debut 17.8.99 vs Sheffield Wednesday, Hillsborough PL 2-1
Appearances 131 **Goals** 5

Another outstanding season as the fulcrum of Liverpool's midfield has earned Didi the respect and affection of team-mates, coaching staff and fans alike. His understated style – breaking up opposition attacks, shielding the back four and redistributing the ball with a minimum of fuss – means he doesn't always grab the headlines but it ensures he is one of the first names on the team sheet.

Schooled at Bayern Munich under such luminaries as Franz Beckenbauer and Giovanni Trappatoni, Hamann won two Bundesliga titles, a German Cup and Uefa Cup before Dalglish tempted him to Newcastle and ended his nine-year association with Bayern. The Geordie fans voted him their player of the year at the end of his first and only season at St James' but Ruud Gullit's arrival gave Houllier the chance to swoop.

Arsenal, Fiorentina and Barcelona were also interested but Hamann had his heart "set on Liverpool.. A then club record £8million brought him to Anfield in July 1999 but a serious injury just 25 minutes into his debut robbed Houllier of an influential presence in his restructured midfield.

Despite an injury-marred first season, Didi quickly emerged as a pivotal, big-game player. His performances in the Uefa Cup run defined Houllier's new Liverpool and he was at his very best in the tumultuous victory over Roma. He finished the season with the best stats for tackles and completed passes and even managed to write his name into history with the last goal at Wembley in Germany's 1-0 victory over England.

In 2001/2002 he continued to exert the calming influence that has won over the sceptics and made him one of the club's most indispensable players. "I think we're on our way to bringing the glory days back here," he says, "and I want to be a major part of that." In that case, Real Madrid can put their cheque book away.

Last season Appearances 48 **Goals** 1

Danny Murphy

Born Chester 18.3.77
Height 5ft 9in **Weight** 12st 8lb
Previous clubs Crewe Alexandra (£3m, 15.7.97)
Debut 9.8.97 vs Wimbledon, Selhurst Park PL 1-1
Appearances 151 **Goals** 24

Another childhood Red, it took Danny Murphy time to win over the Anfield sceptics but his knack of scoring winning goals at Old Trafford certainly helped his cause. An all-action ball player with close control and the ability to create openings, Murphy had an excellent schooling under Dario Gradi at Crewe before being signed by Roy Evans in 1997.

It took him a couple of seasons to progress beyond the fringes of the first team and during one spell out of the side, he sought reassurances from the boss about his future. Houllier's encouraging words, coupled with a renewed desire to knuckle down, bore fruit and Murphy has been one of the revelations of the last two seasons, playing wide on the right or through the middle of the park. Goalscoring midfielders are a prized commodity and Murphy's six goals in 1999/00, 10 in the Treble campaign and eight last year have made him a first choice at club level and brought him to the attention of Sven Goran Erikson. He won his first cap against Sweden in November 2001 but his World Cup was cut short before the tournament had begun when he had to return home after breaking a bone in his foot.

"My priority has always been Liverpool," explains Danny. "They're the club I supported as a kid and to win things with them is a dream." As for the knockers? "The fans are entitled to their opinions. I got stick but in football you have to take these things on the chin." That's what the boss told him and that's exactly what Murphy did. Roll on Old Trafford.

Last season Appearances 56 **Goals** 8

John Arne Riise

Born Molde, Norway 24.9.80
Height 6ft **Weight** 12st 3lb
Previous clubs Aalesund, Monaco (£4.2m, 21.6.01)
Debut 12.8.01 vs Manchester United, Millennium Stadium CS 2-1
Appearances 56 **Goals** 8

Subject of the best new song at Anfield for some years, John Arne Riise's rocket-like free-kick past his former Monaco team-mate Fabian Barthez was guaranteed to secure his place in the hearts of the Anfield faithful. Originating in Anfield's pubs before the Spurs game and sung to the rafters after another thunderbolt at Newcastle, the song can be heard whenever Liverpool have a free-kick in range of Riise's left foot.

"I can never thank the fans enough for that chant," says Riise, "I love it." And Liverpudlians love the red-haired Norwegian with the explosive shot, dangerous long throw and searing pace. His incredible stamina, born out of a fitness regime that saw him spend the summer before he joined Monaco training 24 times a week, has served Liverpool well. Adding balance to the side with his qualities on the left, Riise looks equally comfortable at full back or wide left of midfield.

Liverpool beat Fulham and Leeds to land the Norwegian international and he made a great start, scoring in the Super Cup triumph over Bayern Munich at the Louis II stadium, home of his former club. He went on to make more appearances than any other player on the books last season, scoring some important goals and impressing everyone with the quality of his ball-striking. Hailed as the 'Norwegian Carlos' in France, Riise admits to injuring one of Barthez's fingers in shooting practice at Monaco.

"I just want to hit the ball as hard as possible," admitted John Arne

131

after his 68mph piledriver at Anfield against the reigning champions had brought him to the nation's attention.

"Roberto Carlos is my type of player, his shooting is just brilliant." If you were to ask the Real Madrid and Brazil full back for his opinion, we suspect the feeling just might be mutual.

Last season Appearances 56 **Goals** 8

John Arne Riise proved an instant hit at Anfield and an inspiration to the Kop songsmiths

Vladimir Smicer

Born Decin, Czech Republic 24.5.73
Height 5ft 10in **Weight** 11st 13lb
Previous clubs Slavia Prague, Lens (£4.6m, 21.6.99)
Debut 17.8.99 vs Sheffield Wednesday, Hillsborough PL 2-1
Appearances 109 **Goals** 13

After a first term at Anfield so cruelly ravaged by injury, Vladimir Smicer has slowly established his credentials as the team's supplier-in-chief. In the Treble-winning season, the nimble Czech international was headed only by David Beckham and Nol Solano in goal assists and frequently drew the praise of Houllier and Thompson for his selfless running and perceptive crossing.

Still something of an enigma to many Liverpool fans, Vlad took time to adjust to the pace of the English game but we are now starting to see the form that made him such a force for Lens and makes him such a goal scoring threat for his country. Returning with a vengeance last season, he scored five goals in total, finally emerging from the shadow of Steve McManaman, the player he was bought to replace, in the process.

After again missing the start of the campaign with injury, the tricky, two-footed midfielder was a regular throughout the second half of the 2001/02 season, tormenting opposing defences with his speedy dribbling and array of flicks and tricks. He scored some important goals too, including a memorable last-gasp volleyed winner against Chelsea at Anfield, but in truth he has yet to reproduce the goal-scoring touch that has made him so potent for his country.

Vlad has nevertheless settled in well at Liverpool, is popular with the rest of the squad and is greatly valued by the coaching staff, as Phil Thompson confirms. "He's one of the most creative players at the club, an extremely gifted individual who the other lads respond to well. He's really improved since he arrived and he can get even better."

Last season **Appearances** 35 **Goals** 5

The forwards

El Hadji Diouf

Born Dakar, Senegal 15.1.81
Height 5ft 11in **Weight** 11st 8lb
Previous clubs Sochaux, Rennes, Racing Club Lens (fee undisclosed 1.6.02)
Debut n/a
Appearances 0 **Goals** 0

Described by Gérard Houllier as 'a striker with real talent', El Hadji Diouf scored nine of the 14 goals that earned Senegal qualification for the 2002 World Cup – goalscoring feats that were enough to win him the title of African player of the year for 2001. They also made him a target for Valencia, until Houllier stepped in with a five-year contract.

Nicknamed the 'Serial Killer' for his composure in front of goal, he followed up a barren run in the African Cup of Nations, where Senegal finished runner-up after he missed in a shootout, with a remarkable performance against France in the first game of the World Cup. Playing as the sole front man against an experienced back four, Diouf caused no end of problems with his powerful running, deft touch and trickery.

Despite missing out on the title in the last game of 2001/02, Diouf enjoyed a productive season at Lens, scoring 10 goals, to add to the eight strikes he posted in his first season on loan from Rennes – the Brittany club, who were glad to get rid of him after he crashed a car while driving without a licence in 2000. His off-field problems continued when he later incurred the wrath of Lens after reporting back late from the Cup of Nations having stopped off en route to consult with a witch doctor. The nearest thing he'll get to that at Anfield will be a pint with Dr Fun.

"I know I am not always easy to deal with," Diouf admits of his hell-raising past. "I grew up in a ghetto in Senegal and learnt to fight for everything I wanted. I hate to be taken for a ride but I do respect people, and I crave that respect myself." If his performances in a red shirt match those for Senegal then he'll get plenty of respect at Liverpool.

Emile Heskey

Born Leicester 11.1.78
Height 6ft 1in **Weight** 13st
Previous clubs Leicester City (£11m, 10.3.00)
Debut 11.3.00 vs Sunderland, Anfield PL 1-1
Appearances 124 **Goals** 39

All those who doubt Emile Heskey's qualities as a striker should bear in mind their concerns are not shared by three of the game's leading managers – Martin O'Neill, Gérard Houllier and Sven Goran Erikson. Heskey might not score with the regularity of an Owen or Fowler but his contribution to the team, in both attack and defence, make him an integral part of Liverpool's present and future plans.

The retiring giant from Leicester is a player who thrives on confidence and it was in the middle of a long goal drought last season that a private chat with Gérard Houllier, then recovering from his heart operation, restored that elusive commodity. Heskey suddenly looked like the player Liverpool had paid a club record fee for – direct, muscular and capable of frightening the living daylights out of opposition defenders. A goal against Leicester, two against Leeds and another brace at Ipswich silenced the critics in style. And his decisive header against Roma in the Champions League was the perfect 'welcome home' present for the man who had put him back on track.

Emile Ivanhoe Heskey made his first-team debut for Leicester City as a 16-year-old and first partnered Michael Owen in England's under-18 European Championship team in France, finishing third. They've progressed to the point where their partnership is now first choice for both club and country. He ended his first full season at Anfield as second highest scorer behind Michael Owen with 22 goals and despite the barren run last season, he was again second leading marksman. His superb strikes against Bayern Munich in the Super Cup, Roma in the Champions League and the first at Leeds were the pick of the bunch.

"I can honestly say I never want to leave Liverpool," he says. "This is a great club with great players and great supporters. I feel at home at Anfield and I'd be happy to spend the rest of my career at Liverpool. I love it here." A man of few, but well-chosen, words.

Last season Appearances 56 **Goals** 14

Jari Litmanen

Born Lathis, Finland 20.2.71
Height 6ft **Weight** 12st 2lb
Previous clubs Reipas Lathi, HJK Helsinki, MyPa-47, Ajax, Barcelona (free 4.1.01)
Debut 13.1.01 vs Aston Villa, Villa Park PL 3-0
Appearances 43 **Goals** 9

The Liverpool no7 shirt has a permanent place in Jari Litmanen's heart. "Keegan and Dalglish were extra special to me because they played in my best position, just behind the main strikers," said Litmanen when he signed for the Reds in January 2001. "That is why the no7 shirt always had an attraction for me. It was something I always wanted to wear. I am more than happy to settle for 37 – anything with a 7 in it will do."

The Finn is a player many feel was born to play for Liverpool. Not only is he a walking encyclopaedia on all things Red – ask him the order of penalty takers in the 1984 European Cup final and he will ask you for a proper question – the way Jari plays betrays a childhood watching the great Liverpool teams on television. A superstar in his native Finland and worshipped at Ajax, where he spent seven years and played in two European Cup finals, Litmanen arrived on a free transfer from Barcelona after injury and the departure of Louis van Gaal left him frozen out of the first-team picture. The Nou Camp's loss was Liverpool's gain and despite the fact he has not been able to command a regular starting spot, Litmanen sprinkles magic whenever he appears in a red shirt.

A serious player and a serious individual, he shuns the limelight, preferring instead to plough his energies into refining a technique that has won admirers across Europe. The Finn can operate either as a withdrawn striker or an attacking midfielder, although he has tended to be used from the bench when Liverpool's passing game requires a lift. His use of the ball is never less than considered and while he lacks the pace of his chief striking rivals at the club, he possess one of the sharpest football brains in the business.

In addition to scoring goals and bringing the best out of the players around him, Litmanen has been voted Finnish player of the year eight times, had a postage stamp produced in his honour and a line of Barbie-style dolls made of him in Holland.

Last season Appearances 32 **Goals** 7

Michael Owen

Born Chester 14.12.79
Height 5ft 8in **Weight** 11st
Previous clubs Trainee
Debut 6.5.97 vs Wimbledon, Selhurst Park PL 1-2
Appearances 205 **Goals** 111

Those present at Selhurst Park on a warm May evening in 1997 knew they had seen the future. A 17-year-old Michael Owen came off the bench and scored on his debut to provide an illuminating ray of hope on an otherwise disappointing evening. It was a case of déjà vu a few months later when Liverpool opened the new campaign away to Wimbledon and Owen scored again, this time wrestling the ball from Danny Murphy to equalise from the spot.

Liverpool fans were instantly mesmerised by the kid's confidence and, above all, the pace that left opponents trailing in his wake. We have been watching in astonishment ever since as the boy who broke Ian Rush's schoolboy scoring record and found the back of the net on his debut appearance at every level, became a man. And while the weight of

137

The finest sight a Red can see, Michael Owen's just scored another goal. Hallelujah expectation might have weighed heavy on others it seems only to accelerate Michael's sprint towards immortality.

A scoring record for Liverpool that averages better than a goal every two games does not paint the complete picture. Perhaps more revealing is his knack of finding the net in the biggest games and against the best teams. He's done it for England, never more memorably than with the goal of the tournament in the 1998 World Cup and the hat-trick against Germany in Munich, and, of course, he has done it on countless occasions for Liverpool. Steve Heighway, his mentor as a youth, has spoken of a sixth sense telling him that Owen would pull something out of the fire for Liverpool in the 2001 FA Cup final.

Owen is one of only a few truly world-class players to come out of Britain in the last decade – being the first domestic-based player since Denis Law to be named European footballer of the year. A model professional, his all-round game has improved beyond recognition in the last two years. The variety of goals he scores, his new-found ability to link the play and his talismanic importance to the team make it no surprise that at just 22, he has already signed four contracts with the club. It is these qualities that persuaded Sven Goran Erikson to make him, in David Beckham's absence, the youngest England captain since Bobby Moore. How fitting. Like Moore, Michael Owen is an English football icon.

Last season Appearances 43 **Goals** 28

On the bench

Milan Baros

Born Ostrava, Czech Republic 28.10.81
Height 6ft **Weight** 11st 9lb
Previous clubs Banik Ostrava (£3.6m, 23.12.01)
Debut 13.3.02 vs Barcelona, Nou Camp CL 1-1
Appearances 1 **Goals** 0

Hailed as the 'Ostravan Maradona', Milan Baros was one of Europe's most coveted young stars when he signed for the Reds in December 2001. Blessed with strength, pace and an eye for goal, he scored on his full international debut against Belgium as a 19-year-old, and has already added three more for the Czech Republic. "He's a player with a great deal of ability and potential and I've no doubts he'll go on to prove what a top-class player he is for Liverpool in the coming years," says compatriot Vladimir Smicer.

Last season **Appearances** 1 **Goals** 0

Richie Partridge

Born Dublin 12.9.80
Height 5ft 8in **Weight** 10st 10lb
Previous clubs Trainee
Debut 29.11.00 vs Stoke City, Britannia Stadium LC 8-0
Appearances 1 **Goals** 0

The Dublin-born winger joined Liverpool as a 15-year-old and recovered from his initial homesickness to make excellent progress. He graduated to the first-team set-up in September 2000 after playing in Joe Corrigan's all-conquering reserve side and made his first and only first-team appearance to date in the 8-0 Worthington Cup romp away at Stoke City two months later. He went out on loan to Bristol Rovers in 2000/01 before returning last season to train with the first team at

Melwood and play for the reserves. The Republic of Ireland under-21 was rewarded with a new two-year contract.

Daniel Sjolund

Born Mariehamn, Finland 22.4.83
Height 5ft 11in **Weight** 12st
Previous clubs IFK Mariehamn, IF Brommapojakarna, West Ham (£1m, 30.11.00)
Debut n/a
Appearances 0 **Goals** 0

The junior member of Anfield's Finnish trio, Sjolund joined the club as part of the deal that took Rigobert Song to West Ham United 18 months ago. It was Houllier's second attempt to sign the under-21 international – Sjolund had already agreed terms with the Hammers when he was first approached by the Anfield staff. When his chance came a second time there were no doubts for the striker, another boyhood Liverpool fan. "Deep down I always hoped Liverpool would keep their interest in me," he says. "I came up to Anfield and had a look around. I spoke to the manager and he told me about the club. It was a very easy decision to make." An under-19 regular, Sjolund also scored two goals in four games for the reserves last term.

Le Boss

Gérard Houllier

Manager Joined Liverpool in 1998

"I love football. It is completely in my blood. I sleep football, I eat football and I drink football." The words could easily have been delivered in the Scottish twang of the Ayrshire mining belt but in fact came from the mouth of the man many believe is effecting an Anfield revolution to match that of the great Bill Shankly. And like Shankly's famous quote about football being more important than life or death, this declaration of faith, made on the eve of the Treble-winning 2000/01 season by Liverpool manager Gérard Houllier is now viewed through a lens coloured by subsequent events. The Frenchman's brush with death last season and his victorious return to the hot seat puts into perspective the drive, ambition and total dedication he applies to the job of restoring Liverpool Football Club to greatness.

The former French national-team coach and technical director is credited with establishing the national academy system that paved the way for French domination of the football world. Appointed as joint manager of Liverpool in July 1998 when he returned to a city where he had worked as a school teacher almost 30 years earlier, Houllier took sole charge when Roy Evans resigned in November 1998. He led the club to an unprecedented cup treble in his second full season in charge then added the Charity Shield, European Super Cup and a highest ever finish in the Premiership in his third. For a

The boss points the way to the future

141

man whose high standing within the game owes much to an ability to set out successful blueprints for the future, the pace of development at Anfield must be particularly pleasing.

Gérard Houllier is quite simply the man with the plan. On taking sole charge he set about turning Liverpool into a thoroughly modern, progressive club. Training methods have changed, Melwood is unrecognisable from the days in which Bob Paisley watched the action from his office while, in the words of Terry McDermott, "warming his hydraulics on the radiator", the legendary Boot Room has been replaced by The Bunker. And while Houllier came to the job with the same reforming zeal he used in making France the benchmark for footballing nations, there is still a healthy, if unpreoccupied, respect for Liverpool's past: "When each of my players wears the Liverpool shirt," says Houllier, "I expect him to die for it."

In a coaching career that has spanned almost 30 years, Houllier has built up a fund of knowledge and contacts almost unrivalled in the game. They allow him to keep abreast of the latest developments in tactics, coaching and facilities while also ensuring his antennae remains tuned to the emerging talent across the Continent. The formation of the Hyypia-Henchoz defensive axis perhaps says most about Houllier's ability to evaluate, visualise and realise. Houllier does not invite comparisons with Shankly, although his quote at the end of last season, "I like to make people happy" could almost have been lifted from the inscription at the base of the Shankly statue outside the Kop. Like Shankly, Houllier insists on bringing his influence to bear at all levels of the club and shares the great man's belief that Europe is the yardstick against which the club measures itself. The comparisons, you see, are inevitable.

Both men came to the job at a time of flux for the club, both demand total loyalty from those around them, impress the importance of hard work and instil passion into the men wearing the Liver Bird upon their chests, framed, in Houllier's case, within simple principles for success: respect, being a winner, putting the team first and being a professional, both on and off the pitch. Finally, like Shankly, and all great managers for that matter, Houllier has shown he can be ruthless when the development of the team demands it.

On returning to managerial duties following his five-month absence, Houllier mused, "People asked me if I would give up the game after my illness, but how can you give up something that is your life?" Such devotion has been matched by that of his army of supporters as witnessed by the Kop mosaic against Manchester United, the constant singing of his name while he was recovering from the heart operation and the avalanche of noise that greeted his unexpected return against Roma. They realise that in Houllier they have a man with a similar approach to delivering success as that of a certain Scot who walked into Anfield some 40 years before. Allez, allez indeed.

Gérard Houllier's career

1947	Born in Therouanne
1969	First visits Anfield with former head coach Patrice Bergues to watch the Reds beat Dundalk 10-0 in the Fairs Cup
1973	Appointed player-coach at Le Touquet
1974-76	Made youth coach at Arras
1976-82	Achieves two successive promotions with Noeux Les Mines
1982-85	Leads Lens to promotion and a Uefa Cup place
1985	Turns down approach from Spurs and takes job at Paris St Germain instead. Leads club to its first title a year later
1991	Considered by Liverpool board as a replacement for Kenny Dalglish
1988	Appointed assistant to national coach Michel Platini at French Football Federation
1990	Starts national and regional youth training programme in France
1992	Appointed French national coach. Resigns post after 17 games, the last of which sees France miss out on World Cup qualification when Bulgaria score three seconds before the whistle
1993	Appointed technical director of French Football Federation. "Aimé Jacquet knew he had a good squad at his disposal when he took over from me, and he said at the time he was going to keep the continuity and work in exactly the same way as me."
1996	Coaches France under-18 team to European Championship triumph
1998	Given special medal to mark his contribution to the French World Cup triumph
2001	Wins three trophies with Liverpool in his second full season in charge, followed by Charity Shield and Super Cup at the start of the next. Other awards include BBC Sport's coach of the year, World Soccer magazine's team of the year, World Soccer magazine's manager of the year 2001, Uefa.com coach of the year 2001, British Sports Writers Association team of the year and Merseyside sports personality of the year. Rushed to hospital for emergency heart surgery in October
2002	Returns to the bench for the emotional victory over Roma in the Champions League and leads club to its highest ever Premiership finish. Awarded honourary doctorate from Liverpool University and the Légion d'Honneur, France's highest civilian honour

Back-room Boys

From the generals working under Field Marshall Houllier in The Bunker
to the sergeants grooming the Michael Owens of tomorrow at The
Academy, we introduce the men who make Liverpool tick

Phil Thompson

Assistant manager Former club captain and player from 1971-83. Reserve-team coach
from 1986-92, rejoined Liverpool's back-room staff in 1998

'We love Pinocchio' became a popular reply to the tiresome jibes from
opposition fans last season, as our very own Mr Motivator, former
captain and one of the club's most decorated players, once again
demonstrated his leadership skills when Gérard Houllier was taken ill.
Thommo did a massive job for the club in the boss's absence, even
winning a couple of manager of the month awards in the process, playing
down his own contribution and refusing to claim the credit or to change
a successful formula. Passionate doesn't come close to describing his
attitude towards his job. "If people want to say I'm a young Ronnie
Moran then I'll take that as the biggest of compliments. I do shout but the
players often need to know during games that you're still with them.
Gérard knows what I'm like – I explained that right from the start. I think
we are chalk and cheese in that way, he's more calm, cool and calculated."
A frustrated fan and ex-player, Phil Thompson would walk across broken
glass for Liverpool FC. In 1981, he famously kidnapped the European
Cup and its velvet bag and drove it in the back of his Ford Capri to The
Falcon in Kirkby. Tremendous, as the man himself might say.

Sammy Lee

First-team coach Liverpool Player from 1977-86. Appointed reserve-team coach in 1994
and promoted to joint first-team coach in 1999

Another dyed-in-the-wool Liverpudlian, Sammy Lee rose through the
ranks and eventually displaced Jimmy Case on the right side of midfield.
He went on to win three league titles, two European Cups and three

League Cups in a distinguished playing career for the Reds. In 1986 he left the club to join QPR before enjoying spells with Osasuna in Spain, Bolton and Southampton. He scored on his full England debut against Greece and was a member of the under-21 European Championship-winning side. Appointed reserve-team coach under Roy Evans, Lee endured something of a torrid baptism before earning his spurs with a Pontins League title. Houllier promoted Sammy to joint first-team coach alongside Patrice Bergues and he is now considered one of the country's top young coaches. He's also worked with the England under-21s and was in 2001 invited to work within the full England set-up by Sven Goran Erikson. For the uninitiated, he's the small plump one leading the pre-match warm-ups.

Jacques Crevoisier

First-team coach French Football Federation coach from 1988-2000. Joined the club in 2001.

A youth coach with the French Football Federation for 12 years, Crevoisier arrived at Anfield in 2001 to replace Lens-bound Patrice Bergues. After leading the French under-18s to European Championship victory, the 54-year-old spent 12 months working with the Uefa technical department, focusing on the Champions League and drawing up dossiers on the best teams in Europe. He has PhDs in psychology and physical education and Houllier expressed his delight at being able to recruit such a high-calibre replacement for Bergues. The pair worked together in 1996 when Crevoisier was Houllier's assistant in another victorious under-18 European Championship campaign. "I have lots of things I want to give to Liverpool," says Jacques, "and hopefully I'll be able to do that."

Joe Corrigan

Reserve-team and goalkeeping coach Joined the club in 1994

146 A fine goalkeeper, Joe Corrigan would have won many more England caps had he been around at a different time to Ray Clemence and Peter Shilton. After a distinguished playing career at Manchester City and

Brighton, Corrigan worked on a part-time basis with a few clubs before being offered the chance to become Liverpool's first full-time goalkeeping coach. He was subsequently handed the responsibility of managing the reserve team and after leading the side to a runner-up spot in the Pontins League in his first full season, he landed the FA Premier Reserve Team (North) title in 2000/01. It was the club's first such honour in a decade.

Steve Heighway's emphasis on educating his Academy prospects the right way has paid off

Steve Heighway

Academy director Liverpool player from 1970-81. Became youth-development officer in the 1980s

The man who supplied the crosses for Kevin Keegan, John Toshack, Kenny Dalglish et al over the course of a glittering 10-year playing career is now responsible for supplying the first team with a steady stream of homegrown talent. Director of Liverpool's much vaunted academy, Steve Heighway and his dedicated staff have been responsible for nurturing the likes of Steve McManaman, Robbie Fowler, Dominic Matteo, Jamie

Carragher, Michael Owen, David Thompson, Steven Gerrard and Stephen Wright. He has been in charge of the youth programme since 1989, coaching the youth team to the club's first FA Youth Cup triumph in 1996, and has overseen the conversion from the club's centre of excellence to a purpose-built academy in Kirkby with a staff of 20.

"I would always hope we're doing a good enough job here to unearth players, on a reasonably regular basis, the first team can use," says the man who won five league titles, two European Cups, two Uefa Cups and an FA Cup in his Anfield playing days. Highly protective of his young charges and determined to give them a proper education in both football and life, Heighway is one of the most important men at the club.

Hughie McAuley

Assistant academy director / under-19 coach Joined the club full time in 1990

A member of Heighway's academy inner circle, McAuley spent three years working part time for the club's youth set-up before being offered a full-time position in 1990. His main task is coaching the under-19s but in the course of an average week he will run an eye over all 180 players at the academy. "Our aim is for at least three or four players each season to make the jump from academy league football to the reserves and then maybe into the first-team squad," says McAuley. "It's nice for a big club to have its fair share of local-born players because it pleases the supporters and gives credibility to the youth set-up."

Dave Shannon

Assistant academy director / Under-17 coach Played for Sunderland and Stockport. Joined the club full time in 1998

When the call came from Kenny Dalglish in 1986 Shannon didn't think twice about accepting the offer of scouting work from the club he supported as a boy. Over the next 12 years he became an integral part of the youth and academy set-up and was offered a full-time post in 1998/99 coaching the under-17s. Last season's vintage won the under-17 league.

Alex Miller

Director of scouting Joined the club in 1999

In a typical European week Miller, who organises and oversees the entire scouting network, will clock up more air miles than the average pilot. Saturdays are spent watching an English game, Sundays taken up scouting possible European transfer targets. He's back at home on Monday then off again Tuesday and Wednesday to watch the Champions League, take in a Uefa game on Thursday and return home Friday to study the videos and make his recommendations. "We have a network of people across the world, people we trust and from whom we can find our information," says the man appointed by the boss in December 1999.

Ron Yeats

Chief scout Player and club captain from 1961-71. Rejoined Liverpool in 1986

Signed in 1961 to lead Liverpool into a brave new era, Yeats was the player Bill Shankly famously invited pressmen to 'walk around' when he was unveiled at Anfield. The Aberdeen-born giant captained Liverpool to two league titles and a first-ever FA Cup triumph in 1965. After becoming player, assistant manager, then manager of Tranmere Rovers, Yeats returned to Anfield as chief scout where he has worked under four different managers. He now looks after the British side of the scouting operation, compiling reports on forthcoming opponents and coordinating the club's network of 15 professional scouts.

Mark Waller

Club doctor Joined the club in 1993.

Northampton-born Mark Waller moved to Liverpool in 1977 and has been the club's doctor for the last eight years, overseeing a substantial overhaul of Anfield's medical facilities and compiling a study on injuries. He was appointed England under-21 team doctor in 2000.

149

Dave Galley

Physiotherapist Joined the club in the 1999

One of the top physios in the game, Dave Galley knows all about injuries after his own playing career was cut short as an 18-year-old. He worked part time with Port Vale before spells at Fulham, Luton and Sheffield Wednesday where he combined his club duties with the England under-21 set-up. He joined Liverpool in 1999.

Mark Browes

Assistant physiotherapist Joined the club in 2001

Recruited last year as number two to Dave Galley, Browes is a former non-league centre forward who works out of Melwood helping injured players back to full fitness. He was previously with QPR and Aylesbury.

Gary Armer

Masseur Joined the club in 1998

Liverpool's first full-time masseur joined from Burnley in 1998 and is an integral part of Gérard Houllier's staff. The demands of the modern game mean Armer's healing hands are required to loosen hamstrings and soothe aching muscles on a daily basis.

Graham Carter

Kit manager Joined the club in the 1970s as the players coach driver

Liverpool fan Graham Carter drove the team coach before being employed full-time as the club's kit manager.

Producing the stars of tomorrow

In the last few years Michael Owen, Steven Gerrard, Jamie Carragher and Stephen Wright have all graduated from Liverpool's prolific youth system and the Reds' state-of-the-art academy in Kirkby now ranks alongside any in the world. The facility, which opened in 1998 at a cost of around £13million, was inspired partly by the famous Ajax Academy in Amsterdam. Before plans were finalised, club representatives inspected youth facilities at numerous clubs abroad, and Gérard Houllier introduced many of the ideas that had made the renowned Clarefontaine Academy in France such a success. The site, set in 45 acres just off The Liverpool Way in Kirkby, has an indoor playing hall with a synthetic pitch, 13 outdoor pitches, a weights room, physiotherapy pool and medical centre.

The Academy takes on the best local players at the age of nine and runs sides in 10 age groups, with around 200 boys getting regular two-hour training sessions. When they turn 16 the top youngsters are offered full-time places with the aim that some will graduate at the age of 21 to the first team, while many more will go on to become professional players elsewhere. In addition to producing polished footballers, the Academy aims to ensure the majority of boys who do not make the grade leave the club with academic qualifications to help them get jobs.

Academy director Steve Heighway, Liverpool's legendary winger from the 1970s, is widely regarded as one of the best youth coaches in the business. He's assisted by key men of the various age groups; John Owens (who takes the younger kids), Dave Shannon (under-17s) and Hughie McAuley (under-19s). At under-19 level, several of the better players should be crossing over to make appearances for the Liverpool reserve side, coached by Joe Corrigan. The best of these get the call to train with the first team at Melwood before, they hope, arriving at the Holy Grail of a Liverpool first-team squad number.

Liverpool under-19s

Hughie McAuley's team saw off the likes of Manchester United to become regional Academy Champions in 2002. The under-19s then made it to the final of the national academy play-offs, where they were defeated by a classy Arsenal side. This feat was made all the more impressive by the fact that key players such as Neil Mellor and John Welsh missed several key games after being called up by the reserves.

Players to watch

Neil Mellor U19s games 26 goals 27 | Reserves games 18 goals 19

The son of former Manchester City player Ian Mellor, Neil is a strong forward with an extraordinary record for finding the net, averaging more than a goal a game this season in the process of top scoring for the under-19s and the reserves. He signed a new contract near the end of last season.

John Welsh U19s games 27 goals 9 | Reserves games 15 goals 4

A bustling, all-action midfielder John, like Steven Gerrard, can pass, tackle and score goals. An independent website recently nominated the young Scouser as one of the most promising 20 youngsters in world football.

John Otsemobor U19s games 14 goals 0 | Reserves games 6 goals 0

Liverpool-born Otsemobor has made rapid progress at the Academy. He is a fast, strong centre half who has been capped for England at under-19 level.

Liverpool under-17s

Last year's under-17s side, coached by Dave Shannon, went through the entire season unbeaten. After winning their regional league by a distance, the side progressed to a national play-off against Leicester City, Sheffield United and Reading but did not qualify for the next round.

Players to watch

Jason Massie U17s games 22 goals 18

The forward from Rainhill, Merseyside is the side's main goal getter. He has impressed with his awareness and ability to bring others into the game.

Mark Smyth U17s games 25 goals 16

Another free-scoring forward, the Woolton lad can also play out wide and has been capped for England at under-17 level.

Steven Vaughan U17 games 25 goals 0

The team captain, Vaughan is another England international who is equally comfortable on the left or right of defence.

THE EX-FILES

THE EX-FILES

Close-season departures | Departures last season | Other Reds still playing |
Reds managing and coaching | Obituaries

For most players, the leaving of Liverpool represents stepping onto a footballing escalator marked 'down'. Although many of those released in the last 12 months are still near the top of their profession, a peruse through the list of those that didn't quite make the grade, and what they have achieved since, underlines why players want to stay at Anfield for as long as they can. While it might be a cold, hard world outside the Shankly Gates, former Liverpool players can always expect a warm welcome when they return...

Close-season departures

Nicolas Anelka

Forward
Appearances 22 **Goals** 5
Signed from Paris St Germain December 2001 (loan)
Left for Manchester City May 2002 (£13m).

Signed on loan from Paris St Germain in December 2001, Nicolas Anelka arrived at Anfield looking to revive his flagging international fortunes in time for the World Cup. The Frenchman, who had fallen out with his employers at Arsenal, Real Madrid and PSG, came with his fair share of baggage but he knuckled down and showed no sign of the histrionics that made him so unpopular elsewhere. The sale of Robbie Fowler to Leeds and an injury to Michael Owen meant striking cover was a priority and

155

in typically canny fashion, Le Boss weighed up the pros and cons before figuring a deal until the end of the season, with an option to buy. Despite some excellent displays the goals did not flow as they did during his lethal last season at Arsenal and French coach Roger Lemerre omitted him from the squad that unsuccessfully defended the World Cup. After agreeing personal terms, Houllier then surprised many, not least the player himself, by deciding not to make the move permanent. Kevin Keegan was only too pleased to step in and take the enigma to Maine Road.

Last season Appearances 22 Goals 5

John Miles

Midfield
Appearances 0 **Goals** 0
Clubs Trainee
Left out of contract

A self-confessed 'massive Liverpool fan', John started on Everton's books but joined the Reds as a 14-year-old. A midfielder with an eye for goal, he performed well for the reserves and was promoted to the first-team squad last season. After failing to force his way into Gérard Houllier's plans, he was released at the end of the season when his contract expired.

Last season Appearances 0 Goals 0

Jorgen Nielsen

Goalkeeper
Appearances 0 **Goals** 0
Signed Hvidovre (1.3.97)
Left out of contract

The Danish stopper arrived on the recommendation of former Liverpool reserve keeper Michael Stensgaard. Despite appearing in numerous pre-season tour games, Nielsen never played for the first team and was on the bench for 23 matches during 1999/2000 when he also spent time on loan at Wolverhampton Wanderers. Demoted to fourth-choice keeper when Dudek and Kirkland arrived, he was also released at the end of last season.

Last season Appearances 0 Goals 0

Departures last season

Patrice Bergues

First-team coach
Arrived from the French Football Federation
Left to become director of football at RC Lens June 2001

Gérard Houllier met his longtime right-hand man at school and Bergues played as a semi-pro midfielder under Houllier at Noeux-les-Mines, before following the main man to Lens and later the French Football Federation. When Houllier arrived at Anfield in 1998 he immediately sent for the quiet, likeable Bergues to join his back-room staff and he played a major part in the club's historic treble before taking up an offer to become director of football at Lens in the summer of 2001.

Last season the club narrowly missed out on winning the French championship

Robbie Fowler

Forward .
Appearances 330 **Goals** 171
Youth team
Left for Leeds United November 2001 (£11m)

Robbie Fowler's departure split Liverpool fans down the middle. There were those who felt selling our finest striker since Ian Rush to one of the club's chief rivals was a decision bordering on the criminal, and others who felt he was past his best, his reflexes dulled by niggling injuries. What cannot be disputed is his place alongside Liverpool's greatest strikers. He lies sixth on the all-time list and would surely have overtaken Kenny Dalglish had he stayed. Fowler reached his first 100 goals in just 165 games and went on to score 10 hat-tricks, his last away to Leicester City in October 2001. By that time, he had slipped from being the first name on the team sheet to third choice behind Owen and Heskey. For those who witnessed his meteoric rise from youth-team marksman to consummate striker, this is still hard to fathom. More than just a striker, 'God' as he was known, epitomised Liverpool FC. Kopites could relate to him – he was no angel but more than anyone, the lad from Toxteth with the divine gift of finding the net represented his people. He stood up for the dockers, belly-flopped on a steward after scoring in the FA Cup semi against Wycombe, grabbed a hat-trick in four minutes against Arsenal, sniffed the touchline in front of seething Evertonians and was responsible for moments of pure joy, not least his sublime goal against Alavés in Dortmund. For all these reasons and more, Robbie Fowler will always be one of us. We look forward to giving him a hero's welcome when he returns with Leeds.

Last season Appearances 16 **Goals** 4

Gary McAllister

Midfielder
Appearances 86 **Goals** 9
Signed from Coventry City July 2000 (free transfer)
Left to become player-manager at Coventry City May 2002 (free transfer)

The rapturous ovation Gary Mac received when he came on as sub in the last game of the season against Ipswich demonstrated the impact he made during his short spell at the club. Signed by Houllier to provide guile and experience to the midfield, most observers expected him to be used as little more than cover for Gerrard, Hamann and co. How wrong they were, because without the goals and influence of the stylish former Scotland international in the latter stages of 2000/01, it is doubtful the Reds would have tasted such success. Bald, old but undeniably worth his weight in gold, McAllister became an Anfield legend when he embarked on a five-game scoring streak that encompassed a 44-yard injury-time winner at Goodison. A semi-final clincher against Barcelona and a penalty in the Uefa Cup final in which he also won man of the match, a contribution later recognised when he was shortlisted for the title as Europe's most valuable player.

Last season Appearances 37 **Goals** 2

Alan Navarro

Defender
Appearances 0 **Goals** 0
Youth team
Left for Tranmere Rovers January 2002 (£225,000)

The local born defender-cum-midfielder graduated from the Academy to train with the first-team in September 2000. But after two loan spells at Crewe, he still failed to break into the first team and was transferred.

Last season Appearances 0 goals 0

Jamie Redknapp

Midfielder
Appearances 308 **Goals** 41
Signed from Bournemouth January 1991 (£350,000)
Left for Tottenham Hotspur April 2002 (free transfer)

Redknapp's last years at Anfield are not ones he would want to remember. He made only eight appearances last season after more than a year out with injury, his last outing as a sub in the Champions League against Borussia Dortmund, three days after scoring on his last Premiership start at Charlton. A model professional in his 11 years at the club, despite occasionally being the target for disgruntled fans during the team's fallow years, he never disguised his love for Liverpool. Kenny Dalglish's last major signing, from his dad's club Bournemouth, Jamie broke into the first team under Graeme Souness, the youngest player ever to represent the Reds in Europe. He won his first England cap under Terry Venables and helped turn the Euro 96 match against Scotland before injury hit. Perhaps the most telling insight into his popularity came at Cardiff in May 2001 when as captain he was invited to lift the FA Cup alongside Robbie Fowler.

Last season Appearances 8 **Goals** 2

Sander Westerveld

Goalkeeper
Appearances 103 **Goals** 0
Signed from Vitesse Arnhem June 1999 (£4m)
Left for Real Sociedad December 2001 (£3.49m)

After a superb display in the Charity Shield it was unfortunate the Dutch number two's Anfield career ended in such ignominious circumstances – the soft goal he conceded at Bolton, on the back of a series of costly errors, the final straw for Houllier. It was also suggested he had revealed dressing-room secrets, allegations he furiously denied. Westerveld was undeniably a fine shot stopper but lacked authority in claiming crosses. He was nevertheless an integral part of the Treble-winning side, his finest hour the Worthington Cup final penalty shootout against Birmingham. He also famously lamped Francis Jeffers in the derby.

Last season Appearances 3 **Goals** 0

Christian Ziege

Defender
Appearances 32 **Goals** 2
Signed from Middlesbrough August 2000 (£5.5m)
Left for Tottenham Hotspur July 2001 (£4m)

After one of the most protracted transfers in Anfield history – one that went all the way to the High Court – the classy left-sided utility player could not even win a place among the seven substitutes for the Uefa Cup final. Injury kept him out of the first four games of the 2000/01 season but Ziege won a first-team place before injury and loss of form consigned him to the bench. He then blotted his copybook by claiming he had not moved to Anfield to improve his English, a reference to having to play in the reserves. The ex Bayern Munich and Milan player with the lazy gait left for Tottenham where regular play won him a place in Germany's World Cup squad.

Last season Appearances 0 **Goals** 0

Other Reds still playing

They not have made the grade at Anfield but having been schooled in the Liverpool way, they still have a lot to offer elsewhere...

Ian Armstrong

Midfielder
Appearances 0 **Goals** 0
Youth team
Left for Port Vale 2001 (free transfer)

Prolific for Liverpool's Under-19s in 1999/00, he signed for Port Vale on a free in June 2001. He made 20 league starts last season, scoring three goals.

Phil Babb

Defender
Appearances 170 **Goals** 1
Signed from Coventry City, 1994 (£3.6m)
Left for Sporting Lisbon, 2000 (free transfer)

Babb starred for the Republic of Ireland at the 1994 World Cup, secured a £3.6million move to Liverpool and made 172 appearances in six years for the Reds before seemingly vanishing. He helped Sporting Lisbon to the Portuguese title last term before joining Sunderland.

Stig Inge Bjornebye

Defender
Appearances 184 **Goals** 4
Signed from Rosenborg, 1992 (£600,000)
Left for Blackburn Rovers, 2000 (£300,000)

A sickening training ground injury that resulted in a fractured eye socket provided a gloomy end to an otherwise solid season for Stig at Blackburn. The Norwegian, who spent nearly eight years at Anfield, will pass the career milestone of 300 first games when he returns.

David Burrows

Defender
Appearances 180 **Goals** 3
Signed from West Brom, 1988 (£500,000)
Left for West Ham, 1993 (swap deal involving Julian Dicks)
Now at Sheffield Wednesday

A Dalglish signing from West Brom, 'Bugsy' Borrows was an uncompromising left back who played 180 times for the club before being transferred to West Ham. He subsequently had spells at Everton,

Coventry and Birmingham City before signing for his current club Sheffield Wednesday, in March 2002.

Titi Camara

Forward
Appearances 37 **Goals** 10
Signed from Marseilles, 1998 (£2.6m)
Left for West Ham United, 2000 (£2.2m)

Aboubacar, or Titi for short, was an entertaining revelation during his short spell at Anfield. A combination of elastic-limbed ball skills and wild shooting made him the most unpredictable of Houllier's signings but he still chipped in with some useful goals in the gaffer's first full season in charge. Unfortunately, eight appearances in nearly two years at West Ham suggest he is not long for the Hammers.

Phil Charnock

Midfielder
Appearances 2 **Goals** 0
Youth team
Left for Crewe Alexandra, 1996 (free transfer)

One League Cup start was pretty much the sum of Phil's first-team experience at Anfield but since signing for Crewe in December 1996 the Southport-born midfielder has made over 130 starts. Last season, Charnock and co were relegated from Division One on goal difference.

Peter Crookes

Goalkeeper
Appearances 0 **Goals** 0
Youth team
Left for Halifax Town, 2001 (free transfer)

162

The goalkeeper left Liverpool after one year and signed for Halifax Town after a loan spell at The Shay. He played one game last season as the club was relegated into the Nationwide Conference.

Paul Dalglish

Forward
Appearances 0 **Goals** 0
Signed from Celtic, 1996 (free transfer)
Left for Newcastle United, 1997 (free transfer)
Now out of contract

Being the son of a famous footballing father is never easy but when your dad is the king and you play as a striker you have a lot to live up to. After following his father to Newcastle, where he broke into the first team briefly, Paul moved to Norwich following a loan spell at Bury. He subsequently went out on loan at Wigan but two goals in 30 appearances failed to impress and he is currently out of contract.

Ian Dunbavin

Goalkeeper
Appearances 0 **Goals** 0
Youth team
Left for Shrewbury Town, 2000 (free transfer)

After signing professional forms with Liverpool in August 1999, the Knowlsey-born keeper transferred to Shrewbury Town five months later. He made 36 appearances last season.

Sean Dundee

Forward
Appearances 5 **Goals** 0
Signed from Karlsruhe, 1998 (£2m)
Left for Vfb Stuttgart, 1999 (£1m)

Possibly the worst player ever to pull on the red shirt, Dundee arrived for £2million in June 1998 and left little over a year later for half the amount, having made an extensive survey of Liverpool's 'nite spots'. Incredible as

163

it may seem to anyone who saw Dundee play, he did manage five goals in 12 starts for VfB Stuttgart last season.

John Durnin

Midfielder
Appearances 2 **Goals** 0
Signed from Waterloo Dock, 1986 (free transfer)
Left for Oxford United, 1989 (£225,000) **Now** at Port Vale
Since leaving Liverpool in 1989, Durnin has made more than 330 league starts for seven different clubs. He played for Port Vale last season on a non-contract basis and was virtually an ever present from Christmas.

Jean-Michel Ferri

Midfielder
Appearances 2 **Goals** 0
Signed from Istanbulspor, 1999 (£1.7m)
Left for Sochaux, 1999 (£1.5m)
Another one of Houllier's early signings, the French midfielder made the bench twice during his six months at the club. He was released to Sochaux for £1.5million in July 1999.

Brad Friedel

Goalkeeper
Appearances 31 **Goals** 0
Signed from Columbus Crew, 1997 (£1m)
Left for Blackburn Rovers, 2000 (free transfer)
Released by Gérard Houllier on a free transfer in November 2000, the USA's number one is another ex-Red now playing for former Liverpool boss Graeme Souness at Ewood Park. Friedel enjoyed a fine season before jetting off to represent the USA in the World Cup finals and was outstanding in his country's drawn match with hosts South Korea.

Haukur Ingi Gudnason

Forward
Appearances 0 **Goals** 0
Signed from IB Keflavik, 1997 (£150,000)
Left for IB Keflavik, 2000 (free transfer)
The Icelandic striker was signed by Roy Evans but only ever appeared for the first team in close-season friendlies. He moved back to Keflavik after being unable to force his way into the first-team squad and has subsequently had a loan spell at Groningen.

Steve Harkness

Defender
Appearances 138 **Goals** 4
Signed from Carlisle United, 1989 (£75,000)
Left for Benfica, 1999 (£750,000)
Now at Sheffield Wednesday
After more than 100 appearances for the Reds, Harkness went on loan to Huddersfield and Southend before signing up for a short and ill-fated spell at Benfica. He returned to England with Blackburn before signing for Sheffield Wednesday. Injury kept him out for the whole of last season.

Craig Hignett

Forward
Appearances 0 **Goals** 0
Youth team
Left for Crewe Alexandra, 1988 (free transfer)
Now at Blackburn Rovers
A trainee at Liverpool, Hignett never made a first-team appearance for the Reds but has gone on to become one of the most consistently inventive forward players in England. The diminutive striker has scored 155 goals in a career spanning Crewe, Middlesbrough, Aberdeen, Barnsley and now Blackburn.

Don Hutchison

Midfielder
Appearances 60 **Goals** 10
Signed from Hartlepool, 1990 (£175,000)
Left for West Ham United, 1994 (£1.5m)

The man famous for covering his genitals with the label from a bottle of Budweiser squandered a promising Liverpool career having been signed by Kenny Dalglish. The goalscoring midfielder has been the subject of over £11million in transfer fees but has yet to fulfil his undoubted potential. The Scottish international is in his second spell at Upton Park.

Paul Ince

Midfielder
Appearances 80 **Goals** 17
Signed from Inter Milan, 1995 (£4.2m)
Left for Middlesbrough, 1999 (£1m)

Signed at a time when Liverpool needed a leader in midfield, Ince was forever tarnished by his previous association with Manchester United. After allegedly trying to play the 'Guvnor' in the dressing room, Thommo challenged him to show him his medals and Ince was packed off to Boro.

David James

Goalkeeper
Appearances 214 **Goals** 0
Signed from Watford, 1992 (£1m)
Left for Aston Villa, 1999 (£1.7m)
Now at West Ham United

The man who once blamed a loss of form on playing too many computer games left Anfield in 1999 for Aston Villa where he spent two years before moving to West Ham. Despite injury and some quite horrifying hairstyles, he had a strong second half of the season at Upton Park, forcing his way back into the England reckoning and World Cup squad.

Eifion Jones

Defender
Appearances 0 **Goals** 0
Youth team
Left for Blackpool, 2000 (free transfer)
Released by Liverpool in March 2000, Jones made a total of eight appearances for Steve McMahon's Blackpool last season before having his contract paid up.

Jason Jones

Goalkeeper
Appearances 0 **Goals** 0
Youth team
Left for Swansea City, 1997 (free transfer)
The former Anfield trainee left the club as a 16-year-old in December 1997 and it has taken him five years to amass 10 appearances for Swansea. The keeper conceded 13 goals in three games for the South Wales outfit last season.

Lee Jones

Forward
Appearances 4 **Goals** 0
Signed from Wrexham, 1992 (£300,000)
Left for Tranmere Rovers, 1997 (£100,000)
Now at Wrexham
Signed by Graeme Souness for £300,000 in March 1992, Jones spent five years at the club but only made the bench on four occasions. After spells at Wrexham, Crewe, Tranmere and Barnsley he moved back to his native Wrexham, who were relegated last season.

Mark Kennedy

Midfielder
Appearances 2 **Goals** 0
Signed from Millwall, 1995 (£2m)
Left for Wimbledon, 1998 (£1.75m)
Now at Wolverhampton Wanderers

After becoming frustrated with his lack of first-team opportunities, the occasionally wayward Irish international left for Wimbledon before becoming something of a cult figure at Maine Road. He moved on to Wolves but narrowly missed out on promotion and then the World Cup because of injury.

Frode Kippe

Defender
Appearances 2 **Goals** 0
Signed from Lillestrom, 1999 (£700,000)
Left for Lillestrom, 2002 (free transfer)

Two substitute appearances in three years at Anfield wasn't a great return from one of Houllier's first buys. After loan spells at Stoke he returned to his native Norway with Lillestrom, who were mid-table last time we looked.

Bjorn Tore Kvarme

Defender
Appearances 54 **Goals** 0
Signed from Rosenborg, 1997 (free transfer)
Left for St Etienne, 1999 (£1m)
Now at Real Sociedad

Bought by Roy Evans after John Scales was sold to Spurs, the rugged Norwegian international made a flying start to his Anfield career before a catalogue of costly errors and a change in formation saw him marginalised. Perhaps the one plus was that the club made a cool million on him.

Oyvind Leonhardsen

Midfielder
Appearances 49 **Goals** 7
Signed from Wimbledon, 1997 (£4.5m)
Left for Tottenham Hotspur, 1999 (£3.5m)
Signed by Roy Evans for £3.5million in the summer of 1997, Leo was sold after failing to impress Houllier. Last season, the goalscoring midfielder played almost as many times for Norway as he did for Tottenham.

Jim Magilton

Midfielder
Appearances 0 **Goals** 0
Youth team
Left for Oxford United, 1990 (£100,000)
Now at Ipswich Town
The former Anfield apprentice is now heading into the twilight of his career and while the legs might look weary, the mind is still as sharp as ever. An astute midfielder who gave sterling service to Oxford and Southampton, Magilton was relegated with Ipswich last season.

Mike Marsh

Midfielder
Appearances 101 **Goals** 6
Youth team
Left for West Ham United, 1993 (swap deal involving Julian Dicks)
Now at Accrington Stanley
After emerging through the Anfield ranks as a tough-tackling midfielder, Marsh scored in the famous 3-0 second leg win over Auxerre in the 1992 Uefa Cup. Since leaving Liverpool in 1993, his career has taken him as far afield as Galatasaray and Accrington Stanley. Injury cut short his top-flight career and he last appeared for Boston United, who went up as Conference champions in 2002.

Dominic Matteo

Defender
Appearances 155 **Goals** 2
Youth team
Left for Leeds United, 2000 (£4m)
A quality homegrown centre back who came through the ranks with
Robbie Fowler before being sold to Leeds once the Hyppia-Henchoz
partnership took hold. Matteo has become a first choice for O'Leary's
side and has had plenty of chance to practise his defending while on
international duty with Scotland.

Layton Maxwell

Midfielder
Appearances 1 **Goals** 1
Youth team
Left for Cardiff City, 2001 (free transfer)
The Welsh midfielder left in July 2001 with an enviable 100 per cent
scoring record (he netted on his only appearance for the Reds against
Hull City in the League Cup in 1999). Following a loan spell at Stockport,
he signed for Cardiff City where he made eight starts, scoring one goal.

Jason McAteer

Defender
Appearances 139 **Goals** 6
Signed from Bolton Wanderers, 1995 (£4.5m)
Left for Blackburn Rovers, 1999 (£4m)
Now at Sunderland
'Trigger' was converted into a foraging wing back by Roy Evans but a
combination of bad shampoo adverts and poor crossing curtailed his
Anfield career. Frozen out by Souness at Blackburn, he signed for
Sunderland in October 2001 and was part of the Republic's World Cup
success story, despite threatening to quit after being dropped.

Steve McManaman

Midfielder
Appearances 366 **Goals** 66
Youth team
Left for Real Madrid, 1999 (free transfer)

A second Champions League winner's medal capped Macca's third season at the Bernabeu. Although used mainly as a substitute, the wide man is so highly thought of that his omission from England's World Cup squad was met with disbelief by such illustrious Madrid team-mates as Figo, Zidane and Roberto Carlos. Owns racehorses with Robbie Fowler.

Erik Meijer

Forward
Appearances 27 **Goals** 2
Signed from Bayer Leverkusen, 1999 (free transfer)
Left for Hamburg, 2000 (free transfer)

A minor legend during his two years at Anfield, Mad Erik was never the most prolific of strikers but no one could fault his effort. The big Dutchman scored five goals in 26 games for Hamburg last season, a slightly better ratio than he managed in his 17 months at Liverpool.

Neil Murphy

Defender
Appearances 0 **Goals** 0
Youth team
Left for Blackpool, 2000 (free transfer)

The former trainee played one game at the start of last season for Blackpool before having his contract paid up by Steve McMahon.

Jon Newby

Forward
Appearances 4 **Goals** 0
Youth team
Left for Bury, 2001 (£100,000)

Erik Meijer's striking sidekick in the reserve team that won the title in 1999/00, Newby followed Michael Owen and Steven Gerrard from the Academy but could not break into the first team. Seven goals in 52 games for Bury last term was not enough to save the Shakers from relegation to Division Three.

Chris O'Brien

Midfielder
Appearances 0 **Goals** 0
Youth team
Left for Chester City, 2002 (free transfer)

The Liverpool-born midfielder did not graduate to the first-team squad and was released in October 2001. He is now a member of Mark Wright's set-up at Chester City.

Gareth Roberts

Defender
Appearances 0 **Goals** 0
Youth team
Left for Panionios, 1999 (free transfer)
Now at Tranmere Rovers

The Welsh international defender was a trainee at Anfield before signing for Ronnie Whelan at Panionios in Greece. The move was clearly not to his liking as he was loaned back to Tranmere after just 12 days, making the deal permanent soon after. He has now made well over 100 appearances for the Prenton Park club and is a full Welsh international.

Neil Ruddock

Defender
Appearances 150 **Goals** 12
Signed from Tottenham Hotspur, 1993 (£2.5m)
Left for West Ham United, 2000 (£100,000)
Now at Swindon Town
Sent off in his last game for Swindon in December 2001, Razor missed the second half of the campaign with a knee injury. His managerial partnership at the County Ground with Roy Evans was cut short with Evans' and he is now player-coach under Andy King.

Rigobert Song

Defender
Appearances 38 **Goals** 0
Signed from Salernitana, 1998 (£2.6m)
Left for West Ham United, 2000 (£2.5m)
Now at Lens
We only had one Song but after a year at West Ham he went on loan to Cologne in November 2001, clocking up 16 appearances. He failed in his bid to become the first man in World Cup history to be sent off in three consecutive tournaments during the summer, after dismissals in 1994 and 98, and has since joined French side Lens.

Steve Staunton

Defender
Appearances 147 **Goals** 6
Signed from Aston Villa, 1998 (free transfer)
Left for Aston Villa, 2000 (free transfer)
Having spent his professional life yo-yoing between Anfield and Villa Park, it can only be a matter of time before 'Stan' comes back to Liverpool to finish his career. Following Keano's tantrum, the veteran left-sided defender led his country with distinction in Korea and Japan.

David Thompson

Midfielder
Appearances 56 **Goals** 5
Youth team
Left for Coventry City, 2000 (£3m)

Nine yellow cards, two red and 13 goals were the story of Thommo's season at Coventry. A wide midfielder who has developed a reputation as a dead-ball specialist, Thompson showed real promise at Anfield but let himself down on the disciplinary front.

Tony Warner

Goalkeeper
Appearances 0 **Goals** 0
Youth team
Left for Millwall, 1999 (free transfer)

Tony Bonus, as he was known at Anfield having picked up win bonuses galore without ever playing a first-team game for Liverpool, has settled at Millwall after loan spells at Swindon, Celtic and Aberdeen. He had made nearly 150 appearances for the club by the end of a season in which they pipped for a play-off final place by Birmingham City.

Alex Watson

Defender
Appearances 9 **Goals** 0
Youth team
Left for Bournemouth, 1991 (£150,000)
Now at Exeter City

Dave Watson's brother made nine appearances for the Reds in six years before exploring pastures new with Derby, Bournemouth, Gillingham, Torquay and Exeter City. The defender became assistant manager under Wes Saunders at Torquay before moving to St James's Park to add experience to Noel Blake's defence.

Danny Williams

Midfielder
Appearances 0 **Goals** 0
Youth team
Left for Wrexham, 1999 (free transfer)
Now at Kidderminster

The Wrexham-born midfielder left Liverpool after five years as a trainee, moving back to his hometown club before going on loan to Doncaster. He signed for Jan Molby's Kidderminster in June 2001 and made 40 appearances last term.

Reds managing and coaching

Playing for Liverpool Football Club is akin to furthering your football education. These are the men who are currently passing on those pearls of Anfield wisdom to a new generation of players across the world...

Phil Boersma

Liverpool career 1969-75
Appearances 73 **Goals** 17

Boersma returned to Anfield with Graeme Souness, acting as physiotherapist and first-team coach. Since then he has followed Souness faithfully across Europe, perfecting the art of waddling across the pitch clutching a leaking bag of water.

Nigel Clough

Liverpool career 1993-96
Appearances 44 **Goals** 9

Clough Jnr emulated his father by starting out on the lower rungs of the managerial ladder with non-league Burton Albion in 1998. Last term he led his team into the Nationwide Conference as Unibond champs.

Ray Clemence

Liverpool career 1968-80
Appearances 656 **Goals** 0

A former general manager at Barnet, Clemence was recruited as a member of the England coaching staff by Glenn Hoddle at the start of the 1996/97 season. He has been the national side's goalkeeping coach ever since and was a member of Sven's back-room team at the 2002 World Cup.

Doug Livermore

Liverpool career 1967-70
Appearances 17 **Goals** 0

Livermore has coached at Cardiff City and Swansea City under John Toshack and been assistant manager to Welsh boss Mike England. He was also briefly caretaker manager at Spurs before being brought back to Anfield by Roy Evans as Ronnie Moran's co-assistant. Livermore left when Houllier took sole control in 1999 and is currently at Norwich City with Nigel Worthington.

Kevin MacDonald

Liverpool career 1984-88
Appearances 56 **Goals** 3

The Scottish midfielder who played in the Double-winning side enjoyed spells at Coventry and Rangers after leaving Anfield. When he finished playing he joined Aston Villa as under-21 coach before becoming first-team coach. He currently manages the reserve team at Villa Park.

Steve McMahon

Liverpool career 1985-91
Appearances 276 **Goals** 50

An 18-month gap followed his departure from a first managerial post at Swindon Town, but McMahon got back in the thick of it when he became the boss at Bloomfield Road in 1999. Relegated in his first season, the team bounced straight back via the play-offs before finishing 16th in Division Two last season.

Richard Money

Liverpool career 1980-81
Appearances 17 **Goals** 0

After spells at Derby, Luton Town and Portsmouth, injury forced Money to prematurely curtail his playing career. He has since managed Scunthorpe and worked as a coach at Aston Villa, Nottingham Forest and Manchester City. In April 2002 he was suspended as the club's academy director pending an internal investigation into alleged contact to and from former chairman Bryan Richardson.

Jan Molby

Liverpool career 1984-96
Appearances 291 **Goals** 60

The rotund Dane with the broadest Scouse accent on Merseyside has become a highly rated young manager. After a spell as player-manager at Swansea, he joined Kidderminster in May 1999 and went on to lead the club into the Football League. He left mid way through last season to take charge at Hull City.

Steve Nicol

Liverpool career 1981-95

Appearances 473 **Goals** 46

The legendary Stevie Nic was made interim head coach at New England Revolution for the second time last May. He served as player coach for Notts County in 1995 and was named head coach of the Boston Bulldogs in July 1999 before rejoining the New England MLS side in January 2002.

Steve Ogrizovic

Liverpool career 1977-82

Appearances 5 **Goals** 0

After hanging up his gloves at the end of a long and distinguished playing career, Oggy stayed on at Highfield Road to join Coventry City's back-room staff. He was caretaker manager for a couple of games at the end of last season after Roland Nilsson was sacked.

Dean Saunders

Liverpool career 1991-93

Appearances 61 **Goals** 25

The ex-Welsh international finally hung up his boots after a spell with Bradford City in 1999/2000 and joined his former boss Graeme Souness at Blackburn where is now coach.

Mark Seagraves

Liverpool career 1983-87

Appearances 2 **Goals** 0

Assistant manager to another ex-Red, Steve McMahon at Blackpool, Seagraves played under his present boss at Swindon before ending his playing career at Barrow.

Graeme Souness

Liverpool career 1978-85
Appearances 358 **Goals** 56

A glittering reign at Ibrox was followed by a troublesome spell at his first love, Anfield. But Souness went on to repair the damage with successful spells at Galatasaray, Benfica and Southampton. After then leading Blackburn to promotion he won the Worthington Cup last season.

Mark Wright

Liverpool career 1991-98
Appearances 210 **Goals** 7

After making a series of ill-advised comments to a black referee, Mark Wright parted company with Oxford United in acrimonious fashion. He is currently trying to rebuild his managerial career at Chester City.

Obituaries

Billy Liddell

Born 10.1.1922 **died** 3.7.2001
Liverpool career 1939-61
Appearances 537 **Goals** 229

There was no more fitting tribute to the impact Billy Liddell had on LFC than the one bestowed on him by the fans in the 1940s and 50s when they renamed the club, Liddellpool. For 15 seasons, he was Liverpool, netting 229 goals in 537 matches, a record bettered by just three players since.

Liddell, who died of Alzheimer's disease in July 2001, was born near Dunfermline, the eldest son of a miner. His arrival at Anfield was almost accidental – Liverpool player Matt Busby was in Scotland to play golf but when his partner did not turn up he went to watch local side Lochgelly Violets. The teenage Liddell starred that day, Busby recommended him to the Anfield management and Liddell signed in 1939. "There wasn't a weakness in Billy's game," marvelled Busby. "He was as strong as a bull on the ball. Defenders found him a handful, but always respected him."

Starting out as a raiding winger, Liddell converted to a centre forward. He lost the first six years of his professional career to the Second World War but returned to football in 1946 when his wing-play helped propel the Reds to their first title in 24 years and he won his only medal in a long Liverpool career. The ultimate footballing corinthian, Liddell was also a committed Christian who worked tirelessly for boys clubs. On breaking the club's appearances record he was presented with a cocktail cabinet – an unfortunate choice of gift for a teetotaller.

After tasting Cup final defeat in 1950, disappointment followed four years later when the Reds were relegated. "Billy could have moved on to any club but he stayed with the team he loved," recalls Ronnie Moran. "That was the type of man he was, on and off the field, a true gentleman."

Liddell played 28 times for Scotland, and twice for Great Britain against the Rest of the World. He retired in 1960/61 after helping Bill Shankly propel the club into a glorious new era. "Shanks used to describe him as a strong player, 'who takes a 19-inch shirt collar'," says former team-mate Alan A'Court. Billy became a justice of the peace and a bursar at Liverpool University, remaining an Anfield season-ticket holder throughout.

Joe Fagan

Born 12.3.1921 **died** 2.7.2001
Liverpool career 1958-85.

In 1983, Joe Fagan was presented with the toughest job in football history – following in the footsteps of Bill Shankly and Bob Paisley. So what did he do? He went out and won the League, League Cup and European Cup in his first season. Not that Fagan, who died in June 2001, was a rookie, having been schooled for seasons in the Anfield Boot Room. But it's fair to say no one will ever emulate a managerial debut for which he has never really received full credit. "The players loved him and were desperate to do well for him," recalls Mark Lawrenson. "He was very shrewd, realising when he took over 'this thing was far from broke, so don't fix it.'"

Smokin' Joe was a Scouser who spent the majority of his playing career at Manchester City, starting out as a wing half before moving into the back four. He later played non-league football, before becoming trainer at Rochdale. He made the switch to Anfield in 1958, moving up through the ranks and becoming one of the architects of the Liverpool Way.

Tactically astute, Fagan's philosophy of football was uncomplicated. "You see," he said after lifting the European Cup in Roma's backyard, "we're rather coming to the stage where I'm talking simple, and it's a simple game. We close the space down on them."

Like his immediate predecessor, Fagan was a private man and after two seasons he elected to stand down on the night before the Heysel disaster. The tragic events of the following evening devastated him, but he remained a frequent visitor to Anfield and his beloved Boot Room.

Perhaps the defining image of the Fagan era is the shot of him grinning in a poolside deckchair, one hand on the European Cup, the day after that Stadio Olimpico triumph, flanked by two carabinieri. And perhaps the man is best summed up by another Boot-Room graduate, Roy Evans. "Joe was the best. He was probably the most respected man in football and the guy given the least praise. He will be best remembered for the Treble in 1984, but he was a top coach for 30 years."

Tom Saunders

Born 1921 **died** 8.7.2001
Liverpool career 1970-01

Tom Saunders was a key, if unsung, lieutenant of the Liverpool Boot Room who graduated from youth-development officer to vice-president. After spending his teens serving the Territorial Army in North Africa, the native Liverpudlian started teaching in his home city and played as an amateur footballer for a host of clubs in and around the Merseyside area.

In the late 1960s, Liverpool's departing youth-team coach Tony Waiters recommended Saunders as his successor. Tom took the job and combined developing the club's young talent with scouting the opposition for the first team. Tom also spied for Liverpool in Europe. "A trip behind the iron curtain meant a lot of trouble," he recalled. "I've been to places where it wasn't wise to send one person. But the great thing was meeting so many interesting people. People who couldn't speak English would welcome me and we'd forge a relationship through football."

His contribution to Liverpool's success was a lifetime's work. "He was like my father," said Gérard Houllier. "He was a man of football, not only a figure of the past but a man of the future – a visionary."

THIS IS ANFIELD

THIS IS ANFIELD

Tickets | Matchdays | Around the stadium | Museum & Stadium Tour | A pie and a pint

The unveiling of plans for a new 55,000-seater stadium on Stanley Park suggests the regular pilgrimage to Anfield is set to become a thing of the past for thousands of fans. While our legendary home commands a massive emotional place in hearts, minds and in the history of Liverpool Football Club, the stadium is simply not big enough to satisfy demand for tickets or to generate the sort of gate-receipt revenue that will keep the club competitive within the European elite. Since plans to move from its present site were announced two years ago, the club has investigated a number of options around the city before settling on Stanley Park, with a proposed opening date for the start of the 2005 season. Bill Shankly once said, "As a word Anfield means more to me than I can describe." It is a feeling shared by those who worship there, so here's a guide to sampling the Anfield experience while you still can...

Goin' the match

Getting tickets to see Liverpool can be tricky. From the businessman dining in the luxury of a corporate box through to the lad who picks up a spare from a tout outside, there are numerous ways of getting into Anfield. The simple, old method of queuing up at the turnstiles and paying your cash is now largely a thing of the past, apart from the occasional cup game that hasn't sold out. Of course, this is especially sad for the fully bearded men who would regularly be seen in the queue for the kids' turnstile.

Ways and means – getting a home ticket

The safest way to guarantee a place at Anfield for every home game is to get a season ticket. Of the 45,000 seats at Anfield, roughly 27,000 are filled by season-ticket holders. Unfortunately, the waiting list of applicants is now 16,000 strong and the ticket office reckon it'll take 10 years for the most recent applicants to get their hands on one of these prized assets. The turnover is agonisingly slow due to the fact most people who no longer require their ticket pass it on to family or friends. This will change with increased capacity, but in the meantime, the chances of getting one are low. However, if you think you'll still be around in 2012 and want to get on the list, send your name, address and phone number to the LFC Ticket Office, PO Box 204, Liverpool L69 4PQ. They'll call you back to inform you you're on the computer files.

More realistic for fans who want to see the Reds play as often as possible is the club's Priority Membership Scheme, which is in effect a semi-season ticket. The scheme has 10,000 members and 5,000 seats available for every match. It costs £34.50 to join and members can apply for home-game tickets two weeks ahead of the general public. While chances of success are only 50-50 for the glamour fixtures like Manchester United and Everton, they improve for the so-called lesser games when not all the 10,000 apply. Despite the frustratingly random nature of the scheme, the odds are better than those of applying through general sale and, almost inevitably, there is now a waiting list to get on this scheme – although nothing like the length of the season-ticket queue. To apply for 2003/04 membership (this year's quota is full), call 0151 261 1444. Each

Reds Against Racism

Re-enforced at every home game by announcements over the PA system, LFC is extremely proactive in its action against racism. Racist abuse or chanting is not tolerated at Anfield and it's likely to meet with ejection from the stadium, arrest, or a life-long cancellation of season tickets.

With the vile imagery of former Reds legend John Barnes back-heeling a banana thrown from the Goodison terraces in the 1980s still fresh, racism in football has not totally disappeared. Last season Emile Heskey suffered a shameful torrent of racist abuse from a large section of fans away in Boavista during the first group stage of the Champions League campaign.

Racist chanting from Liverpool fans has not been heard for decades and fans of every colour, creed and nationality are able to watch the game in complete comfort and safety. Racist abuse at football matches is now illegal and all Anfield supporters are encouraged to report any incidents they come across to the stewards or police on duty.

successful applicant receives a membership card, Liverpool video and CD.

Another way to maximise chances of getting tickets is to join the Association of International Branches of the Liverpool Supporters Club. There are AIB branches nationwide from Glasgow to London, and worldwide from Norway to Australia, so wherever you live, there's likely to be one nearby. As well as the bonus of getting together with local Reds, every branch has a ticket allocation for every game. Most clubs also run coach trips or flights to games, which takes the hassle out of organising it yourself. Call the AIB on 0151 261 1444 to find your nearest branch.

If you don't want to join a club or waiting list, the lottery of postal and phone applications is the next option. To buy tickets this way you must apply 23 days in advance of the game. Send a letter stating the match and number of tickets required with a SAE to LFC Ticket Office, PO Box 204, Liverpool L69 4PQ. You can pay by cheque (payable to Liverpool Football Club), postal order, credit or debit card (include your card number, expiry date and debit-card issue number where applicable). Or use the credit-card hotline on 0870 220 2345. You can buy a maximum of four tickets. Book more than three days in advance and they'll be sent out by post, otherwise collect them from the ticket office where you must produce the card used to book them – although it's rare there will be unsold tickets so close to a game. However, it's sometimes worth calling the office on the day of the match even if the game is sold out and asking if they have any returns (tickets people have booked but no longer want). For smaller Premiership games there are often a few left – but don't bother calling if it's the derby, or United are in town.

Applications almost always exceed the number of tickets available so they are allocated through a ballot. For the bigger games, stubs from previous fixtures often need to be enclosed with applications. This system rewards loyal fans who get to most games, so hang on to all your stubs. Any remaining tickets go on sale direct through the Liverpool Ticket Office (situated next to the Kop McDonalds), 16 days in advance.

If all else fails and desperation sets in, there are always the touts around Anfield on matchday. Easy to spot, they hawk through the crowds, requesting "swaps or spares". Buying from touts can be expensive, risky and it is illegal – if you're unlucky you could find yourself alongside the tout in the back of a Merseyside Police van. If you insist on buying from a tout, be careful. If it's a season-ticket stub, make sure you check the number corresponds with the match it's for (this is advertised above the

187

entrances) – it's a common rip-off to sell unsuspecting fans vouchers for last week's game. Try to give touts the exact money as they don't tend to deal with giving change and don't flash too much cash about. Remember you're participating in an illegal activity, so the police aren't likely to be too understanding if you get ripped off.

Disabled fans

There are 79 disabled spaces within Anfield all located in the Paddock although less than 20 of these are available on a match-by-match basis. Tickets for last season were £3 for wheelchair users and £21 or £24 (dependent on fixture category) for helpers. A maximum of two helpers per wheelchair is permitted, but second helpers must pay the full match-ticket price. Season tickets for one wheelchair user and one helper cost £445 in 2001/02, but there is a waiting list of several years. In addition, Liverpool offer 40 tickets for visually impaired fans – 24 season tickets, 16 individual match tickets. Ticket prices were the same as for wheelchair users. Fans must apply to the ticket office 26 days in advance of the match, enclosing a copy of their BD8 form and appropriate payment.

Corporate hospitality and boxes

The idea of watching the match from a lavish executive suite while dining on chicken liver parfait is anathema to many fans, who'd rather be on the Kop with a Scouse pie. But Anfield's 32 executive boxes and hospitality suites are a huge money spinner for the club and certainly provide a superb venue for businessmen entertaining clients and the odd lucky lottery winner.

Hospitality rates vary according to a client's need. The cheapest package is £45 per person, which will get you a match ticket with half-time snacks in the Reds Bar, while £5,000 will accommodate 20 guests in the TV studio suite to watch a match with fine food and wine. The club can also arrange museum and stadium tours, parking and hotels.

Various corporate hospitality packages will once again be available at Anfield from the start of next season. A new matchday hospitality brochure detailing all the packages is available from the club, please write to **Corporate Sales Dept, Liverpool Football Club, Anfield Road, Liverpool, Merseyside L4 OTH**, or call the conference and banqueting department of the club on **0151 263 7744**.

The new Anfield?

Out with the old...

Football has been played at our Anfield home since 1884 when Everton became tenants on land owned by local brewer John Orrell. In 1892, just a year after winning the first of 19 league titles to be paraded at Anfield, Everton upped sticks and moved to Goodison following a rent dispute. Liverpool FC was formed, the Kop terrace was built in 1906 and soon after a legend was born.

But after 110 glorious years in which the worldwide fame of the club has been synonymous with its Anfield home and the supporters that flock to it, the board has decided it's time to move on and move away – even if it only the distance of a couple of Jerzy Dudek goalkicks. The plans for the new 55,000-seater Anfield Stadium on Stanley Park, the result of a two-year process and informed by a desire to stay close to the club's spiritual home, have been presented to Liverpool City Council and discussion has begun with the local community. The agreement is that there will be no loss of public space, so the boundaries of Stanley Park will most likely be redrawn to incorporate the site of the old Anfield.

What happens to the existing site is a sensitive area as many fans have had the ashes of family and friends scattered on the pitch and of course there is the location of the Hillsborough Memorial and Shankly and Paisley Gates. "It's a very emotional issue and moving from Anfield is not a decision that has been taken lightly," says Liverpool's chief executive Rick Parry.

The club explored the viability of staying put but the cost and disruption involved with replacing the old Main Stand, built in 1973, to increase the capacity by the requisite 11,000 seats was deemed to be more problematic than building a brand new stadium just 300m from the existing site. The look of a revamped Anfield, with a dramatically enlarged Main Stand and Anfield Road End was also said to have disappointed even the most ardent pro-stay members of the board. Original plans for a 70,000 all-seater stadium were scaled back because the cost involved would have compromised investment in the team and saddled the club with a large debt. Parry admits there is a still a lot of work to do and plans will doubtless be refined to take into account feedback and opinions of local residents and fans. Good news for the sceptics, and there are many, is that the club has a firm commitment to retaining the Kop end with an enlarged, single tiered, covered terrace.

189

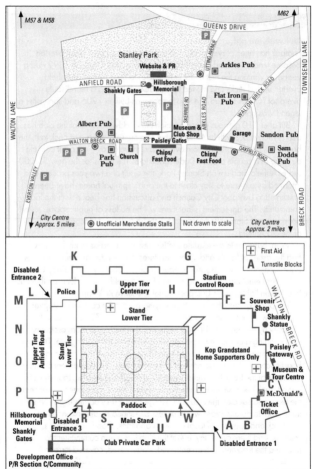

190

Away matches

Virtually all tickets for away games go to season-ticket holders. Allocations differ according to the away club concerned and demand from the regulars usually outstrips supply. The club tries to keep the distribution fair for aways by alternating who can apply for the tickets according to their season-ticket serial number – so again it's a bit of a lottery to get tickets for the matches you want. The numbers of those who can apply can be found at the ticket office, on the information line, in the local press and on the Liverpool website www.liverpoolfc.tv In the unlikely event of there being tickets available on general sale for an away match, they are sold in the same way as home tickets – but don't hold your breath.

The ticket office is open from 9.15am to 4.45pm weekdays, 9.15am to kick-off on matchdays and for 45 minutes after the final whistle. It often opens at 8.15am on the first day of sale of away-match tickets. While this information was accurate at the time of going to press, sales methods can change, so keep in touch with the latest ticket situation on the Liverpool Ticket Information Line on 09068 121 584.

Champions League and cup games

The sale of FA and Worthington Cup tickets depends entirely on the opposition and whether it's a home or away draw – so check the local press or Liverpool website. If we've got Everton in the FA Cup, you're looking at full uptake from the season-ticket holders and a queue made up of stubs holders, while Shrewsbury in the Worthington probably means you'll be able to walk up and buy your ticket on the gate five minutes before kick-off.

For European games, the group fixture list is already known and ticket arrangements are straightforward. A season-ticket holder is sent a form and provided they respond in time, their applications are guaranteed a ticket (although it won't necessarily be in their normal seat). The uptake from season-ticket holders dictates how many tickets go on general sale. The bigger matches in later rounds (such as Roma last year) often require ticket stubs from previous games and can lead to suitably massive queues on the day they go on sale.

To apply for match tickets for away fixtures in Europe, you must be a member of the **LFC European Travel Club**. The scheme is intended to keep potential trouble-makers away and to prevent fans journeying to

You will see at Anfield

Doctor Fun an insane, long-serving Kopite whose matchday outfit consists of hand-painted red shoes, red top hat and tails and a glove puppet named Liverpool Charlie. Avoid when drunk.

Sporting applause for every visiting goalkeeper when he runs to the Kop and for any side that wins by playing quality football. Kopites have always respected class.

Flags Huge ones at the front of the Kop, smaller versions all round the ground.

Rousing renditions You'll Never Walk Alone before kick-off and near the end, Scouser Tommy (though action on the pitch will determine whether it reaches the end) and, more recently The Fields Of Anfield Road (see songs, in The Directory).

The Kemlyn Arm a peculiar hand gesture practised by the Anfield equivalent of the Politburo in the lower Centenary Stand.

Lacoste shellsuits worn with bottoms tucked into socks in low-slung plus-four stylee. Modelled by a significant percentage of the Anfield public.

Scandinavians some decked in specially emblazoned boiler suits, some in jester hats, some with scarves round their wrists. No, really.

You won't see at Anfield

Team mascot we have no desire to spend pre-kick-off being waved at by an enormous nylon Liver Bird.

Giant foam hands best left to Gladiators and Boro fans.

Pre-match entertainment we're here to support the team, not watch police dogs jump through hoops.

Cheerleaders inanely grinning schoolgirls, silvery giant pom-poms? No ta.

Ballboys why bother when the crowd does the job anyway?

Supporters band Kopites sing and instinctively know when to start a song.

Stand up if you... songs They belong to a lower class of fan.

Obese, topless men our proud sartorial heritage precludes this kind of low-grade Geordie-esque behaviour.

away games without tickets. Last season's membership fee was £5 and fans need two passport-sized photographs along with their money when applying. You must quote a membership card number when applying for tickets abroad.

Details for this season are available on the club's official website **www.liverpoolfc.tv** or by writing to the membership office at **PO Box 205, Anfield Road, Liverpool L69 4PS** or call **0151 261 1444** for further information. Fans should note that membership of the official supporters club is not sufficient to purchase tickets for away games in Europe.

Matchdays

The roof of the Kop usually provides the first glimpse of Anfield for the visiting fan. Whether approached by walking up Walton Breck Road from Everton Valley or by strolling past the numerous ale houses on Oakfield Road, the facade of Liverpool's mythical home end is the vista that quickens the pulse and heightens the sense of anticipation.

As the full extent of this hulking end looms into view so the streets become busier with the human flow of matchday traffic. Stalls selling unofficial souvenirs such as flags, badges and scarves can be found outside the petrol station at the junction of Walton Breck Road and Oakfield Road, while individual vendors bark out adverts for their This is Anfield replica signs or T-shirts reminding Manchester United of their inherent inferiority, albeit with any number of topical twists.

Fanzine sellers clutching bundles of the latest issues of Through The Wind And Rain, Red All Over The Land and The Liverpool Way can be found at their usual specs outside the Kop, on Anfield Road or at either end of the walkway behind the Main Stand.

Around the ground

There are plenty of historical points of interest around the stadium, including the statue of Bill Shankly in messianic pose outside the entrance to the club museum at the Kop end. The bronze figure with the outstretched arms, bearing the legend 'he made the people happy', serves as a useful pre and post-match meeting point.

On the corner of the Kop and Centenary Stand can be found an enormous flagpole that originally adorned Brunel's trans-Atlantic steamer, The Great Eastern. This is where Liverpool's championship flags have been flown from on matchdays and is, funnily enough, known as

flagpole corner. Halfway along the Kop is the Paisley Gateway opened in 1999 to honour the remarkable achievements of Britain's most successful manager. The archway of the gates, honouring the wishes of his wife Jessie, includes representations of the three European Cups he won and the coat of arms for Hetton-le-Hole, Paisley's birthplace.

Turn right at the end of the Kop, through a cramped alleyway and it opens up on to a car park behind the Main Stand. Past the gleaming cars belonging to the players and coaching staff, past the player's entrance (always ringed by well-wishing fans and autograph hunters) and you come to the second famous set of gates at Anfield. The imposing Shankly Gates, with the wrought iron legend You'll Never Walk Alone across the top, bar the way to Anfield Road and were erected in 1982 in tribute to the great Bill Shankly, who died the year before.

On the right of the Shankly Gates is the poignant Hillsborough Memorial. An eternal flame is framed by the names of the 96 people who lost their lives on 15 April 1989. Scarves, flowers and cards are laid at the foot of this simple but powerful symbol throughout the week, peaking on matchdays when tokens from opposition teams and fans can be found interspersed with the red of Liverpool. A smaller memorial was erected at Hillsborough after 10 years of pressure from relatives of the victims.

LFC Official Club Store

The modern club store could not be further removed from the cramped cabin that served as the nerve centre of the club's merchandising operation in the 1970s. Located at the corner of the Spion Kop, next door to The Albert, the old shop carried a tiny range of flags, caps, posters, keyrings, player mug shots and LFC v-neck polyester sweaters.

In the 1980s the shop moved to larger premises next to the Shankly Gates before being relocated to its present spacious home beneath the Kop. Refurbished in August 1998, the **Anfield club store (0151 263 1760)** is now an impressive 6,500sqft emporium selling over 1,000 different Liverpool products, ranging from mugs to LFC motor scooters. What's more, if you can't find on display the Alan Hansen souvenir jockstrap you're after you can fill out a customer-comment card to suggest the merchandise team get on the case.

On matchdays between 7,000 and 10,000 supporters pay a visit which means you might be required to queue for a short while before getting in. Such has been the demand that in April 1999 a 4,400sqft store was opened in **Williamson Square (0151 330 3077)** in the city centre before a second smaller on-site LFC store was opened on the old site next to the Shankly Gates at the start of the 2000/01 season. If you're bringing kids to Anfield, expect to be carted inside one of these outlets and be prepared to spend or have a good excuse not to lined up in advance.

The good news for those intent on bagging themselves a LFC mountain bike but who cannot make it to Anfield, is that you can shop online through the **www.liverpoolfc.tv** website or by using the direct **mail-order hotline** on **0870 6000532**.

Opening times Saturday 9am to 6pm, Monday to Friday 9am to 5pm, Sunday 10am to 4pm. Evening kick-offs 9am to 11pm.

Museum & Tour Centre

Opened in December 1997 by Nessie Shankly, Jessie Paisley and Ron Yeats, the Liverpool Museum attracts in the region of 50,000 visitors a year. Sharing an entrance with the official club store behind The Kop, the museum houses a remarkable collection of trophies, shirts, medals and assorted artefacts, from players, managers and fans, that chart the history of our proud club.

195

It's goose-pimples aplenty once you begin the museum walk, but you can't help thinking it's all a bit shadowy and cramped – certainly it can feel claustrophobic on a busy day. A club of Liverpool's stature deserves a more lavish exhibition, but the current dimensions are severely constrained by the limited space available at Anfield. No doubt it'll be addressed at the new stadium – something along the lines of Ajax's commodious, state-of-the-art museum at the Amsterdam ArenA wouldn't go amiss.

Curator and lifelong Reds fanatic Stephen Done has nevertheless done a superb job in adding to the collection that used to be tucked away in the Main Stand. After passing the ceramic memorial to the 96 who lost their lives at Hillsborough, the fascinating journey takes you through the different eras with mementoes of the personalities that came to embody them, plus various trophy cabinets, one of which holds scale replicas of the club's four European Cups. There's a waxwork exhibit recreating a typical scene from the home dressing room in 1965, the year Shankly inspired Liverpool to its first FA Cup. Shirt and medal collections from the Liddell, Shankly, Paisley and Dalglish eras make for a glittering wander down memory lane, while those not old enough to have swayed with the masses on the old, terraced Kop can get a feel of what it was like by leaning against a graffitied crash barrier and listening to a soundtrack of the noise generated by 25,000 Kopites.

Done has also ensured that fans are represented in the collection and the assorted scrapbooks, badges, rattles and scarves give a feel for the passion of the people who have done more than anyone to make the club what it is today. There's Craig Johnstone's surf board and fittingly, next to the case housing Ian Rush's Juventus shirt is the memorial plaque commemorating the 39 Juventus fans killed at Heysel in 1985. Flowers are laid here each year on the anniversary.

When you begin the **stadium tour**, you and your multinational party are met by a bona fide Scouse sherpa next to the Shankly statue. You get to see the dressing rooms, touch the This Is Anfield sign, walk down the players' tunnel and sit in the dugout and you can take as many photographs as you like. The guides are friendly and informed and as well as fielding your questions on the history and dimensions of the stadium, they'll fill you in on all the little details. Did you know, for example, there used to be two smaller baths next to the large communal one in the home dressing-room? And that Souey and Brucie liked to fill them with iced water immediately after a game and dive straight in?

Museum opening times Monday to Sunday 10am to 5pm, last

admission, 4pm or one hour before kick-off on matchdays – there are no stadium tours on matchdays. Museum and stadium tour costs £8.50 adults, £5.50 children/OAPs, £23 family of four (2 adults, 2 children). Museum only £5 adults, £3 child/OAP, family of four £13. There are special deals for schools and groups. Advance bookings for stadium tours are strongly recommended. **Booking hotline 0151 260 6677.**

Banners, flag days and mosaics

The Kop's long standing as the home of the noisiest, most passionate fans in football began in the 1960s. Inspired by their club's renaissance under Bill Shankly and the city's burgeoning reputation on the world stage, Kopites pioneered the rhythmic singing and clapping that quickly became the hallmark of British supporters.

As many as 27,000 people used to squeeze on to the old Kop, creating a carnival of noise and colour, with scarves, flags and homemade banners providing the red backdrop for You'll Never Walk Alone. The Kop has stayed at the forefront of fan culture, perhaps more so since terraces were abolished following the Hillsborough disaster, by celebrating its heritage with regular flag days and demonstrating its loyalty with fan mosaics that cover one whole end of the ground.

By the end of last season, Liverpool fanzine Red All Over the Land had organised nine Kop mosaics, requiring 12,500 fans to hold up pieces of coloured paper at a certain time. The French Tricolour featuring Gérard Houllier's initials before the home game against Manchester United was perhaps the most memorable of last season. "They're a way of creating a spectacle and adding to the atmosphere. That's why the club always help us out," says RAOTL's Andy Knott.

The flag days started back in 1994 when, with the demolition of the old Kop imminent, a group of like-minded fans decided the most famous end in world football should not, like so many other home terraces across the country, be allowed to bow out with a whimper. Leaflets were handed out and notices published calling for fans to turn up to the game against Norwich with their flags, scarves, shirts, mementoes, anything from past eras of watching the Reds. As a result The Last Stand Of The Kop on Saturday 30 April was a cacophony of colour and noise as the old terrace was given a fitting send-off. Since then Flag Days have been organised to

197

recognise all sorts of anniversaries and achievements, as well as to lift the team on big occasions. "The flag events really distinguish this club from all others, it's brilliant the way we celebrate our legends," says John Pearman, editor of RAOTL.

Since the halcyon days of the club's early triumphs in Europe, Liverpudlians have always led the way in colourful, witty and downright bizarre banners. The Treble-season witnessed a renaissance in Scouse originality, continuing a heritage that can be traced back to a balmy night in Rome in 1977 when Joey Jones was immortalised on the greatest of them all. Below, we celebrate Scouse DIY culture by cataloguing 25 years of the most memorable slogans

1973 Without a doubt Zurich Zur-Out

1977 Joey ate the frog's legs, made the Swiss roll, now he's munchen Gladbachs

1978 Kenny's From Heaven

2001 Wine for my men, we ride at dawn; What we achieve in life echoes in eternity

2001/02 Back in the USSR with Liverpool's Fab Four; Welcome to hell – my arse! If you think this is hell try the Grafton on a Friday night

Nosebag – food around Anfield

Anfield – where the chippy reigns supreme. You'll find loads of them as you walk to and from the stadium, especially on Breck Road, Oakfield Road and Walton Breck Road. As well as fish, fish cakes, pies, chicken portions and sausages to go with your chips, trays of chips generously smothered with gravy or curry sauce are very popular and cheap. A limited Chinese menu will be available in many and you should be able to order a kebab should you prefer. If it's a burger you want there's a McDonalds in front of the Kop and opposite is a takeaway pizza establishment. Dotted around the ground, there are a few mobile vendors selling hot dogs, burgers and chips. You'll also come across a few local sandwich and cake shops where you can buy pasties, pies, sandwiches and cobs – filled rolls to the uninitiated. If it's something more exotic you're after then head for the town centre where'll you find countless excellent places to eat, catering for all tastes and budgets. You may even be able to locate a pub selling the famed delicacy – a plate of Scouse, basically a tasty local version of Irish Stew.

Get 'em in – pubs around Anfield

Within a mile of Anfield there are a host of pubs for that all-important pre or post-match jar. The atmosphere will be friendly so don't be surprised to see away fans in there as well. Prices compare favourably with the rest of the country and average out at a couple of quid for a pint of lager, a little more for a double shot, £1.80 for a pint of bitter and around £1 for a soft drink, though most pubs usually have some promotion or other going on. Other than a packet of crisps, peanuts or occasionally a sandwich don't bank on getting something to eat in a local pub. You might have to be patient getting served, especially in the pubs nearest to the stadium, and persistence is advised although shouting too loudly at bar staff to attract attention is likely to get you blanked. When you do get served, use the phrase, "Take your own love/mate" and a small tip will be taken, which might just get you served quicker next time. Although far from comprehensive, here's a list of some of the more popular ale houses within walking distance of Anfield.

The Albert
185 Walton Breck Road

The Kopite watering hole and a must for first-time visitors in search of a pint. Stands adjacent to the Kop gates and an excellent pre-match singsong and electric atmosphere is guaranteed. LFC flags, scarves and photos adorn the walls, but not recommended for the claustrophobic.

The Park
194 Walton Breck Road

Standing directly opposite the Kop and another fans' favourite, you'd struggle to find more Reds packed into a pub on matchdays. The bar staff cope admirably, but getting served frequently requires a triumph of human spirit and endeavour over adversity. Great atmosphere, not a bad pint, but little elbow room when busiest.

Sam Dodd's Wine Bar
166/172 Oakfield Road

Don't be put off by the wine bar moniker. Dodd's attracts a younger crowd, it's spacious with a split-level interior but is still usually standing room only. Also boasts a Cellar Bar, which gets chocker as well. For post-match highlights, there are TVs throughout.

The Sandon
182 Oakfield Road

Fancy having a drink where the Reds used to get changed a hundred years ago? Liverpool's first chairman John Houlding once owned the Sandon Hotel and you will find LFC memorabilia on display. Within earshot of the Kop and usually packed to the rafters, this huge pub's five bars are more than able to cope.

The Salisbury
93 Granton Road

Can be a bit difficult to locate if you're not local, but this small corner boozer is five minutes walk from the Kop, off Oakfield Road. It has a recently done up Tudor-style lounge, but the bar room is lined with some special LFC memorabilia, including autographed players' shirts, photos and programmes from the 1970s and 80s when it was frequented by the players in the days when a post-match warm-down meant a few pints.

The Arkles
77 Anfield Road

A very popular boozer for home and away fans, it's on the adjacent corner to the Centenary Stand/Anfield Road. For post-match analysis and results elsewhere, you'll find satellite sports channels on the big screen. Real ales are also on sale.

The Breckside (Flat Iron)
377 Walton Breck Road

How often do you get the chance to have a bevvy in a triangular pub? The Breckside's unique shape is why locals call it the Flat Iron and it's very much a traditional Liverpool pub. Always packed on matchdays and only a five-minute walk from the Kop.

The Cabbage Hall
20 Breck Road

Walk another five minutes on from the Flat Iron away from Anfield down Walton Breck Road and you'll come to the Cabbage. The larger floor space allows for more comfort although it does get busy. There's big-screen football and limited car parking outside if you get there early enough.

The George
124 Breck Road

Traditional Scouse alehouse, reasonably busy when Liverpool are at home with two small seated bars. A 10-minute walk along Oakfield Road from the ground.

The Oakfield
49 Oakfield Road

Two bars, a pool table, dartboard and fine selection of Reds paraphernalia on the walls. What more could you want? Ten minutes walk to the ground, the Oakey gets quite busy and serves good ale for a traditional owl fella's pub.

The Grove
145 Breckfield Road North

A comfortable two-bar hostelry, 15 minutes' walk from the Kop. Not one for the real-ale connoisseur, despite the traditional feel of the place, but there's a pleasant atmosphere and it's worth a visit.

The King Harry
55 Blessington Road

A less than 10-minute walk along Anfield Road in the direction of Goodison and you're there. Keg-only ales, two quite small bars but comfortable and decorated within living memory – unlike some others in the locale. There's also a good selection of Reds items on display.

The King Charles
60 Grasmere Street

Set back from the main drags of Breck Road and Oakfield Road, so easier to get served and find somewhere to sit. A good mix of locals and matchday regulars from all over the country, there's a vibrant and friendly atmosphere at the King Charlie.

The Liverpool Supporters Club
212 Lower Breck Road

A 15-minute stroll from the ground along Priory Road or Walton Breck and naturally very popular on matchdays. It's been totally independent from the club for many years and is housed in what was once a cinema, so there's loads of space. If you can get in, you'll find an interesting array of Reds memorabilia together with very reasonably priced drinks.

201

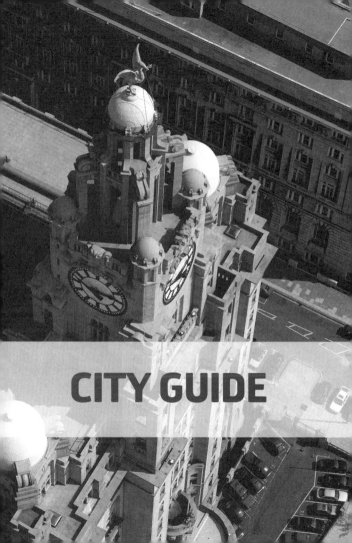

CITY GUIDE

CITY GUIDE

History of Liverpool I Famous Merseysiders I Getting there I Getting around
I Accommodation I Pubs and bars I Nightclubs

What does the rest of the world think of Liverpool and Scousers? Harry Enfield's comic stereotype of argumentative, moustachioed men sporting shellsuits and perms has a lot to answer for, as does Alan Bleasdale's Yosser Hughes. While the area around Anfield with its tight rows of terraced houses has hardly changed at all over the years, those who take the time to explore the recently redeveloped city centre and its diverse, vibrant nightlife will discover that Liverpool is anything but the 'slum' depicted in the tragically retro terrace jibe. The city has undeniably had it tough over the last 40 years, but now there is a new optimism and confidence about the place. In the words of one Kop chant: they all laugh at us, they all say our days are numbered. This 'us-against-the-world' philosophy, coupled with the sharpest wit in the business, mean that tired slurs get very short change. Liverpool is a great city, full of resilient, innovative people. We're proud of it and we'd like to show you around...

Liverpool

The pool of life

Perceptions are notoriously difficult to change but after 60 years of economic hardship and decline, the ongoing renaissance of Liverpool continues to confound those who like nothing better than to write the city off. Halfway through the 20th century, Liverpool found itself on the wrong side of an economic faultline: the world's pre-eminent commercial port went into steep decline, unemployment rose sharply and many of the city's wonderful buildings fell into disrepair. But throughout this long depression, Liverpool's cultural, social and sporting heritage, coupled with the unique and indomitable spirit of its people, ensured that the proud heart of this famous city never stopped beating. Today, economic and social regeneration, allied to serious investment and huge EU regeneration grants, have combined to give a never-less-than confident city a fresh swagger. While poverty is still a genuine problem across Merseyside, the Scouse Republic of Liverpool is undeniably back on the up.

Once the empire's second most powerful city and the gateway to the west for millions of European emigrants, Liverpool has long been a leader in music, humour and, of course, football. It is home to The Beatles, Europe's oldest Chinatown, Britain's largest cathedral and some of the most famous waterfront buildings in the world, but the modern Liverpool no longer has to look to its past to justify the present. A new, progressive self-confidence and civic pride is now evident throughout a city that, against the odds, has done so much to reinvent and rejuvenate itself in recent years.

Widescale redevelopment of the city centre has given rise to a vibrant nightlife, supported by countless bars, restaurants, cafes and nightclubs (notably Cream), that are both the envy of its metropolitan neighbours and a magnet for visitors of all nationalities. The superb Albert Dock redevelopment (Britain's largest collection of Grade I listed buildings) now provides a fitting face for Liverpool's historic waterfront. The pace with which old warehouses are being turned into desirable city centre dwellings is relentless, the city's universities are constantly over-subscribed and new service industries are making inroads into the city's higher than average unemployment statistics. Underpinning all these welcome improvements, however, is the bedrock of Liverpool's enduring legacy: the wit, pride, passion and sense of community that makes being Scouse such a badge of honour for its people.

Around town

One of the great things for the first-time visitor to Liverpool is the fact that many of the city's showpiece attractions can be reached easily on foot. The first stop is right on the doorstep of Lime Street Station – the Greek revival splendour of St George's Hall, a testament to the wealth once generated through transatlantic trade. Beyond the sculptures and pillars of Liverpool's former concert hall and courts – also the last stop on open-top bus tours for triumphant Liverpool teams – you have the choice of either turning back up the hill towards the cathedrals, universities and Georgian terraces of the Hope Street district or to travel along William Brown Street to the Walker Art Gallery, home to one of the country's finest provincial art collections, and the Liverpool Museum, housing a suitably eclectic and curious range of artefacts.

A stroll through the city centre will then acquaint the visitor with the bustling shopping areas of Bold Street and Church Street, and take them on a Beatles Magical Mystery Tour of the Cavern Quarter around Matthew Street. Venturing towards the waterfront, you pass the beautiful Georgian Town Hall on Water Street before spying the visual landmarks of the city, the twin Liver Birds on the Gotham-esque Royal Liver Building. Interestingly, the clock faces on the building are the largest in the world. Perhaps the best way to gain an appreciation of this dramatic cityscape and skyline is to see it from the water. Indeed, a ride of the ferry across the Mersey (bookings: 0151 330 1444), immortalised in the song, gives a romantic flavour of the first sights that greeted visitors from across the world and a taste of what first made Liverpool great. While down at the water's edge we also strongly recommend a visit to the Tate Gallery, the Museum of Liverpool Life and the Maritime Museum.

All the tourist information you could possible want – including timetables, maps and the comprehensive Visitor Guide, are available from two handy offices: the Queen's Square Centre centrally located in Queen's Square (Mon-Sat 9am-5.30pm, Sun 10.30am-4.30pm) and the Albert Dock Centre at the Atlantic Pavilion (daily 10.30am-5.30pm), which both share the same telephone enquiries number (0906 680 6886) and website (www.visitliverpool.com). Both also sell the National Museums and Galleries on Merseyside (NMGM) Eight Pass that gives unlimited access into eight local museums for twelve months.

Capital City of Culture 2008?

Sport aside, Liverpool is internationally famous for producing top musicians, writers, film and TV makers, actors, artists, designers, media personalities and comedians. So, it's hardly surprising that the city is among the favourites to become European Capital of Culture in 2008, a year after the city celebrates its 800th birthday.

Together with rival cities Newcastle/Gateshead, Belfast and Bradford

Liverpool as a World Heritage Site

Liverpool's magnificent water front could soon join the Taj Mahal, Pyramids, Great Wall of China, plus British sites Stonehenge, Durham Cathedral and the cities of Bath and Edinburgh as one of the world's most important historical landmarks if it is successful in its attempt to be granted official recognition – as a world heritage site – by UNESCO. But why?

Liverpool was the country's pre-eminent commercial port of the 19th century at the time of Britain's greatest global influence. It carried most of the trans-Atlantic trade, saw much of the emigration from Northern Europe, and the docks and commercial district of offices and exchanges are evidence of the importance and prosperity of the city at the time.

The bid to become a world heritage site is being put together by Liverpool City Council and English Heritage. Liverpool has been placed on a tentative list of 15 sites by the government and once all the applications have been submitted, they will decide which nomination to forward to UNESCO in June 2004. UNESCO then considers all the entries over an 18-month period. The man responsible for compiling the documents is John Hinchliffe, a Kop season-ticket holder for almost 20 years. "We basically have to prove the case that Liverpool is of outstanding universal value, so we'll be looking at the history of the site, including a statement of world significance, the potential pressures on the area, tourism considerations and so on," says John.

While the bid is founded on the city's mercantile history, it won't be confined to the dock wall and extends to include the warehouse structures of Albert, Wapping and Stanley Docks as well as business areas like Dale and Victoria Streets and the William Brown Street quarter. World-heritage-site status is a great honour that will bring recognition of the international importance of Liverpool in world history and such promotion of the city would lead to increases income for regeneration. Contact the Liverpool City Council's Conservation Team on 0151 233 5678 for further details.

among others, Liverpool submitted its bid in March 2002. A government shortlist was then drawn up in September 2002 and a final decision is expected in March 2003.

Providing a significant injection of wealth into the local economy, the creative industries account for almost five per cent of Merseyside jobs and generate an estimated annual turnover of almost half a billion pounds. A successful bid would lead to more jobs and growing wealth within the city's creative sector. A positive financial knock-on effect in commerce, retail and tourism is also predicted. To spearhead and coordinate the bid on behalf of the city, the Liverpool Culture Company was set up as an independent organisation with campaign veteran Sir Bob Scott as chief executive.

Born to be a Scouse

Famous Merseysiders

Liverpool's Fab Four – **John Lennon, Paul McCartney, George Harrison** and **Ringo Starr** – have been joined by plenty of other famous Scousers down the years. BBC newsreader **Peter Sissons** went to school with **Jimmy Tarbuck** and John Lennon, while former Liverpool Echo journalist and TV quiz 'mistress' **Anne Robinson** was born and raised in Crosby.

Famous Scouse thespians include Sex In The City's **Kim Catterall**, who grew up in Mossley Hill, and **Malcolm McDowell** – star of controversial 1970s flick A Clockwork Orange – was born and raised in Anfield. Celebrated actor Sir **Rex Harrison** (1908-1990), of Dr Doolittle and My Fair Lady fame, was Huyton-born and Rising Damp and Reggie Perrin comic genius **Leonard Rossiter** (1926–1984) grew up in Toxteth. The Royle Family's **Ricky Tomlinson** lived his boyhood years in Everton, while **Keith Chegwin** and his sister, broadcaster **Janice Long** came from Bootle, as did former glamour model **Kathy Lloyd**.

From the world of politics, four times British prime minister **William Ewart Gladstone** MP (1809-1898) was born in Liverpool. The current PM's wife, Cherie Blair QC, was born and raised in Crosby.

Famous Merseyside writers include successful author of children's fiction **Brian Jacques**, and film maker and writer of sci-fi classics like Hellraiser, **Clive Barker**. Comedian, actor and author **Alexei Sayle** is a son of Anfield. Playwright **Alan Bleasedale** (Boys From The Blackstuff) is a Scouser and **Willy Russell** (Blood Brothers, Educating Rita) is Whiston-born. Brookside supremo **Phil Redmond** grew up in Huyton as did comedian **Freddie Starr**.

Leading the way: Liverpool firsts

- The Lyceum building in Bold Street once housed Europe's first lending library, opening its doors in 1757
- Diabetes was first recognised as such in 1776 by Dr Matthew Dobson who practised in Liverpool's Harrington Street
- In 1776, the world's first lifeboat service set up just up the coast from Liverpool in Formby
- The world's first chemist (or dispensary) opened in Liverpool's Princess Street in 1778
- The world's first animal-welfare centre opened in Liverpool in 1809 – the organisation went on to become the RSPCA
- The world's first passenger railway opened in 1830 and ran between Liverpool and Manchester
- The world's first school of tropical medicine opened in Liverpool in 1898 and was responsible for discovering malaria could be spread by mosquitoes
- Alder Hey, in West Derby, is Europe's largest children's hospital
- Both Littlewoods and Vernons pools competitions were started in Liverpool The Moores family – forefathers of the current Liverpool chairman, David – started Littlewoods –
- Liverpool's China Town is the oldest in Europe

Getting there

Liverpool's historic position as the 'Gateway to the West' means it has traditionally been one of the UK's most accessible cities. And despite the best efforts of Virgin Trains and those responsible for upping the UK population of traffic cones, this still remains the case.

Trains

Mainline trains pull into Lime Street Station to the north of the city centre. Trains from Liverpool Lime Street to London's Euston run hourly (2 hr 55min) and there are direct rail links with most other UK cities. Manchester is less than an hour away, while Leeds and Birmingham can be reached in two hours or less. For timetable and fare information, call 08457 484950.

Merseyrail, Liverpool's underground network, is very small (four stations:

Central, Moorfields, James Street, and Lime Street) and although it can be a quick way of getting across the city, as most places are within walking distance it's not really needed unless it's raining. Trains also serve other suburbs of the city and across the River Mersey to the Wirral which in turn connects to the Roman city of Chester, North Wales and beyond. For local timetable and fare information, call 0151 236 7676.

Coaches

National Express (0900 808080) coaches arrive at the city's station on Norton Street, just north east of Lime Street. Local buses depart from a variety of terminals: Queen Square (for city centre, Pier Head and Chester services); Paradise Street (southbound and a few northbound services); and St Thomas Street (eastbound and cross-river).

Flights

Liverpool's John Lennon Airport (0151 288 4000) is situated in Speke, seven miles south east of Liverpool city centre and just five minutes from the nearby motorway network serving the rest of the UK. It has direct flight connections to Luton, Ireland, the Isle of Man and nine major European destinations thanks to EasyJet. There are regular bus and train links to the city centre or you could jump in a taxi and expect to pay up to £12.

Driving

Anfield gets very busy on matchdays and we do not recommend you drive to the ground unless you intend to arrive early. The main problem is parking around the stadium, although finding Anfield is fairly straightforward.

From the north take the M6 until junction 28 then follow signs for Liverpool on A58. Continue straight on into Walton Hall Avenue past Stanley Park and turn left into Anfield Road for the ground.

From the south take the M6 then M62 until the end of motorway. Turn right at signs for the A5058 into Queens Drive. After three miles, turn left into Utting Avenue, then right into Anfield Road for the ground.

From the west take the Mersey Tunnel into Liverpool city centre, then follow signs for Preston A580 into Walton Hall Avenue. This becomes Walton Lane, take a right into Anfield Road for the ground.

From the east take the M6 until junction 28 then follow signs for Liverpool on A58. Then as from the north.

211

Parking around the ground

Anfield is surrounded by tight, terraced streets which can make parking a real problem. The main matchday carpark is found in Stanley Park, behind the Anfield Road end. Conversely, if you arrive early enough you might be able to find a space in one of the surrounding roads where you are advised to accept the charge for having your car 'minded' by a young, tracksuited urchin. You should not have to pay more than £3 for the pleasure. There are also a few unofficial carparks along Walton Breck Road that charge around £5.

Getting around

Buses, local trains and taxis

Liverpool Lime Street is about three miles from the ground. To catch a local train take Merseyrail to Sandhills station, just over a mile from the stadium. A shuttle bus runs from the station to Anfield on matchdays costing just 50p extra return when you buy your ticket. Merseyrail prepaid tickets are also accepted. Call 0151 330 1066. If you prefer to walk, turn right out of the station along Sandhills Lane. At the lights go up the hill along Lambeth Road with the park on the right. Turn right before the Lambeth pub and 100 yards further on hang a left into Whittle Street. At Kirkdale Road turn left, then right and up the hill. Continue straight over the lights then turn right into Walton Breck Road when you see a signpost to Anfield. The ground is a little way up on the left.

Bus numbers 17, 17c, 17d, or 217 will take you from Queen's Square by Liverpool Lime Street station to Anfield. Or numbers 26 and 27 run from Paradise Street. Fares and routes vary; for more information visit the Queen Square Information Centre or call the Merseytravel information line 0151 236 7676.

Black cabs are easily available. There are taxi ranks across the city but you'll probably be quicker to hail a passing cab. It should cost no more than a fiver from the city centre.

Hotels, food, drink, clubs

Accommodation

City-centre accommodation has improved over recent years and there's a fair choice of hotels, from budget chains and small-scale guest houses to business-orientated four-stars. There's also an excellent youth hostel a short walk from Albert Dock for those who don't mind dorm-style accommodation. The tourist offices can help with specific recommendations but you're unlikely to beat the prices at the budget chains in the centre. Both tourist offices will book rooms for you for free and can supply details of their special-offer weekend breaks and packages, call 0845 6011125.

Hotel prices below are for a double room for two persons per night, including breakfast. They were current as of June-2002.

Budget (under £70)

Aachen Hotel
89-91 Mount Pleasant
Tel 0151 709 3477; 17 rooms; £54
Award-winning hotel located at the heart of the city and handy for Lime Street. Famous for its 'eat as much as you like' breakfast.

Alicia Hotel
Aigburth Drive
Tel: 0151 727 4411; 39 rooms; £65
A country house-style hotel located in Sefton Park, close to the picturesque Lark Lane and a fiver in a taxi from the city centre. It boasts a late bar for residents.

Antrim Hotel
73 Mount Pleasant
Tel: 0151 709 5239; 20 rooms; £55
A friendly family-run hotel popular with football fans, probably because the bar stays open late. Book early to avoid disappointment.

Campanile Hotel
Wapping and Chaloner Street
Tel: 0151 709 8104; 100 rooms; £54.85
Situated next to Albert Dock and overlooking the water front, the Campanile is competitively priced but its bar closes at 11pm.

Devonshire Hotel
Edge Lane
Tel: 0151 263 2109; 54 rooms; £58
Packed with football fans during the season, the Devonshire is 10 minutes by car from Anfield and 2½ miles from the city centre. The social bar stays open until the last person leaves!

Gladstone Hotel
Lord Nelson Street
Tel: 0151 709 7050; 154 rooms; £57
Turn right out of the side entrance of Lime Street Station and walk up the hill. Modest rooms but a quite marvellous breakfast.

Henry's Premier Lodge
45 Victoria Street
Tel: 0870 7001422; 39 rooms; £62.45
Perfect location for museums, shopping, nightlife and Beatles fans, this competitive Premier Lodge is close to the Cavern Quarter.

Hotel Ibis
Liver Street
Tel: 0151 706 9800; 127 rooms; £53.50
If you don't mind sharing a double bed with a mate then the Ibis is a good option. A bar, restaurant and close proximity to Albert Dock make it a popular choice.

Howard Johnson Hotel
Ribblers Lane, Knowsley
Tel: 0151 549 2700; 86 rooms; £68
214 Located 7 miles out of town and close to junction 4 of the M57, this modern hotel is conveniently placed for Anfield and features a late-night resident's bar.

Lord Nelson Hotel
Lord Nelson Street
Tel: 0151 709 4362; 58 rooms; £48 B&B
Right opposite the Gladstone, it boasts a 24-hour bar for residents and easy access to many and varied delights of Liverpool on a Saturday night.

YHA
Tabley Street
Tel: 0151 709 8888; 15 rooms; £38
Dormitory-style accommodation with rooms for six, four or two people. Ideally placed for a pint at the Baltic Fleet pub.

Mid-range to expensive (£70 – £140)
Britannia Adelphi Hotel
Ranelagh Place
Tel: 0151 709 7200; 402 rooms; £116
One of the city's landmarks, the Adelphi was the subject of BBC's Hotel series. Crystal chandeliers and the odd four-poster bed adds to the feeling of faded grandeur.

Crowne Plaza
St Nicholas Place, Princes Dock
Tel: 0151 243 8000; 159 rooms; £100
A stylish haunt popular with the 'beautiful people', The Plaza is set on the water front and boasts excellently-appointed rooms and leisure facilities including great swimming pool with view of the Mersey.

Feathers Hotel
Lord Nelson Street
Tel: 0151 709 9655; 75 rooms; £90
Access to the neighbouring university's gym and pool mean guests can work off the excesses of the bar, restaurant and 'help yourself' breakfast.

Marriott Hotel
Queen Square
Tel: 0151 476 8000; 146 rooms; £130
Panoramic views of the city, a selection of bars and restaurants and even the chance to top up your Big Ron suntan (additional extra).

Thistle Hotel
Chapel Street
Tel: 0151 227 4444; 226 rooms; £87
Ship-shaped hotel a stone's throw from the Liver Buildings on the water front, it is ideally placed for Albert Dock and a night on the town.

Restaurants
The renaissance of the city centre means it now successfully caters for all tastes and budgets. Lovers of Chinese food will be pleased to discover Liverpool has its own Chinatown beginning at Berry Street and following down to Nelson Street. As cosmopolitan as you would expect from the UK's first genuinely multi-ethnic city.

Beechers Brook
29a Hope Street. Tel: 0151 707 0005
European restaurant serving fresh food prepared daily on the premises. Listed in Good Food, Egon Ronay and Michelin Guides.

Blue Bar and Grill
17 Edward Pavilion. Tel: 0151 709 70 97
An eclectic menu and expansive balcony attract the city's fashion conscious. Popular haunt of the players.

Caesar's Palace
5 - 9 Renshaw Street. Tel: 0151 708 7787
Situated in the heart of Liverpool city centre, the dazzlingly designed Caesar's Palace offers a varied and competitively priced menu.

Chung Ku
Columbus Quay. Tel: 0151 726 8191
Only a few minutes north along the dock road, this split-level, avant-garde eaterie has a relaxed atmosphere and panoramic views of the river.

De Coubertin's Sports Bar & Restaurant
43 North John Street. Tel: 0151 284 1996
A sports-themed restaurant and bar full of interesting memorabilia with an American-style menu and a wide range of wines, cocktails and beers.

El Macho Cantinas
Hope Street. Tel: 0151 708 6644
This famous haunt in the university quarter serves up traditional Mexican food in a lively atmosphere. Frozen margaritas are recommended.

Everyman Bistro
9-11 Hope Street. Tel: 0151 708 9545
Egon Ronay recommended, this theatre-basement venue has been a firm favourite among musicians, artists and actors for 30 years. Late bar.

Life Café
1a Bold Street. Tel: 0151 707 2333
Modern restaurant set in one of Liverpool's most beautiful historic buildings, the Lyceum. With a varied menu and lively café bar next door, serving everything from cocktails to cappuccinos.

Little Asia
9 Victoria Street. Tel: 0151 227 9009
Found on one of the trendiest and up-and-coming streets in Liverpool, this innovative new venue combines Indian, Thai and Chinese foods. Lively cocktail bar downstairs.

Newz Brasserie
18 Water Street. Tel: 0151 236 2025
A lively after-work bar atmosphere combined with a superb à la carte menu courtesy of Stewart St John, one of Merseyside's most distinguished chefs.

Not Sushi
4-24 Exchange Street East. Tel: 0151 709 8854
Situated in the basement of Modo, Not Sushi was one of first noodle bars in the north west. An excellent selection in stark, reflective surroundings.

Number 60
60 Hope Street. Tel: 0151 707 6060
A stylish but unpretentious new restaurant in the heart of Liverpool. While the more expensive restaurant is a favourite with Gérard Houllier, the basement Cafe Bar is perfect for a more informal meal.

217

Simply Heathcote
Beetham Plaza. Tel: 0151 236 3536
At the top end of the range, Michelin-starred chef Paul Heathcote's acclaimed eaterie offers modern British cooking in stylish surroundings.

St Petersburg
7 York Street. Tel: 0151 709 6676
If Russian cuisine is your thing we recommend you try the borsch and beef stroganov. Good, authentic food in a relaxed atmosphere. Late bar.

The Living Room
Victoria Street. Tel: 0151 236 1999
Trendy, airy piano bar with an à la carte grill menu. Excellent food and a huge range of cocktails makes this a popular place to be seen in.

The Pan American Club
Britannia Pavilion, Albert Dock. Tel: 0151 709 1156
Cocktails, US beers and spirits, the best of regional American cuisine and an authentic daytime deli cafe menu. Set in the Grade I listed Britannia Pavilion with club menu on ground floor or à la carte on the mezzanine.

Valparaiso Restaurant
4 Hardman Street. Tel: 0151 708 6036
Offers Latin American specialities, seafood, vegetarian menu and Chilean wines. Reservations recommended.

Chinatown
If you're in the mood for a Chinese meal the best bet is to head for Chinatown (Berry Street and Nelson Street). Liverpool boasts the oldest Chinese community in Europe and a whole host of excellent restaurants, plus it's a great place to go after the pubs and clubs have closed.

The Far East
27-35 Berry Street. Tel: 0151 709 3141
A cavernous dining room run by the Cheung family. Tony the boss can regularly be seen chatting with customers and making sure everyone is happy. They invariably are.

Yuet Ben
1 Upper Duke Street. Tel: 0151 709 5772

Liverpool's first and original Peking style restaurant was established in 1968 just a stone's throw from its present premises. Authentic flavours of northern Chinese cuisine.

Pubs and bars
The success of the nightclub Cream has revolutionised Liverpool's nightlife in the last decade, attracting thousands of new visitors and encouraging entrepreneurs to cash in on the hordes of clubbers who throng the streets each weekend. The traditional ale house culture characterised by clouds of cigarette smoke and owl fellas crooning to the juke box still exists in the city's superb and numerous old-school pubs, but fashionable new bars featuring DJs, stripped pine floors and fancy sofas seem to be springing up each week. The result is a city that while it has never needed an excuse to party now finds itself with a feast of venues to choose from (over 250 in the city centre alone). We start our tour of Liverpool's rich and abundant nightlife with a few fine ales in traditional surroundings before following the conga of exposed female flesh in search of a cocktail and a boogie.

Traditional Liverpool pubs
Drinking has traditionally had an important place in Scouse culture and few cities can rival Liverpool's selection of grand old ale houses, most within walking distance of Lime Street Station.

Around the station
McHales Bar
Lime Street

More commonly known as the Yankee Bar, this historic boozer was popular with US servicemen during the war but is now home to Liverpool's 'ard knocks'. Not recommended for out-of-towners.

The Dispensary
Renshaw Street

Formerly known as The Grapes, this famous city-centre pub has been refurbished to provide the ambience of a traditional Victorian ale house. Its cask-drawn ales are also highly rated.

The Globe
Cases Street
A long, narrow old-school pub that is traditionally lively before and after games. Watch out for the sloping floor if you've had a few.

The Vines
Lime Street
Situated on the corner opposite The Adelphi, this sumptuous Edwardian building features an interior enhanced by ornate plasterwork, copper sheeting and its own art collection.

Towards the river
Doctor Duncans
St Johns Lane
The redesigned interior reflects a traditional Victorian ale house and celebrates the life of local legend Dr Duncan, a GP who fought for better living conditions for the working classes of Liverpool.

Ship And Mitre
Dale Street
Voted pub of the year in 2001, the Ship And Mitre offers an excellent choice of real ale and the finest sausages in Liverpool.

The Baltic Fleet
Wapping
Located opposite the Albert Docks, this Grade II listed building is one of the last of the old dockers' pubs in the city. The nautical interior is split into three floors.

The First National
James Street
Originally a banking hall with ornate gothic pillars, The First National has been modernised to reflect a comfortable pub atmosphere.

The Railway
Tithebarn Street
Open plan pub with smaller rooms at the back and a TV showing sport. Not a great selection of beers but the finest toasted sandwiches around.

Around the university
The Philharmonic
Hope Street
A popular and incredibly beautiful Victorian pub near the university, The Philharmonic was one of John Lennon's favourite watering holes, possibly because of the gents amazing marble urinals.

The Pilgrim
Pilgrim Street
Very studenty and very loud, this two-floor pub boasts live music, karaoke and decent prices. Quality atmosphere guaranteed.

Ye Olde Cracke
Rice Street
Excellent and reassuringly dark pub at the top of the hill. Loads of guest beers, a circular bar but not many tables. Lennon used to drink here when he was an art student.

Cavern Quarter
The spiritual home of the Merseybeat revolution, offering a riotous and inebriated night on the tiles. References to the Beatles abound as you stagger through the tight alleys and lanes towards the next pint.

Flanagan's Apple
Matthew Street
Superb Guinness, guaranteed singalong on a Saturday night and top live music make for the original, and still the best, Irish pub in town.

Lennon's Bar
Matthew Street
Another Beatles-themed watering hole that serves food. Usually packed to the rafters with a lively crowd enjoying good music.

Rubber Soul
Matthew Street
Reasonably modern and more spacious than many of its Matthew Street neighbours, Rubber Soul is a popular local's' boozer.

The Cavern Pub
Matthew Street
This themed pub highlights all the bands that played at The Cavern between 1957 and 1993. There's a statue of John Lennon outside. Natch.

The Grapes
Matthew Street
As The Cavern did not have a license to serve alcohol, The Beatles used to duck into The Grapes for a pint before and after gigs. A certain American student by the name of Bill Clinton is also rumoured to have once broken up a fight between Ringo Starr and a local drunk.

The White Star
Rainford Gardens
When rowdy musicians were chucked out of The Grapes, they'd inevitably seek refuge in The White Star. The Beatles were no different.

Bold Street/Concert Square/Wood Street
When the **Baa Bar** opened in 1992, few could've predicted the influence that the city's first pre-club hangout would have on Liverpool's bar scene. Trendy establishments with late licences are springing up everywhere, neatly filling the vacuum between pubs and clubs, and the mixture of exotic spirits and dance music caters for those who can't be bothered to stand shivering in the queue for Cream. Welcome to the human zoo.

Bar VR
Bold Street
A busy bar that does a roaring trade with its midweek cheap drink offers and quality in-house DJs.

Life Café
Bold Street
Modern and spread over two floors, this café bar has become very popular in the last year. Packed with dressed-to-kill twentysomethings.

222 ### Mello Mello
Slater Street
Probably past the height of popularity, Mello Mello is still a great place

to chill out and features possibly the most comfortable chairs in the city.

Baa Bar
Fleet Street
The first of Liverpool's new wave of pre-club bars, it's now something of an institution, even if its popularity has waned slightly.

Beluga
Wood Street
The basement bar Beluga avoids commercial sounds in favour of a more chilled music policy. Less dressy than others it's still very busy at weekends.

Chillies 2
Wood Street
The cod Tex Mex decor, bright lights and loud music make Chillies a popular early evening haunt. Hosts Salsa classes during the week.

Qube
Wood Street
Generally booming over the weekend, Qube is a local's' favourite that also attracts the occasional footballer. DJs and cheap Stella are the key.

Revolution
Wood Street
Fight your way through the Concert Square crowds to sample the multitude of vodkas. Another cool bar with a funky music policy.

RSVP
Wood Street
Nice food, friendly staff and pounding music mean RSVP's three rooms are packed. Big chairs mean you can enjoy your vodka jelly in comfort.

Edwards
Concert Square
There are three Edwards in Liverpool City Centre. The one in Concert Square has three floors and attracts a trendy clientele.

Rococo Modo
Concert Square

A mix between bar and club, Modos has an upfront music policy that centres on house at the weekends and pop during the week. Massive and very popular with the club crowd.

The Arena
Concert Square

A massive venue featuring a dance floor that's invariably rammed at the weekends and a patio that's chocker in the summer. Comes into its own on a warm evening when the windows are flung open.

Albert Dock

If Concert Square proves too hot to handle then a short stroll will lead you to the impressive Albert Dock redevelopment which serves up an altogether more laid-back vibe.

Blue Bar
Edward Pavilion

The city's flagship-style bar opened in 1998 with a fine restaurant on the first floor. The light, airy and minimalist bar area is popular with footballers and celebs alike.

Bar Monaco
Atlantic Pavilion

The wonderful views of Albert Dock are the main feature of this chilled, stylish bar populated by a young professional crowd. The music policy leans towards jazz, funk and soul which makes it less hectic than others.

The Pumphouse
Albert Dock

A large, fairly standard boozer housed in a striking building was once the pumping station for the Dock.

Hardman Street
With the Philharmonic on the corner, you could do a lot worse than getting your weekend started in one of many lively venues on Hardman Street.

The Magnet
Hardman Street
Lively mix of local's and minor celebrities, combined with some strange decoration, make the Magnet a quality venue for a post-match session.

Kirklands
Hardman Street
Once vied with Plummers for the pre-club crowd but since the explosion of new venues downtown, the queues have not been so formidable.

Plummers
Hardman Street
Formerly a regular haunt for the in-crowd, the stripped wood floors and fancy stools provided a template for many of the city's fashionable bars.

Nightclubs
The coachloads of clubbers that pour into Liverpool each weekend are evidence of the city's pre-eminent position in danceland's pecking order. Cream is still the hot ticket, but with new venues and nights opening up with head-spinning regularity there's no shortage of alternatives. Most places operate a smart/casual dress policy – a world removed from the seminal days of dancing on the bar at the city's first rave venue, the legendary Quadrant Park in Bootle (sadly closed some years ago).

Aquarium
Seel Street
Two dance floors bossed by Lee Butler and Pez Tellet make the Aquarium's 2Tasty Thursday nighter an absolute must for house heads.

Barcelona
Renshaw Street
Packed out week after week, Barcelona has an amazing interior design but a small dance floor occasionally leads to problems usually sorted by the scariest bouncers in Liverpool.

Club 051
Mount Pleasant
One of the city's longest-running clubs, the 051 was there at the start and is still running top-quality deep-house nights featuring the best DJs.

Cream
Wolstenholme Square
One of the most famous clubnights in the world, Cream is held at the massive Nation Complex. The club that blazed the trail and continues to lead the way, attracting clubbers from all over the world.

Garlands
Erberle Street
A mixed-gay crowd throngs every Friday to bouncy house and tough beats. Garlands welcomes the 'the black, the white, the gay and the straight'.

Krazy House
Wood Street
Three floors, an eclectic music policy and the biggest collection of grinning nutters in the north west make the Krazy House an attitude-free Saturday night with a difference

Lomax L2
Hotham Street
Live-music venue that tends to showcase indie favourites, rock monsters and classic funksters. A big favourite with Liverpool's students.

Society
Fleet Street
In the heart of the city's café/club quarter, Society is a sumptuous New York warehouse venue that attracts a sexy, dressed-up crowd and showcases visiting DJs from the UK's top club nights.

The Velvet Lounge
Bold Street
226 Every Friday and Saturday chill out to The Elements of Life which serves up the best jazz, funk R&B and disco.

AWAY DAYS

AWAY DAYS

The guide to Premiership away grounds 2002/03 | Bogey teams | Lucky teams

Last season Anfield was voted the ground away fans most enjoy visiting, but what of Liverpool's famous travelling support? The stories of mass mobilisations of Kopites are legend, from the red army that descended on Molineux for the title decider in 1976 to the human convoy of 30,000 Liverpudlians that snaked across Europe for the night of nights in Rome a year later. Then there was Stamford Bridge in 1986 when Chelsea's crumbling away end was turned into a temporary Kop to see Kenny land the first half of the Double and, of course, Dortmund in 2001 when red swamped three-and-a-half sides of the Westfalenstadion for the unforgettable 5-4 beating of Alavés.

The days of huge terraces are gone and the opportunity for major turn-outs for away games are few and far between these days. However, the spirit of the trans-Alpino veterans, those intrepid fans who blazed a trail across Europe in the 1970s and established Liverpool's support as the Continent's best, still lives on. Now that the club has re-established itself as a force in Europe, Liverpool's travelling fans regard every tie, every round as the opportunity for new adventure. The obscure hats, badges, shirts and flags seen on the Kop the week after European trips visible reminders.

But it is the more familiar destinations of the Premiership that take up the travel plans of most fans. Last season Houllier's men won 12 times away from home, a massive improvement on the previous campaign and inspired, as the manager would testify, by the incredible support the team enjoys on its travels. Getting tickets for Premiership away games can be as difficult as planning an overland route to Kiev, but the craic, the camaraderie and the 'us against the world' spirit produced by travelling Kopites often make away games the most memorable. So, with this in mind, we present the essential guide to following Liverpool on the road.

229

Arsenal

Stadium Highbury
Capacity 38,500
Away allocation 2,800 (Clock End and West Stand Lower)
Address Avenell Road, London N5 1BU
Telephone 020 7704 4000 (tickets 020 7704 4040)
Website www.arsenal.co.uk
Independent website www.arseweb.co.uk, www.arsenal-world.com
Fanzines The Gooner, Up The Arse, Highbury High, Gunflash
Eats The Exquisite offers half-price food and wine before 7pm and the Moonshine Cafe serves a great fry-up, both on Blackstock Road; Golden Fish Bar in Gillespie Road offers, you've guessed it, top-class fish'n'chips; for your normal reconstituted meat stuff try the burger vans outside the Arsenal World Of Sport shop in Station Place, next to Finsbury Park tube.
Drinks The Auld Triangle, St Thomas's Road; Arsenal Tavern, Blackstock Road (don't wear colours); The Drayton Park, behind the away end, is a popular haunt for visiting fans, as is the World's End at Finsbury Park.
By car From NORTH M6, M1 and exit at junction 2. Follow signs for City. After Holloway Road Station (6¼ miles) turn third left into Drayton Park, after ¾ mile turn right into Aubert Park and second left on to Avenell Road. **From SOUTH** at London Bridge follow signs to Bank of England, then Angel. Turn right at traffic lights towards Highbury roundabout on to Holloway Road, and third right into Drayton Park. Then as from north. **From WEST** M4 exit at Junction 1, take A315 towards Chiswick, left after 1 mile to M41, then A40 (M) to A501 ring road. Turn left at Angel then as from south.
Parking On street only and very restricted at that. Best option is to park near Caledonian Road or Bounds Green, either side of Arsenal tube station on the Piccadilly Line.
By bus Victoria Coach Station, then Victoria Line tube to Finsbury Park.
By rail Euston Station, then Victoria Line to Finsbury Park or Piccadilly Line to Arsenal station.
Last season 1-2 (h) 1-1(a). Champions
Premiership record P20 W11 L4 D5 F25 A10

230 **Traveller's notes** Something of a regular early season away trip in recent years, the visit to Highbury is rarely less than incident packed. If the referee is not brandishing red cards at anything that moves (three players

have been sent off in two of the last three matches between the clubs at Highbury) then something similarly surreal will probably be taking place, like Jamie Carragher returning fire at the Gooners in the Lower East Stand. Last season saw our successful run against the Londoners come to an end and they will be the benchmark against which Houllier's class of 2002/03 measure themselves.

Did you know Liverpool have faced Arsenal in four major cup finals, winning only once. The Gunners came out on top in the Reds' second FA Cup final in 1950, and again when they came from behind in 1971 to complete the Double. In the 1987 League Cup final the Londoners then spoilt a 144-game record by beating Liverpool in a game where Ian Rush had scored. Sweet revenge came in 2001 when Michael Owen's late double won the FA Cup at Cardiff.

ARSENAL FOOTBALL CLUB PLC

FA CUP 4TH RD SPONSORED BY AXA
ARSENAL V LIVERPOOL
27 JAN 2002 01:00 AFTERNOON

SOUTH STAND CLOCK END BLOCK 20
BLOCK   ROW   SEAT   PRICE
20   29   106   £24.00

TO BE RETAINED   SEGA   VISITORS SECTION   SEGA

Aston Villa

Stadium Villa Park
Capacity 42,500
Away allocation 3,000 (North Stand)
Address Trinity Road, Birmingham B6 6HE
Telephone 0121 327 2299 (tickets 0121 327 5353)
Website www.avfc.co.uk
Independent website www.heroesandvillains.net, www.villa.org.uk
Fanzines Heroes And Villains, The Holy Trinity

Eats Villa Fish Bar on Manor Road is handy from Witton station; otherwise try the Aston Lane Fish Bar on the corner of Aston Lane and London Road; for a taste of the West Indies (or, in contrast, a full English breakfast) call in at Silver Sands Caribbean Takeaway on Witton Road; on the novelty tip, sample a Villa balti inside the ground… but only once. Post match, get a cab to the Balti Triangle of Moseley, Sparkhill and Sparkbrook.

Drinks Near Witton station The Harriers and the Yew Tree are decent pubs for away fans, as is the Witton Arms; Broad Street is Birmingham's 'golden mile' for pubs, including the Sports Cafe, Key Largo, All Bar One, Tiger Tiger, The Figure of Eight and Bakers.

By car From NORTH exit M6 at junction 6 (Spaghetti Junction) on to the A38 (M) Aston Expressway towards the city centre. Take first exit right on to Victoria Road. At roundabout take right exit into Witton Road for Villa Park. **From SOUTH** take M1 to junction 19 then M6. Exit at junction 6 then as from north. **From EAST** M42 to junction 8. M6 heading towards Birmingham then as from north. **From SOUTH EAST** at the end of the M5 the road divides, keep left and follow signs for London M1 M40 on to M6 eastbound. Exit junction 7 or 6 and as from north.

Parking Car parks at Aston Villa Leisure Centre on Aston Hall Road and Brookvale Road at the junction with Tame Road. On-street parking is restricted around the ground.

By bus Take no7 from outside Marks & Spencer in city centre to the ground – you'll know when you're there by the queue of claret and blue.

By rail From Birmingham New Street take a local train to Witton station, it's a two-minute walk from ground, or Aston station, 10 minutes away.

Last season 1-3 (h) 2-1(a). 8th

232

Premiership record P20 W10 L8 D2 F34 A24

Traveller's notes Traditionally one of the best awaydays of the season, Villa Park always seems to attract a particularly voluble and large Reds following. We have enjoyed many happy times at Villa in the last 20 years, ranging from Ian Rush's seminal hat-trick on a frost-bitten night in 1982 to winning FA Cup semi-finals against Portsmouth and Wycombe. Better still, we've won three of our last four Premiership matches at Villa Park – a ground that has undeniably lost some of its charm with the erection of the soulless, new Doug Ellis Stand. Much like the Villa team, it could be said.

Did you know In May 1980 Israeli defender Avi Cohen scored the one and only goal of his Liverpool career in a championship-clinching 4-1 victory over Aston Villa at Anfield. Earlier that afternoon, Cohen had put Villa ahead with an own goal.

Blackburn Rovers

Stadium Ewood Park

Capacity 31,500

Away allocation 4,000 (Darwen End)

Address Blackburn BB2 4JF

Telephone 01254 698888 (tickets 01254 671666)

Website www.rovers.co.uk

Independent website www.4000holes.org.uk, www.brfc-supporters.org.uk

Fanzines 4000 Holes, Colin's Cheeky Bits

Eats Opposite the ground on Bolton Road visiting fans can gorge themselves at the Mother Riley Cafe, or there's a 'walk-thru' McDonalds at Ewood Triangle. Whatever that is.

Drinks The Fernhurst on Bolton Road is close to the away end; The Ewood Park, The Ewood Arms, The Aquaduct, The Moorings, Angel, Brown Cow and the Waters Edge are all within a short stroll of the ground.

By car From NORTH leave M6 at junction 29 and join M61. At first exit join M65 and head east to Blackburn. At junction 4 join A666 Blackburn. Ewood Park is well signposted and about 1 mile away on the right. **From SOUTH** exit M6 at junction 29 for M65. Head east to Blackburn then as from north. **From WEST** from M6/M62 or M60 join M61. Exit at M65 and head east. Then as from north or south. **From EAST** from Yorkshire, either B6234, A56 Haslingden bypass or the Skipton Road, join M65 and head west. Then as from north, south or east.

233

Parking Behind The Fernhurst in the Youth Aid car park off Albion Road; Albion Mill car park on Albion Street; industrial estate car parks on Branch Road. All within a stone's throw of the stadium.

By bus Blackburn Central bus station is next to the railway station. Services 3, 3A, 3B, 46, 346 all go from Blackburn to Darwen. Ewood Park is about 1½ miles into the journey.

By rail Manchester Piccadilly, then change for Blackburn. The ground is a couple of miles from the station.

Last season 4-3 (h) 1-1 (a). 10th

Premiership record P16 W7 L4 D5 F24 A23

Traveller's notes Blackburn Rovers are normally generous with their allocation which makes for a decent atmosphere in what is one of the shortest away trips of the year. The frisson between former team-mates and colleagues, Graeme Souness and Phil Thompson, made for some interesting touchline viewing last season in what was the first head-to-head since the former sacked the latter during his time in charge at Anfield. Blackburn itself is possibly one of the least exciting places on the planet but Rovers have some tasty players in Damian Duff, David Dunn and the Turkish midfielder Tugay to compensate. Our record at the impressively redeveloped Ewood Park is reasonable and nothing more.

Did you know In 1994/95 Liverpool came from behind to beat Blackburn 2-1 in the final match of the season at Anfield. But as Manchester United failed to beat West Ham, Rovers boss Kenny Dalglish was presented with the Premiership trophy at his beloved Anfield.

Birmingham City

Stadium St Andrews
Capacity 30,200
Away allocation 2,600 (Railway Stand)
Address Birmingham B9 4NH
Telephone 0121 772 0101 (tickets 0709 111 25837)
Website www.bcfc.com
Independent website www.PlanetBlues.co.uk

Fanzines The Zulu, Made In Brum, The Penguin
Eats McDonalds is two minutes from the ground on Bordesley Park Road; a flourishing Chinatown in the city centre and balti shops galore on A34

route into the city; Fat Terry's hotdog stand near Kingston Road; plenty of chip shops along Digbeth.

Drinks Avoid most pubs around St Andrews but for the determined among you check out The Ibis Hotel, Bordesley Park Road or The Brewer and Baker on Camp Hill; otherwise head for city centre and New Street.

By car From NORTH exit M6 at junction 6 on to A38 (M) for Birmingham city centre. Exit at 2nd junction and bear left at the roundabout, following signs to Birmingham City FC. **From SOUTH EAST** exit M40 at junction 3A on to M42 northbound. Exit at junction 4 and turn left at roundabout on to A34. Continue over 4 roundabouts (the road becomes A41) to Camp Hill Circus roundabout. Take 3rd exit on to A4540 Sandy Lane. Follow signs for Small Heath and Bordesley Green for ground. **From SOUTH WEST** M5, M42 and exit at junction 3a. Follow signs to The North, B'ham East, North and Central to M42 then as from south east.

Parking St Andrews Street behind the garage but get there early. From Bordesley Circus roundabout, follow signs to Ring Road North and M6 into Watery Lane, first left into Adderley Street – there's an industrial area with plenty of unrestricted parking. Side streets off Coventry Road. **Last**

By bus Birmingham New Street take 15, 15a or 17 along Coventry Road. Despite the maze of subways, it really is quicker to walk.

By rail Birmingham New Street, then see above for buses.

Last season n/a. 5th in Div One, won play-off final

Premiership record n/a

Traveller's notes After such a long time away, Birmingham City's fans will be looking to make a mark in the Premiership. They have consistently travelled in numbers and those present at the Worthington Cup final or last season's Cup match at Anfield will testify that they certainly know how to get behind their team. They are not, however, the friendliest bunch so beware of large packs of Zulus when travelling to St Andrews. Steve Bruce's side are workmanlike at best and unless the man with a triple-jointed nose can bring in quality reinforcements, they are surely destined to return from whence they came.

Did you know Liverpool's biggest ever league defeat was against Birmingham City on 11 December 1954. In 1983/84 Anfield witnessed its third lowest attendance for a League Cup tie when only 11,638 turned out to see the Reds play City.

Bolton Wanderers

Stadium Reebok
Capacity 27,400
Away allocation 4-5,000 (South Stand)
Address Burnden Way, Bolton BL6 6JW
Telephone 01204 673673 (tickets 01204 673601)
Website www.bwfc.co.uk
Independent website www.boltonwfc.com, www.wanderersways.com
Fanzines Tripe'n'Trotters, White Love

Eats Stuart's Bakery near the station on Newport Street for pies, pastries and rolls; Mahoney's Pie Shops inside the ground; an unholy quartet of Pizza Hut, McDonalds, KFC and Burger King to the east of the ground.

Drinks Most of the pubs around the ground are home only but if you've got a thirst try Barnstormers or Bromilow Arms on Lostock Lane.

By car From NORTH M6 to junction 29. M65 towards Blackburn to junction 2 and M61 towards Manchester. Exit M61 at junction 6, turn left at roundabout into Burnden Way. **From SOUTH** exit M6 at junction 21a on to M62. Take junction 12 on to M60 northbound. After 2½ miles on to M6. At junction 2 road divides, bear left staying on M61. Exit at junction 6 and turn right at roundabout into Burnden Lane. **FROM EAST** M62 becomes M60 just north of Manchester. Leave M60 at junction 15 on to M61 then as from south.

Parking Parking at stadium – follow signs – £6 and 30-minute wait to get out. Victoria Road, off the Chorley New Road or restricted spaces on Lostock Industrial Estate, Lostock Lane.

By bus 539 runs twice an hour from Bolton station to the ground.

By rail Bolton and Wigan are the nearest mainline stations to the Reebok.

Last season 1-1(h) 1-2 (a). 16th

Premiership record P6 W3 L1 D2 F11 A7

Traveller's notes We had never lost to Bolton in the Premiership before last season's debacle. The Reebok is an attractive ground with its own unique character although like so many other new stadiums, it's stuck on the outskirts of town. The locals share our dislike for Manchester United although theirs occasionally borders on the obsessional.

236 **Did you know** Liverpool's defeat at the Reebok last August was their first in the League against Bolton since 1962/63 – beforehand, the Trotters were one of only four teams never to have beaten the Reds in the Premiership.

Charlton Athletic

Stadium The Valley

Capacity 26,500

Away allocation 2,000 (Jimmy Seed Stand)

Address Floyd Road, London SE7 8BL

Telephone 020 8333 4000 (tickets 020 8333 4010)

Website www.cafc.co.uk

Independent website www.NetAddicks.com

Fanzines Goodbye Horse

Eats A top all-day nosebag can be had at the Valley Cafe opposite Charlton station; Seabay Fish Bar in Floyd Road will cater for your cod and saveloy needs; drive-thru McDonalds on Bugsby's Way.

Drinks The Antigallican, just seconds from Charlton Station, is the main away fans pub; The Bugle Horn in Charlton Village (right out of the station up Charlton Church Lane); Charlton Liberal Club welcomes away fans for small entry fee at the door.

By car **ALL DIRECTIONS** exit M25 at junction 2 and follow A2 towards London for 10 miles. When A2 becomes A102 (M) Blackwall Tunnel approach road, take A206 Woolwich Road towards Woolwich. Ground is on the right.

Parking Around the ground is no-go unless you want your motor towed away. Best bet is Thames Barrier car park near The Antigallican pub or book in advance with the club for a space at Fossdene School.

By bus From North Greenwich tube take 161, 472 or 486.

By rail Euston Station and Jubilee Line underground to North Greenwich or Northern Line tube to London Bridge, overland to Charlton station.

Last season 2-0 (h) 2-0 (a). 14th

Premiership record P6 W4 L1 D1 F14 A4

Traveller's notes Like Charlton's former temporary home, Selhurst Park, The Valley is a pain in the backside to get to. But once the wilds of South East London have been successfully negotiated, visitors are rarely afforded anything less than a friendly welcome. Why? Well for starters, Charlton fans do not have ideas above their station. Alan Curbishley has put together a solid, hard-working side that is capable of playing attractive football on its day. Built on sound, if modest, financial foundations, Charlton have also demonstrated that it is possible to buck current trends by achieving relative success without breaking the bank.

Did you know Ronny Rosenthal scored a hat-trick on his full Liverpool debut away to Charlton in 1989/90. Scoring with his left foot, right foot and head, the Israeli maestro continued a sequence that has seen the only Reds hat-tricks against the Addicks scored away from Anfield.

Chelsea

Stadium Stamford Bridge

Capacity 42,449

Away allocation 3,086 (East Stand Lower)

Address London SW6 1HS

Telephone 020 7385 5545 (tickets 0891 121011)

Website www.chelseafc.co.uk

Independent website www.blueandwhitearmy.net

Fanzines Chelsea Independent, Matthew Harding's Blue And White Army

Eats Uncle Ken's eateries in the grandiosely titled Chelsea Village: Arkles, Fishnets and King's Brasserie – all pricey. Usual fish'n'chips and kebab shops around the ground, for more up-market eateries try King's Road.

Drinks Slug and Lettuce and Bootsy Brogan's on Fulham Broadway (near Fulham Broadway tube); The Blackbird, Earls Court tube. Otherwise, in true Peter Osgood style, treat yourself to an overpriced fancy foreign lager up the King's Road. Don't wear colours, mind.

By car From NORTH and **EAST** M6, M1, M25 and exit at junction 15. Take M4 which becomes A4, following signs to Central London. Over Hammersmith flyover, still on A4 (Talgarth Rd) and take 2nd available left-hand turn into Earls Court Road. Go past Earls Court station to next major junction and straight across into Redcliffe Gardens. At next traffic lights, turn right into Fulham Road and Stamford Bridge is about ½ mile on right-hand side.

Parking Underground car parks are part of Ken's west London white elephant but we advise you arrive before 2pm. You will have to be willing to pay £15 for the privilege. Otherwise there are some pay-and-display spaces around ground and off King's Road.

By bus 14 from Tottenham Court Road, 211 from Waterloo to Hammersmith, or 11 from Liverpool Street station.

238 **By rail** Euston, Victoria Line to Victoria and change to District Line, direction Wimbledon, for Fulham Broadway. Turn left out of station and ground is 200 yards away.

Last season 1-0 (h) 0-4 (a). 5th

Premiership record P20 W8 L7 D5 F27 A28

Traveller's notes Since Kenny Dalglish wheeled away to celebrate the goal that delivered the first half of the league and cup double in 1986, Stamford Bridge has become the House of Pain for Liverpool fans. We've had bogey team and bogey grounds in the past but few, if any, compare to the torture inflicted at Stamford Bridge. The locals are not the nicest either but regular home successes against the Reds, and large ones at that, have meant they've been too busy celebrating to think about extending their reputation for violence. A masochist's outing in recent years, the awayday to Chelsea traditionally dents both pride and the bank balance.

Did you know The Reds have yet to win at Stamford Bridge in the Premiership. Last season's 4-0 defeat made it 11 games without a victory in west London, with Liverpool having won just twice in the last 17 visits. One of those two wins, however, was in 1986 when Kenny Dalglish scored the only goal to secure the first half of the League and Cup Double.

Everton

Stadium Goodison Park

Capacity 40,260

Away allocation 3,075 (Bullens Road)

Address Liverpool L4 4EL

Telephone 0151 330 2200 (tickets 0151 330 2300)

Website www.evertonfc.com

Independent website www.whenskiesaregrey.com, www.toffeeweb.com

Fanzines When Skies Are Grey, Speke From The Harbour

Eats Chippies, pie shops and cake outlets galore on County Road. Tea and cakes at St Luke's church on the corner of Gladwys Street, honestly. Normal home-game pies and the like in ground.

Drinks If you don't fancy your regular matchday local, The Spellow on the corner of Gladwys Street, The Blue House at the Park End and The Winslow in between are sure to get you in the 'derby spirit'. Go easy on the gloating and don't mention Ian Rush.

By car From NORTH exit M6 at junction 23 and follow signs to Liverpool A580 for 10 miles. Pass under M57 and after 3½ miles turn left on to A5058 then right into Utting Avenue (signposted Liverpool FC, Everton

239

FC). Go under railway bridge and turn right at crossroads into Priory Road. Car park is on the left. **From SOUTH** exit M6 at junction 21a on to M62. Take junction 6, turn right at roundabout on to M57 until junction 4. Turn left at roundabout on A580 for 2 miles, left on to A5058 and then as from north.

Parking Same as for Reds home games, Stanley Park car park – 1,000 spaces, secure and cheap.

By bus No19 from Queen's Square to Walton Lane; no20 from St Thomas Street along Spellow Lane.

By rail From Liverpool Lime Street walk to Central station and catch an Ormskirk or Kirkby train. Get off at Kirkdale and follow the crowds.

Last season 1-1 (h) 3-1 (a). 15th

Premiership record P20 W6 L6 D8 F22 A21

Traveller's notes A souring in relations in recent years has made the 'friendly derby' look like a media myth. Evertonians could largely ignore the moribund tat that masqueraded as a side while they were regularly beating Liverpool, but since the Reds restored the status quo, banter has turned into bitterness. And nobody does bitterness better than the Blues. Flags on sale in the city centre celebrating the appointment of David Moyes and Everton's latest escape from relegation tell you all need to know about how far the Bluenoses have sunk. Don't expect a return to the days of half-Liverpool, half-Everton scarves any time soon.

Did you know Ian Rush scored four goals in a 5-0 win against the Blues in a 1982 league game at Goodison Park. He holds the all-time record for goals in the Merseyside derby with 25.

Fulham

Stadium Loftus Road while Craven Cottage is being redeveloped
Capacity 19,300
Away allocation 3,000 (School End)
Address South Africa Road, Shepherds Bush, London W12 7PA
Telephone 020 7893 8383 (tickets 020 7384 4710)
Website www.fulhamfc.com
Independent website www.toofif.com, http://members.tripod.com/~cravencottage/
Fanzines There's Only One F In Fulham, Where Were We When We Were Skint
Eats Uxbridge Road offers travelling Reds possibly the widest variety of

the season, from cafes, burger bars, fried chicken outlets and chippies to Caribbean, Indian, Chinese, Thai and Lebanese restaurants.

Drinks The Fringe and Firkin on Goldhawk Road offers an eclectic mix of backpackers, woollybacks and pseuds; Moon on the Green on Uxbridge Road serves decent food but turns its nose up at football shirts; The Springbok on South Africa Road is the main away pub but get there early.

By car From NORTH M6, M42 and M40 into London where it turns into A40. Exit at junction signposted White City and Harlesden. Turn right off the sliproad, under A40 flyover into Wood Lane and take a right at the first lights into South Africa Road. Ground is on the left. **From WEST** exit M4 at junction 4b and stay in lane for Watford M1, Oxford M40 on to M25. Exit at M40 eastbound. Then as from north. **From SOUTH** from Hammersmith roundabout take exit with Lloyds Bank on corner and follow Shepherd's Bush Road to Shepherd's Bush past Fringe and Firkin on the left, on to Wood Lane. Pass BBC Television Centre and turn left at lights on to South Africa Road.

Parking BBC car park in Wood Lane costs £5. On-street parking is scarce.

By bus From Victoria Coach station take District Line tube to Hammersmith – direction Ealing Broadway or Richmond – then no293 bus. Or change on to Hammersmith & City Line for Goldhawk Road or Shepherd's Bush – 15-minute walk to ground.

By rail Turn right out of Euston Station, walk 300 yards to Euston Square and catch Hammersmith & City Line to Shepherd's Bush. Alternatively, take Northern Line from Euston south to Tottenham Court Road and change on to Central line westbound until White City. From here it's five-minute walk.

Last season 0-0 (h) 2-0 (a). 13th

Premiership record P2 W1 L0 D1 F2 A0

Traveller's notes Those that missed out on last season's journey into the past – terraces, wooden stands, odd cottages, will have to settle for an alternative wander down memory lane this season. The Reds have not visited QPR's Loftus Road, Fulham's temporary home while Craven Cottage is being redeveloped, since 1996. A tight, compact ground, it should make for a decent atmosphere, even if some older travellers are still haunted by the memory of Ian Rush and co serving up passable impersonations of Robin Cousins on that awful plastic pitch. Fulham's fans have the smallest repertoire of songs in the Premiership, but they're harmless enough.

Did you know Robbie Fowler scored on his Reds debut against Fulham in a 1993 League Cup tie. In the return leg, Robbie went four better, becoming one of only four Reds to score five goals in a game. Ronnie Moran chastised the youngster afterwards, insisting it should have been eight!

Leeds United

Stadium Elland Road

Capacity 40,204

Away allocation 3,500 (South Stand or enclosure between East and South Stands)

Address Leeds LS11 OES

Telephone 0113 226 6000 (tickets 0113 226 1000)

Website www.lufc.co.uk

Independent website www.ToEllandBack.com

Fanzines The Square Ball, To Elland Back

Eats Cracked Egg Cafe on Elland Road does a decent all-day breakfast; United Fisheries is the chip shop favoured by most regular patrons of LS11 – get there early to avoid the queues.

Drinks The Grove near the station; The Old Peacock on Elland Road; The Britannia on Top Moor Side and Bulls Head in St Matthews Street both in Holbeck, five minutes from the ground; in town head for the Corn Exchange and juicers such as Norman's, Oporto or The Elbow Rooms. As ever, be wary of wearing colours in city centre.

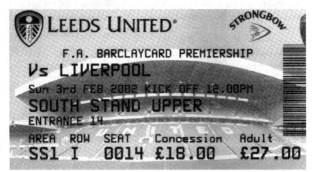

Bogey teams

The memories of **Arsenal** are all too painful. Charlie George on his back in 1971, Brian Talbot scoring the winner in a third FA Cup semi-final replay in 1980, Charlie Nicholas wrecking Rushie's record at Wembley in 1987, Michael Thomas snatching the title at Anfield with the last kick of the 1988/89 season. Thank God for Michael Owen.

Since knocking the European Cup holders out of the FA Cup in 1978 and again in 1982, **Chelsea** have beaten Liverpool 12 times in 20 home matches. The Reds have lost their last seven games at Stamford Bridge, conceding 20 goals and scoring just four. Ouch.

Inspired by the brilliance of Gordon Banks, **Leicester City** won six out of seven games against Liverpool from 1957. They also won three consecutive matches at Anfield in the early 60s and again between 1998 and 2000. In 1981 they did the double over Liverpool, ending the Reds' three-year, 85 game unbeaten home record in the process.

Nottingham Forest were promoted under Brian Clough and promptly stole our title and beat us in a controversial League Cup final replay before knocking us out of the European Cup as holders a season later. Don't mention them to Thommo.

Wimbledon won in their first match at Anfield in 1987 before Aldo's penalty miss wrecked our double ambitions in the FA Cup final of 1988. The Wombles went on to win twice more at Anfield, knock us out of the League Cup and extinguish faint title hopes in 1996 and 1997.

In March 1983 **Brighton**'s shock 1-0 win against Bob Paisley's men at Anfield marked the start of a short but painful hoodoo. A season later, The Seagulls repeated the feat in the third round of FA Cup before completing the hat-trick in another televised Cup encounter, winning 2-0 at the Goldstone in 1984.

By car From NORTH WEST and **WEST** exit M62 at junction 27 on to M621 direction Leeds. Take junction 2 and first left A643 on to Elland Road. Ground is on the right. **From SOUTH** and **EAST** at end of M1 keep in lane for Manchester M621. Exit at junction 2 then as from north west and west.

Parking Visitor's car park at the ground or on industrial estate on Lowfields Road.

By bus First Leeds run matchday shuttle buses from Neville Street to the ground, £1 return. Come out of railway station, across car park and down steps. The buses are on the right under railway bridge.

By rail From Leeds station, see above. Otherwise, it's a half-hour walk.

Last season 1-1 (h) 4-0 (a). 5th.

Premiership record P20 W11 L6 D3 F40 A19

Traveller's notes David O'Leary and his unlikeable band of babies (Robbie Fowler excluded) didn't merit much sympathy last season and were certainly not given any in the awesome 4-0 win at Elland Road. We've enjoyed a decent run of success against the Peacocks away from home, if you ignore the 4-3 defeat in 2000/01, and that should continue if O'Leary is forced to shed a few of his biggest wage earners during the close season. Leeds supporters don't have a great reputation and the existence of a boorish, bully boy fringe suggests this will not change soon.

Did you know Liverpool have twice been on the wrong end of 4-3 defeats to Leeds in the last decade. The first was in the 1992 Charity Shield when Eric Cantona scored a hat-trick, the second was in 2000/01 when Mark Viduka scored all four. The Reds have nevertheless scored more Premiership goals against Leeds than any other side in the top flight.

Manchester City

Stadium Maine Road

Capacity 33,100

Away allocation 3,000 (North Stand)

Address Mosside, Manchester M14 7WN

Telephone 0161 232 3000 (tickets 0161 226 2224)

Website www.mcfc.co.uk

Independent website www.blueview.co.uk. www.mcfconline.co.uk

Fanzines King Of The Kippax, Bert Trautmann's Helmet

Eats Wilmslow Road, otherwise known as the 'curry mile' offers, unsurprisingly, an extensive range of Indian food; footie burgers and radioactively hot pies on sale from vans in and around ground; The City Chippy, Claremont Road and Blue Moon Chippy, Maine Road for, er… chips.

Drinks Whitworth Hotel, Whitworth Lane is the best bet, or drop in at City's training ground on Platt Lane. Avoid pubs on Claremont Road.

By car From **NORTH** and **EAST** M61, M63 and exit at junction 9, following signs to Manchester A5103. After 2³⁄₄ miles turn right at the crossroads into Claremont Road and right into Maine Road after ¹⁄₃ mile. From **SOUTH** exit M6 at junction 19, follow A556, then M56 and take junction 3. Then as from north and west. From **WEST** exit M62 at junction 17 and take A56 to A57, following signs to Manchester Airport. Follow Birmingham signs to A5103 and turn left into Claremont Road for 1¹⁄₃ miles.

By bus Buses 11, 41, 42, 43, 44 and 46 from Piccadilly Station to Platt Lane.

By rail Manchester Piccadilly or Victoria stations.

Parking On street in Rushholme or off Wilmslow Road; some local schools also offer matchday parking.

Last season n/a. Div 1 champions

Premiership record P10 W4 L1 D5 F20 A11

Traveller's notes The Platt Lane End at Maine Road was one of the best away ends in the land, featuring a huge roof that amplified the noise and protected visitors from the inevitable Mosside downpour. More recently, away fans have been housed in the rickety temporary seating in one corner of the ground which, when it rains, is akin to being strapped to the mast of Ellen Macarthur's sailing boat. City make a welcome return to the Premiership under Kevin Keegan and despite some eye-catching summer signings, not least Nicolas Anelka, we fully expect to collect our mandatory three points from Maine Road. Whether King Kev will still be around to see it remains to be seen.

Did you know Ian Rush scored the last of his 364 goals for the Reds against City at Maine Road in 1996. The game ended 2-2 which, due to Alan Ball's faulty mathematics, was enough to relegate City to Division One.

Manchester United

Stadium Old Trafford

Capacity 67,000

Away allocation 2,973 (South East Quadrant)

Address Sir Matt Busby Way, Manchester M16 0RA

Telephone 0161 872 1661 (tickets 0161 868 8000)

Website www.manutd.com

Independent website www.UWSonline.com, www.RedIssue.co.uk

Fanzines United We Stand, Red Issue, Red News

Eats Lou Macari's chippy at the junction of Chester Road and Sir Matt Busby Way; Legends, so called because of the painted mural of United 'legends' on the facade.

Drinks It's not exactly common for Reds to share a convivial pint with their rivals from down the East Lancs Road, but if you do need a snifter keep your head down, accent under wraps and try one of the following: The Tollgate or The Throstles Nest on Seymour Grove, Old Trafford; Hanrahans, Merchants Quay, Trafford Road.

By car From NORTH and EAST take M61 to M60 and exit at junction 4, following Manchester A5081 signs. Turn right after 2½ miles into Sir Matt Busby Way. **From SOUTH** exit M6 at junction 19 and take Stockport A556 road then Altrincham A56) From Altrincham follow Manchester signs for 6 miles and turn left into Sir Matt Busby Way. **From WEST** exit M62 at junction 17 and take A56 to Manchester. Follow signs for the South then Chester for 2 miles and turn right into Sir Matt Busby Way.

Parking A park-and-ride system operates from Carrington or you can park up at Altrincham and catch the tram. Some school parking but club car parks around stadium are reserved for the prawn sandwich brigade.

By bus From Piccadilly take nos 252-257, 17, 114 and 236 to Old Trafford.

By tram Jump aboard a Metrolink from Piccadilly (Altrincham Line) to Old Trafford or (Eccles Line) to Pomona.

By rail The Metrolink goes from Manchester Piccadilly to Old Trafford station and it's a 10-minute walk to the ground.

Last season 3-1 (h) 1-0 (a). 3rd

Premiership record P20 W6 L8 D6 F27 A30

Traveller's notes Undoubtedly the biggest away game of the Premiership season, visits to Old Trafford, the self-styled 'Theatre of Dreams', have hardly been the stuff of nightmares in recent seasons. Danny Murphy's one-man crusade to put the legions of crowing Mancs and prawn-sandwich munching, plastic glory-hunters and the red-faced one in their place has helped erase the memory of regular defeats at the home of our arch rivals. United fans are a highly amusing lot, what with their mocking of our 'Mickey Mouse treble', their bandy swagger and their banners on the West Stand, but it now looks like they'll have to come to terms with the truism of a famous Liverpool banner, "Form is temporary, class is permanent".

Did you know Liverpool have won their last five games against Manchester United to reverse a sequence of 23 defeats and 23 draws in 58 games from 1976/77 to 1999/00. One of the 12 wins in that time was the 1983 League Cup final – a Wembley victory that completed a hat-trick of League Cup wins for the Reds.

Middlesbrough

Stadium Cellnet Riverside

Capacity 35,100

Away allocation 2,866 (South Stand)

Address Middlesbrough TS3 6RS

Telephone 01642 877700 (tickets 01642 877745)

Website www.mfc.co.uk

Independent website www.fmttm.co.uk

Fanzines Fly Me To The Moon

Eats Basically its burger vans and more burger vans along the chilly dockside trek.

Drinks Away fans are welcome at The Cornerhouse, below Middlesbrough station and Yates Wine Lodge near bus station; The Bridge on Bridge Street East is small but only five minutes from the ground.

By car From SOUTH exit A1 (M) at signpost Thirsk A168, Teesside A19 on to A19 for 32 miles. Turn right on to A66 Middlesbrough bypass for 3 miles until first roundabout. Turn left into Forest Road, the ground is straight ahead. Conversely, head straight into town and park up. **From NORTH** approaching town on A19, cross River Tees and turn left on to A66 Middlesbrough bypass. Then as from south. **From WEST** leave A1 (M) at junction 57 on to A66 (M), then as from south.

Parking There is no parking around the stadium, your best bet is to park up in the town centre.

By bus Nos 36, 37 and 38 go from central bus station to North Ormesby, a short walk from the ground.

By rail Change from GNER East Coast mainline at Darlington for Middlesbrough station, 1 mile from the ground. Leave station from back exit, follow the crowds right along Bridge Street East, past The Bridge pub and swing right into Windward Way which, as the name suggests, offers a fairly blustery walk to the stadium.

Last season 2-0 (h) 2-1 (a). 12th

Premiership record P14 W8 L3 D3 F26 A13

Traveller's notes Stuck in the middle of nowhere, The Cellnet Riverside Stadium is a desert of atmosphere where the only distraction tends to be the ships occasionally passing by or the multitude of foam hands in the crowd. To be fair, the Boro faithful (or unfaithful, as their dwindling crowds last season suggests) got behind their team in the match last season but you can almost excuse them for not making the long, windy trek along the bank of the Tees when they're force-fed such tedium most weeks. The Riverside is a world removed from the old Ayrsome Park and while at least there are no darts and snooker balls lobbed at the away fans anymore, this soulless, design-and-build bowl is everything Liverpool should avoid when they come to build the new Anfield.

Did you know Liverpool have not lost at home to Boro since the Premiership started and have tasted defeat just four times in the last 28 league matches between the teams.

Newcastle United

Stadium St James' Park

Capacity 52,193

Away allocation 1,800 (north-west corner of Sir John Hall Stand)

Address Newcastle NE1 4ST

Telephone 0191 210 8400 (tickets 0191 261 1571)

Website www.nufc.co.uk

Fanzines Talk Of The Tyne, Number 9, True Faith

Eats Stowell Street is handy for St James' and features a variety of decent Chinese restaurants and takeaways; Cafe Sol in Pink Lane for bocadillos and butties; Eat Out on Westgate Road promises the usual mix of burgers, kebabs and pizzas.

Drinks Head for the Quayside for any number of pubs and clubs; Free Trade Inn, City Road is a short cab ride from the station; Rafferty's on Pink Lane is walkable from Newcastle Central.

By car From NORTH exit A1 on to A167 Ponteland Road towards city centre. After 1½ miles at fourth roundabout turn left on to Jedburgh Road, right on to Grandstand Road and left on to A189 Ponteland Road which becomes Barrack Road. Carry on until roundabout. St James' is on the left. **From SOUTH** turn off A1 (M) at junction with A184. Carry on and bear left on to A189. Go over Redheugh Bridge, straight over roundabout and on to Blenheim Street until you meet Bath Lane. Turn left into Bath Lane, right into Corporation Street and left at the roundabout into Barrack Road. The ground is on the right. **From WEST** take A69 towards city centre, go past Newcastle General Hospital and at traffic lights turn left into Brighton Grove. After 70 yards turn right into Stanhope Street, then into Barrack Road.

Parking On-street parking and council-run car parks around the ground.

By bus Gallowgate Bus Station is 1/4 mile from the ground.

By rail Newcastle Central railway station is 3/4 mile from the ground. The Metro runs every 3 to 4 minutes to St James' station.

Last season 3-0 (h) 2-0 (a). 4th

Premiership record P18 W11 L4 D3 F37 A24

Traveller's notes St James's Park is a magnificent stadium (at least on two sides, anyway) and a happy hunting ground for Liverpool teams. Other than an Andy Cole-inspired 3-0 win for the Geordies in 1993, we have only lost once at Newcastle in the last 10 years, and last season a comfortable 2-0 victory put Bobby Robson's championship ambitions into perspective. As for the locals, they're an enthusiastic bunch who seem to think that being labelled the most passionate fans in the land relies on each and every one of them wearing a home shirt. The effect is to turn the towering stands into a giant bar code, which is strangely appropriate given the infamous attitude certain board members had towards them.

Did you know The Reds have scored 23 goals in eight straight home wins over the Toon. Michael Owen has scored 11 including two hat-tricks.

Southampton

Stadium Friends Provident St Mary's Stadium

Capacity 32,000

Away allocation 3,200 (Northam Stand)

Address St Mary's, Southampton, SO15 2XH

Telephone 0870 220 0000 (tickets 0870 2200150)

Website www.SaintsFC.co.uk

Independent website www.TheUglyInside.com

Fanzines The Ugly Inside

Eats Plenty of choice in and around the station or you could try one of the pies sold at the various outlets around the impressive new stadium.

Drinks Arriving by train, most away fans will probably go in The Victory opposite the station. Around the corner in Commercial Road is The Rat & Parrot and dead opposite is a converted church called Cafe Sol. The Giddy Bridge, a large Wetherspoons pub in London Road, The Prince of Wales, The Bevois Castle and The Station all welcome away fans too.

By car From NORTH follow A34 or M3 until it meets M27. At Eastleigh head off on A33 sliproad marked Southampton. Go straight over roundabout into Upper Avenue, left at next roundabout and straight until big roundabout. Take 2nd exit, stay in left-hand lane until Six Dials junction. Go over Northam Railway Bridge and turn right into Britannia Road. **From WEST** exit M27 at Junction 3 and join M271 south bound. Turn left at roundabout to join A35 towards city centre. Continue on West Quay Road (shopping centre is on the left) until roundabout. Go straight across towards Town Quay, Isle Of Wight Ferry Terminal on right-hand side. Follow one-way system round park then turn left into Canute Road. At main set of traffic lights with Ocean Village on the right, turn left and up to roundabout. Go straight over into Albert Road North, this becomes Marine Parade, St Mary's is on the left. **From EAST** exit M27 at junction 7 and turn left on to A334 (Charles Watts Way). At next roundabout take 2nd exit into Thornhill Park Road which becomes Bitterne Road East then Bitterne Road West. Go over Northam Bridge with Meridian TV studios on the right, at next set of traffic lights turn left into Prince's Street (Prince of Wales pub on corner) round into Millbank Street and straight on into Belvidere Road. St Mary's is on right-hand side.

Parking Public car parks are scattered 10, 15 and 20 minutes from stadium. Plus park-and-ride scheme, see below. Parking tickets are available on request from Liverpool FC and must be displayed for the duration of your stay.

By bus St Mary's free shuttle bus from opposite Railway station. Match tickets come with free return park-and-ride bus tickets specifically for away supporters. The car park is situated just off M27 at junction 8 and is clearly signposted from motorway exit. The journey takes about 20 minutes and buses line up waiting for away fans after match has finished.

By rail From Euston take Northern Line to Waterloo and mainline train to Southampton Central – it takes about an hour.

Last season 1-1 (h) 0-2 (a). 11th

Premiership record P20 W9 L4 D7 F39 A29

Traveller's notes The Dell traditionally provided one of the worst views but one of the most enjoyable awaydays of the season, even if Liverpool's record there was hardly formidable. If this season's trip to St Mary's is anything like the first then Liverpool supporters will be hoping to get a restricted view ticket, rather than having an unbroken view of another clueless collapse. Southampton's fans are a curious bunch, seemingly content to while away 90 minutes singing outdated songs about Pompey rather than celebrating the fact that Gordon Strachan is quietly building a side to do justice to the club's impressive new stadium.

Did you know In the 1985/86 FA Cup semi-final at White Hart Lane, Saints defender Mark Wright broke his leg in a 2-0 defeat to the Reds. Six years later Liverpool captain Mark Wright lifted the FA Cup at Wembley after a 2-0 win over Sunderland.

Sunderland

Stadium Stadium of Light
Capacity 48,300
Away allocation 3,128 (Metro FM Stand)
Address Sunderland SR5 1SU
Telephone 0191 551 5000 (tickets 0191 551 5151)
Website www.sunderland-afc.com
Independent website www.thewearsideroar.com
Fanzines A Love Supreme, The Wearside Roar
Eats There's a McDonalds opposite the stadium; Roker Cafe on Roker Avenue for sandwiches and all-day breakfasts; Bridge Street, leading from the city to the ground, boasts a variety of cheap and cheerful food outlets; Indian, Italian or fish'n'chips at the seafront.
Drinks William Jameson on Fawcett Street, 10 minutes from the ground, is massive and a top pub for away fans; Terminus and The Wheatsheaf on Roker Avenue; quarter-mile of bars around concourse of ground.
By car From SOUTH exit A1 at junction 64, signposted Washington, Birtley A195. Get on to Western Highway, after 1½ miles at roundabout follow signs for Sunderland A1231 on Washington Highway. Take 2nd exit for A1231 and follow road for 4½ miles, heading for city centre. Follow signs for Queens Road B1289, turn right at roundabout and follow signs for Stadium of Light.
Parking Spaces for 1,100 cars are reserved by season-ticket holders but visitors can book a space in advance through ticket office. Or try multi-storey on St Mary's Way in town centre.
By bus From town centre nos 27, 2 and 29 run from station to

Lucky teams

The Stadio Olimpico is Liverpool's lucky second home. After winning the 1977 European Cup there, the Reds defeated **Roma** on home soil to lift the trophy again in 1984 before repeating the dose with a memorable 2-0 Uefa Cup win in 2001. A draw in the Italian capital in last season's Champions League tie preserved our unbeaten record. **Borussia Mönchengladbach**, **Dynamo Dresden** and **Benfica** have been our other lucky European opponents, all losing three ties against Liverpool.

After 20 years of domestic pain, Old Trafford has become something of a lucky ground. Solitary strikes by Danny Murphy have defeated **Man United** twice in the last two seasons, contributing to a run of five straight victories over the bitter enemy.

Highbury has not been a source of many points in the last couple of seasons but after winning only one of 16 league games there from 1966, Liverpool enjoyed a purple patch between 1994 and 2000, beating **Arsenal** four times and drawing twice in six visits to North London.

Since the start of the Premiership, Liverpool have not lost in four visits to **Sunderland**. Ten wins in 14 visits from 1976, 27 goals and a 7-1 victory in 1991 also made Derby a happy hunting ground.

In the FA Cup, we'd be happy to draw **Grimsby**, **Stockport** and **Stoke** because we've beaten all three on the four occasions we have been paired. **Fulham** are Liverpool's ideal opponents in the League Cup, losing all five ties against the Reds.

Wearmouth Bridge; 131 and 538 from main Park Lane bus station to ground.

By rail Sunderland station is just 10 minutes walk from stadium.

Last season 1-0 (h) 1-0 (a). 17th

Premiership record P8 W4 L0 D4 F9 A4

Traveller's notes Sunderland's travelling support is famously raucous and the atmosphere at the amusingly titled Stadium of Light is similarly impressive. Over zealous stewards are the only drawback as they like nothing better than to chuck people out for standing up. Sunderland's fans have puzzled many with their unrealistic and inflated expectations and while Peter Reid may not be everyone's cup of brew, he has undeniably done well for the Mackems, and he is, of course, a boyhood Red. Liverpool's supporters were in arguably their finest voice of the campaign for last season's victory at the Stadium of Light and if you can last the 90 minutes without being ejected, Sunderland is an away trip well worth making.

Did you know Liverpool's record home league defeat came at the hands of Sunderland on 19 April 1930. Memories of that 6-0 defeat have been emphatically erased since, with the Mackems winning just twice at Anfield since 1936. They have not beaten Liverpool at home since 1958.

Tottenham Hotspur

Stadium White Hart Lane

Capacity 36,289

Away allocation 2,480 (South Stand)

Address Bill Nicholson Way, 748 High Road, Tottenham N17 OAP

Telephone 020 8365 5000 (tickets 08700 112222)

Website www.spurs.co.uk

Independent website www.TheSpursWeb.com, www.SpursWeb.com, www.mehstg.co.uk

Fanzines My Eyes Have Seen The Glory, One Flew Over Seaman's Head, Cock-A-Doodle-Doo

Eats The hike along Seven Sisters Road takes you past any number of Turkish, Indian, Italian, Chinese and Greek restaurants, plus the usual fast food chains. If it's a more traditional taste of Tottenham you're after go for a bagel in or outside the ground.

Drinks The Railway Tavern, White Hart Lane; O'Mara's, Tottenham High Road; The Beehive, Stoneleigh Road; The Park, Park Lane; The Two

253

Brewers and The Victoria, Scotland Green.

By car **From NORTH** from M1 (A1 at junction 2/3) or M40 (A40 at junction 1) join A406 North Circular eastbound until you hit Edmonton junction. Take sliproad signposted Tottenham to A1010, Fore Street. Continue 1 mile and ground is on the left. **From SOUTH** go through Dartford Tunnel on M25 and exit at junction 31, turning left at roundabout on to A13. Exit at North Circular A406 and continue until you see sign for Tottenham, Brimsdown A1055. Follow signs for 1 1/2 miles until you pass Tesco on the left. Filter right at lights into Leeside Road and straight on into Brantwood Road, turn left at T-junction into Tottenham High Road. Ground is on the left.

Parking Like the match tickets, parking is pricey. If you can't find a spot on a neighbouring street, try Gibson Business Centre at the junction of White Hart Lane and Tottenham High Street.

By bus Victoria Coach Station, Victoria Line to Seven Sisters and bus no259 or 279 to ground. Or 25-minute walk.

By rail Euston then Victoria Line to Seven Sisters or Tottenham Hale.

Last season 1-0 (h) 0-1 (a). 9th

Premiership record P20 W9 L6 D5 F36 A34

Traveller's notes Over-priced, a long way from the station and populated by beauts who seem to believe they still support a big club, Tottenham is developing a reputation as a graveyard for the Reds. The inside of the modern White Hart Lane is reminiscent of a outsized leisure centre, an effect that only a few inflatable palm trees and signs warning against running, bombing and petting could enhance. A lone drummer in one corner has the unenviable task of lifting the atmosphere which, though improved of late thanks to the improvements Glenn Hoddle has made to the side, is still infused with the pessimism that has characterised much of the last decade.

Did you know Liverpool have scored four own goals against Tottenham since the start of the Premiership. Jamie Carragher bagged one in both games in 1998/99. John Barnes and Neil Ruddock were the other culprits.

West Bromwich Albion

Stadium The Hawthorns

Capacity 27,200

Away allocation 3,000-5,200 (Smethwick End)

Address Halfords Lane, West Bromwich, West Midlands B71 4LF

Telephone 0121 525 8888 (tickets 01021 525 8888)

Website www.WBA.co.uk

Independent website www.WBAunoffical.com, www.baggies.com

Fanzines Grorty Dick

Eats The Grill House, Birmingham Road, for good, cheap meals; The Fish Inn, West Bromwich High Street; KFC, Pizza Hut and McDonalds in the pedestrianised shopping centre on West Bromwich High Street.

Drinks The Black Eagle, Factory Road, Hockley (1½ miles from ground, near Benson Road metro station); The Vine, Roebuck Lane, West Bromwich (½ mile from ground, near Kenrick Park metro); The Old Cross, Causeway Green Road, Langley (2 miles away, off Wolverhampton Road).

By car **From NORTH, EAST** and **WEST** exit M6 at junction 8 on to M5. After ¾ mile exit at junction 1, signposted to A41 West Bromwich, Sandwell, Birmingham. Turn left at roundabout (Birmingham A41) into Birmingham Road. **From SOUTH** M40 to M42 and follow signs to M5 the South West, Birmingham S & W. After 12 miles, M42 ends at junction 4a of M5 – follow signs to M5, the North West, Birmingham W, N and Cent on to M5 northbound. Exit at junction 1, 4th turning on roundabout (Birmingham A41) into Birmingham Road.

Parking Halfords Lane, follow signs off M5 to A4182 Matchday Parking; on-street quite near to ground or club has small, paying car park.

By bus M74, M78 and M79 go from Bull Street in Birmingham city centre to Wolverhampton, via The Hawthorns.

By rail Birmingham New Street, Moor Street or Wolverhampton and then metro to The Hawthorns. Trains run to The Hawthorns metro station from Birmingham Snow Street station and to Smethwick Rolfe Street (10 minutes from the ground) from Birmingham New Street.

Last season n/a. Div 1 runners-up

Premiership record n/a

Traveller's notes Other than a Coca-Cola Cup tie a few years back, it's been

255

a long, long time since the Hawthorns featured on the annual roster of awaydays. Back in the days when almost every West Brom players seemed to be called Brown and sported either a hazardously dry perm or a handlebar moustache, the Baggies were a realistic threat to the all-conquering Reds. A long spell outside the top flight followed but Gary Megson has worked a minor miracle by winning promotion on a tiny budget. The former Evertonian, a man who during his playing career threw up before every game with nerves, seems intent on telling the whole world about how hard he's had it, but even if he finds a way to resolve the differences with his chairman he will surely struggle to keep them up this season.

Did you know On 23 September 1978 Kenny Dalglish scored at the Hawthorns by kicking the ball out of goalkeeper Tony Godden's hands and rolling it into an empty net. The game finished 1-1 and West Brom finished the season third behind Liverpool in the table.

West Ham United

Stadium Boleyn Ground
Capacity 35,647
Away allocation 2,200 (Centenary Stand)
Address Upton Park, London, E13 9AZ
Telephone 020 8548 2748 (tickets 020 8548 2758)
Website www.westhamunited.co.uk
Independent website www.kumb.co.uk
Fanzines Over Land And Sea, The Water In Majorca

Eats Burger, kebab, fish'n'chips and pie'n'mash vendors line the road from Upton Park tube to the ground. Take your pick but be warned: liquor on the latter means your meal will be covered in a curious green gravy – it's a cockney thing.

Drinks Best to avoid boozers around the ground (besides, the police escort back to the tube will prevent you grabbing a post-match bevvy in the locale), so head for The Green Man on Plashet Grove or The Central, Barking Road. Or sample a traditional east-end welcome (no, seriously) in the West Ham Supporters Club bar under the Bobby Moore Stand.

By car From NORTH M6, M1, A406 east, A124 (Barking Road) towards East Ham and Upton Park for two miles, turn right at lights into Green Street. **From WEST** M40, A406 east to A124 (26 miles). Then as from north. **From SOUTH** M25 approaching Dartford Tunnel, exit at junction 31, turn left on to A13. Follow signs to London A13 (10 miles) then signs to The City, Woolwich Ferry. Keep in right-hand lane for The City, East Ham A117 and turn right under flyover. After 1 mile at T-junction turn left into Barking Road and ¾ mile on left into Green Street.

By bus Victoria Coach Station then District Line tube to Upton Park.

By rail Euston station then Northern Line to Moorgate. Change to Hammersmith & City Line east to Upton Park. Turn right from tube station and the Centenary stand is about 500 yards on the left.

Parking Very restricted around ground. You can park near Upminster underground station and hop aboard for a quick tube ride to the ground.

Last season 2-1 (h) 1-1 (a). 7th

Premiership record P18 W8 L4 D6 F25 A15

Traveller's notes Traditionally backed by one of the loudest crowds in the Premiership, West Ham have stayed true to their roots. Upton Park (or the Boleyn Ground, if you prefer) has been enlarged and improved but the ground has retained its unique atmosphere. The patrons, loveable cockney geezers one and all, have good reason to cheer because West Ham like to play good football, and with players such as Cole, Carrick, Kanoute and Di Canio on board, the passing style that has long been the Hammers' hallmark is still very much in evidence today. The main drawback of an awayday to West Ham, however, is the price which puts the Hammers on a par with Chelsea and Tottenham in the rip-off stakes.

Did you know The first colour broadcast of BBC's Match Of The Day came from Anfield on 15 November 1969. The opponents were West Ham and the final score was 2-0 to the Reds.

HISTORY

HISTORY

Origins | Feast and famine | Shankly the messiah | Paisley the shy genius
The torch is passed | Hillsborough and beyond | Houllier and the new Liverpool

When a rain-soaked Gérard Houllier, cradling the Uefa Cup, looked up into the stands to acknowledge the acclaim of Liverpool's jubilant fans in Dortmund, he was following in some illustrious footsteps. Not only had he just led his side to an unprecedented cup treble, he had put Liverpool firmly back on the map of Europe, a map it once dominated under Bill Shankly, Bob Paisley and Joe Fagan. After a decade spent languishing in the doldrums, Liverpool once again have a young, hungry team fashioned in the manager's own image. And as you shall see, the story of the most successful club in English football history is punctuated by just such watershed moments...

In the beginning...

Origins
Out of the blue

Had the members of Everton FC not fallen out with their landlord over rent in 1892, it's more than likely that Anfield would be synonymous with blue rather than red. The origins of our neighbours lie in the consecration of St Domingo's church on Breckfield Road North and the enthusiasm of its parishoners to form a football club. That club became Everton FC in 1879 and under the energetic leadership of John Houlding, a self-made man who would later become Lord Mayor of the city, moved to a playing field on Anfield Road in 1882 before becoming founder

261

members of the Football League four years later.

But Houlding and Everton's members fell out and when the powerful brewer gave them notice to quit Anfield, he was left with a ground but no team. His response was to hit back: he registered the name of Everton Football Club, thus ensuring for a short time there were two clubs of the same name in simultaneous existence, rounded up a rump of Anfield loyalists and set about forming a football club of his own. Thankfully, he decided to ditch his plans for a second Everton and instead called his new team Liverpool Association Football Club. Made up of Scots recruited by the club's first 'manager' John McKenna, the team played its first match in the Lancashire League on Thursday 1 September 1892, beating Rotherham Town 7-1. A handful of spectators saw Malcolm McVean, wearing the club's colours of blue and white quarters, score the historic first goal.

News soon spread of the goal-scoring exploits of this new team and the club won the Lancashire League and Liverpool District Cup in its first year. McKenna applied for membership of the Football League Division Two and somewhat surprisingly, the application was accepted. On 2 September 1893 Liverpool played its first Football League match, beating Middlesbrough Ironopolis 2-0 away with McVean again opening the scoring. The goal was the first step on a journey that would take Liverpool to greatness beyond the wildest dreams of its early founders.

Feast and famine

Liverpool ended their first season in league football as they did their last, by bettering their rivals from the other end of the East Lancs Road. An unbeaten Division Two campaign culminated in a 'Test match' victory over Newton Heath (later to become Manchester United) that secured promotion to the top division. They would be relegated a year later but after bouncing straight back in 1895/96, with William Barclay working alongside McKenna as manager/secretary, the club enjoyed eight years in the top flight, reaching an FA Cup semi-final in 1897, seeing the first of many players awarded international caps and winning a maiden league title in 1901. Alex Raisbeck, one of seven brothers from Stirlingshire and the club's first star player, was chaired from the Hawthorns pitch with the trophy after clinching the title on the last day of the season.

In 1905/06 the club won its second championship before securing an FA Cup semi-final against Everton. Football fever gripped Merseyside, leading to a mass exodus for Villa Park. Everton triumphed 2-0 and went

Liverpool Firsts

The original and the best, the mighty Reds were the first to...

Play every possible match in a domestic season **2000/01**
Win five trophies in a calendar year **2001**
Have a shirt sponsor **1979**
Play in front of a reigning monarch **1914**
Inflict a home defeat on Barcelona by an English side **1976**
Keep the European Cup in England in successive seasons **1977 and 1978**
Have six players selected for England in a post-war international **1977**
Play an English league match on colour television **1969**
Concede just four goals at home in a league campaign **1978/79**
Have an English-born manager of a European Cup-winning team **1977**
Play an FA Cup tie on closed-circuit TV **1967**
Remain unbeaten in 60 successive home league games **1980**
Play in a live televised Premiership game **1992**
Win the League using just 14 players **1966**
Win every home league game in a season **1893/94**
Win an FA Cup semi-final on penalties **1992**
Win the FA Cup without an Englishman in the side **1986**
Win the first, last and only Screen Sports Super Cup **1986**
Win the European Cup on penalties **1984**
Have eight different players on the scoresheet in a single match **1989**
Win a European final with a golden goal **2001**
Provide a manager who has won three European Cups **1977, 78 and 81**
Represent England in two World Club Championships **1981 and 1984**
Win a domestic trophy in four successive seasons **1981-84**
Be involved in an FA Cup semi-final that went to three replays **1981**
Do a treble **1984**

on to win the final, meaning both major trophies were in residence on Merseyside for the first time. Liverpool rewarded its growing legion of supporters by building the Spion Kop that summer, but as a new era opened on the most famous end in world football another closed on the pitch. It would be another 16 years before Anfield celebrated another trophy. Stalwarts Raisbeck and goalkeeper Sam Hardy left to be replaced by new heroes such as Elisha Scott, a charismatic keeper signed from Ireland in 1912. However, defeat at the hands of Burnley in the 1914 FA Cup final was the one beacon amid a period of mediocrity. And as the dark clouds of war gathered over Europe, Liverpool fought their own grim battles against relegation.

Evolution of Anfield

The Kop

In the early 1900s an expanded Anfield Road stand was introduced, but it was in 1906, following Liverpool's second league win, that the most significant terrace in football history was to come into being – the Spion Kop. Designed by Archibald Leitch, the Kop consisted of a mound of ash rubble topped with wooden steps and crush barriers. Holding 20,000, it boosted the ground's capacity to nearly 60,000. It was named after the famous Boer war battle of Speonkop in Natal, South Africa, where many Liverpudlians were killed fighting for the Royal Lancashire Fusiliers (later immortalised in the song Scouser Tommy). The new stand gave Anfield such a reputation it was able to attract international fixtures and cup semi finals. In 1928 the Kop was given a roof, and the old Main and Kemlyn Road stands were extended to meet the new covering. A distinctive flagpole from a transatlantic steamer was then added at the corner of the Kop and Kemlyn Road stand.

Football resumed in earnest in 1919 after the war and Liverpool made steady progress before capturing a third league title in the 1921/22 season. Harold Chambers and Dick Forshaw scored the goals while Elisha Scott represented an often unpassable barrier in goal. The title was successfully defended a year later in a campaign that saw the Reds win 26 of 42 games, before the pendulum swung in favour of the team across Stanley Park. Everton, inspired by Dixie Dean, won three further titles and an FA Cup before 1939 while Liverpool, under the stewardship of one-legged Matt McQueen and later George Patterson, struggled to recapture past glories.

The outbreak of the Second World War saw the 1939/40 season cancelled after just three games. Liverpool played in the hastily reorganised West League and drafted in guest players, including one Bill Shankly, who made a solitary appearance for the Reds in 1941/42. Billy Liddell made his debut in 1940 and in a curious system, the club won one half of the season's two championship titles in 1942/43.

When football resumed in earnest in 1946 Albert Stubbins tossed a coin to decide whether to join Liverpool or Everton, called right and teamed up with Liddell and Jack Balmer in attack to shoot Liverpool back to the summit for a fifth league title. Playing alongside that early triumvirate of striking talent were two men who would later go on to manage the club: Phil Taylor and Bob Paisley. A tough-tackling wing half, Paisley starred in the 1950 FA Cup semi-final victory over Everton but was left out of the team that lost to Arsenal in the final. He later admitted it was the lowest point of his career but the experience at least allowed him to empathise with players he dropped for important games years later.

The 1950s was a barren decade for the club and Don Welsh, who took over in 1951, became the first manager in the club's history to be sacked after leading the team to relegation in 1954. He was replaced in 1956 by a former long-serving captain and player, Phil Taylor. New players such as Ronnie Moran, Alan A'Court and Jimmy Melia were blooded but there

Greatest signings in Liverpool history

1 **Kenny Dalglish** £440,000 from Celtic in 1977
2 **Ron Yeats** £30,000 from Dundee United in 1961
3 **Kevin Keegan** £35,000 from Scunthorpe in 1971
4 **Sami Hyypia** £3million from Willem II in 1999
5 **Graeme Souness** £352,000 from Middlesbrough in 1978
6 **Ian Rush** £300,000 from Chester City in 1980
7 **Alan Hansen** £100,000 from Partick Thistle in 1977
8 **Ray Clemence** £18,000 from Scunthorpe in 1967
9 **Ian St John** £37,500 from Motherwell in 1961
10 **John Barnes** £900,000 from Watford in 1987

was heartache and frustration before Liverpool regained their first Division status. Indeed, for large swathes of the 50s only the shining genius of Billy Liddell illuminated a dejected Anfield. A moribund decade for the club ended in ultimate ignominy: defeat to non-league Worcester City in the FA Cup of 1959. Taylor resigned soon after to be replaced by a single-minded Scot named Bill Shankly. Liverpool Football Club would never be the same again.

Evolution of Anfield

From toilet to fortress
In 1957, the radical decision to install £12,000 worth of floodlights was made to enable night football to be played at the ground. Bill Shankly's arrival in 1959 was, however, to herald huge changes. He condemned the ground as "the biggest toilet in Liverpool" and set about transforming facilities. Ground-watering equipment at a cost of £3,000 was introduced, followed by the new cantilever Kemlyn Road Stand in 1964, costing £350,000 and seating 6,700 supporters. The next year, the Anfield Road end was demolished and replaced with a brick terrace – which still supports the current 'Annie Road' stand today.

Shankly
The messiah
Appointed on 1 December 1959 on an annual salary of £2,500, Bill Shankly had managed Grimsby, Workington and Huddersfield before arriving at Anfield like a one-man whirlwind. One of 10 children from the mining town of Glenbuck, he immediately set about transforming a club in decline. He upgraded training methods and the Melwood training ground, demanded a programme of stadium improvements to make Anfield fit for its public, cleared out 24 unwanted players and, most importantly, insisted on control of all team matters. Anfield had never seen anything like Shankly. But for all this sudden change, Shankly decided not to tinker with the existing back-room staff, made up of lieutenants such as Bob Paisley and Reuben Bennett. It was to prove a wise choice and a benchmark for future successions.

266

On the pitch, a youthful Roger Hunt was given his start, as was Ian Callaghan who was plucked from the ranks of Anfield apprentices. But

A brief history of the home shirt

Liverpool AFC played its first match in 1892 and players wore blue and white quartered rugby-style jerseys, knee-length white shorts and blue socks.
In the early 1900s, shirts and socks became maroon which soon gave way to ruby red with black shorts. The 1950 FA Cup final defeat against Arsenal saw the Liverpool jersey first feature a club crest. Later on in the decade, tighter-fitting red short-sleeved shirts were introduced, featuring a white V-neck and white cuffs.

The shirt changed to a crew neck as Liverpool lifted the Division One title in 1963/64. Bill Shankly was responsible for the introduction of an all-red kit the following season – he felt it made his players look more intimidating. It changed little until the mid 1970s, when Umbro became kit manufacturer. Shirt badges were golden for the League and European Cup-winning 1976/77 campaign and a few months later Liverpool became the first British club to secure a shirt deal when Hitachi signed on as sponsors.

A white pinstripe was introduced for the 1982/83 season, but the sponsor had changed to Crown Paints. Adidas became kit maker in the 1984/85 season and the company's trademark three stripes appeared in white on the shoulders and down the side of the shorts. Over the next few seasons, the collar became more rounded and in 1987/88 Candy became sponsors.

To mark the club's centenary year in 1992, Adidas reverted back to an all-red shirt but for three blocks of white across the right shoulder. The away kit became green for the first time. A year later Carlsberg took over as shirt sponsors and green featured for the first time on the collars and cuffs of the home shirt. The mid 90s also saw the introduction of the squad numbering system and players' surnames appearing on the back of shirts.

Reebok became Liverpool's third kit manufacturer in 1996 and its first shirt incorporated a red and white collar. The late 1990s brought a very Shankly-esque jersey before Reebok designed a collared V-neck with white piping for the treble-winning season. In another first, a special Champions League jersey was issued for 2001/02. Its white cuffs and V-neck, together with gold logos and fours stars echoed the days of European domination in the 70s and 80s.

still Liverpool could not escape Division Two and with attendances dropping below 30,000 Shankly's blueprint came under closer scrutiny. The Scot stuck to his guns and in 1961 completed the signings of Ian St John from Motherwell and a defender called Ron Yeats from Dundee United. They were the twin totems upon which a new era would be built.

Ninety-six goals, a club record 41 of them coming from Roger Hunt, saw Liverpool romp to the Division Two title in 1961/62. An ecstatic Kop insisted on the players reappearing for a lap of honour after the title-clinching home game against Sunderland. The rhythmic clapping and singing that greeted them confirmed that Shankly had stirred dormant passions inside his adoring public. The manager then persuaded the board to part with a whopping £40,000 for winger Peter Thompson and after an erratic start to the 1963/64 season, Liverpool's blossoming team of internationals hit their stride, beating Everton at Anfield and ramming six past visiting teams on four occasions. Three wins over Easter secured the club's sixth championship and, more importantly, the first major trophy of the Shankly era.

Times were changing on Merseyside and a wave of optimism engulfed Anfield. The Beatles were conquering the world and the Kop adopted a Merseybeat anthem as its own. You'll Never Walk Alone became the hymn that Shankly's team marched to as it embarked on its first campaign in the European Cup and set about filling the one conspicuous

Honours

League champions 1900/01, 1905/06, 1921/22, 1922/23, 1946/47, 1963/64, 1965/66, 1972/73, 1975/76, 1976/77, 1978/79, 1979/80, 1981/82, 1982/83, 1983/84, 1985/86, 1987/88, 1989/90
European Cup 1977, 1978, 1981, 1984
Uefa Cup 1973, 1976, 2001
Uefa Super Cup 1977, 2001
FA Cup 1965, 1974, 1986, 1989, 1992, 2001
League Cup 1981, 1982, 1983, 1984, 1995, 2001
FA Charity Shield 1966, 1974, 1976, 1979, 1980, 1982, 1988, 1989, 2001
Division Two champions 1893/94, 1895/96, 1904/05, 1961/62

hole in its burgeoning record by winning the FA Cup.

Liverpool progressed to the semi-finals in Europe after winning on the toss of a coin at the end of a replay against Cologne. In the FA Cup, a win over Leicester set up a semi-final against Chelsea, won thanks to goals from Peter Thompson and Willie Stevenson. Don Revie's experienced Leeds United were waiting in the final and on a damp, grey day, brightened only by the songs and pageantry of the Kopites massed at one end of Wembley, Liverpool won 2-1 in extra time. Roger Hunt gave the Reds the lead, Bremner equalised before Ian St John scored the goal that brought the most famous trophy in English footballing to Anfield for the first time. Gerry Byrne broke a collar bone early in the game but stayed on until the end. The reward for Shankly, Byrne, St John et al came when half-a-million people lined the streets of the city to welcome home their victorious team.

Liverpool 1965
The FA Cup final team vs Leeds United
Tommy Lawrence
Chris Lawler
Gerry Byrne
Geoff Strong
Ron Yeats
Willie Stevenson
Ian Callaghan
Roger Hunt
Ian St John
Tommy Smith
Peter Thompson

Two days later Inter Milan came to Anfield for a night that has gone down in the folklore of the club. The Kop was closed two hours before kick off as 25,000 swaying fans generated a wall of noise. The injured Gordon Milne and Byrne paraded the FA Cup before the game, the crowd erupted and Inter, as Shankly had hoped, froze in the din. Liverpool won 3-1 on the night but went out a week later amid controversy and unsubstantiated allegations of a bribed referee.

By now, Shankly had built a seemingly unstoppable momentum at the club, harnessing the passion of the supporters to a team that they could be truly proud of. Another League title followed the next season, along with a losing appearance in the Cup Winners Cup final at Hampden Park. But like any top manager, Shankly was conscious that his first great side was approaching its sell-by date. A heavy defeat to Ajax in the fog of Amsterdam, stuttering form in the League and a shock cup exit at Watford signalled the watershed. Shankly accepted the time was right to dismantle his side and start again.

Over the course of the following six, trophyless seasons, Shankly lowered the average age of his side, introducing fresh young talent like

Emlyn Hughes, Ray Clemence, John Toshack and Steve Heighway, while St John, Hunt and Yeats all faded from view. The team that walked out to contest the 1971 FA Cup final against Arsenal had an average age of 22 and although Liverpool lost 2-1 after extra time, Shankly took great encouragement from a season in which the mighty Bayern Munich, boasting the core members of the West German World Cup team, were dismantled 3-0 in the Fairs Cup at Anfield. More significantly perhaps, in the week before the Wembley defeat Shankly spent £35,000 on the final piece of his new jigsaw – an enthusiastic bundle of energy named Kevin Keegan.

Keegan became a superstar at Anfield, impressing from the start by scoring on his debut in the opening game of the 1971/72 season. And although his time at Anfield is best remembered as one half of a classic little 'n' large strike partnership with John Toshack, Keegan started out as a midfield dynamo. Indeed, it was from this deeper position that Keegan fired Liverpool to an unprecedented 'double' in 1972/73. In the League, the Reds were simply masterful and wrapped up the title on Easter Monday by beating old rivals Leeds in front of 55,000 delirious fans. Then, after 62 games of an arduous season, they dug in and conjured up two more big performances to beat the highly fancied Borussia Mönchengladbach over two-and-a-half legs – the first leg at Anfield was abandoned due to torrential rain – in the Uefa Cup final. It was the first time an English side had won the League title and a European trophy in the same season.

The trophies continued to come. In the next season's FA Cup competition, Shankly's team came alive, shrugging off a close shave against lowly Doncaster to progress to the final against Newcastle. In the

Evolution of Anfield

The Main Stand

The early 1970s saw further improvements as £400,000 was spent on a redeveloped Main Stand, which was expanded and given a new roof. Better dressing rooms, a players' restaurant, lounge, a club shop and superior roof-top floodlighting were all added to the construction, which opened in March 1973. It also had a tailor-made TV gantry, making Anfield the best ground in the land for televised football.

build-up Malcolm 'Supermac' MacDonald boasted about what he was going to do to the Liverpool defence, but for most of the game he was a frustrated spectator as an Emlyn Hughes-led Reds side put on an exhibition performance to win 3-0 at a canter. Keegan scored twice and Shankly, who had fans worshipping at his feet on the Wembley turf at the end, declared his team "the best in England and probably the world". Little did those fans know their leader would soon be gone.

Liverpool 1974
The FA Cup final team
vs Newcastle United
Ray Clemence
Tommy Smith
Alec Lindsay
Phil Thompson
Peter Cormack
Emlyn Hughes
Kevin Keegan
Brian Hall
Steve Heighway
John Toshack
Ian Callaghan

Bob Paisley
The shy genius

On 12 July 1974 Liverpool called a press conference to unveil new signing Ray Kennedy from Arsenal... and to drop the bombshell that the great Bill Shankly had intimated his desire to retire from league football. Shankly, the master psychologist, motivator and charismatic talisman, wanted to bow out at the top and no amount of persuasion, it seemed, could get him to reconsider. The news left his thousands of disciples in deep shock and fearful for the future. They need not have worried because, although he did not initially want the job, Bob Paisley, right-hand man to Shanks and loyal servant to the club since 1945, would take Liverpool to even greater heights.

The pressure on the quiet, retiring Paisley was intense and when his first season finished without a trophy, there were those who doubted the wisdom of the board's appointment. However, solid foundations were in place and when Shankly left, the other members of the now famous Anfield Boot Room – Joe Fagan, Reuben Bennett, Ronnie Moran, Roy Evans and Tom Saunders, moved up and the tradition of succession from within had begun.

Paisley added Phil Neal and Terry McDermott to his squad and a rejuvenated John Toshack saw his strike partnership with Keegan finally bear fruit. Ray Kennedy was transformed from a striker into one of the most cultured midfielders in the country, while David Fairclough and Jimmy Case emerged from the reserves. Liverpool began fluently and got

271

Bob Paisley, Liverpool's most successful manager with one of his three European Cups

stronger, finally seeing off QPR's challenge to land the League title in the last game of the season at Molineux, watched by a vast army of travelling fans. In Europe, Dynamo Dresden, Barcelona and Bruges, among others, were beaten on the way to a second Uefa Cup triumph. It was a second League and European double in three seasons and confirmed to any remaining sceptics that Paisley was a worthy heir to Shankly.

This was proved emphatically in Liverpool's unforgettable 1976/77 season. Chasing an unprecedented League, FA Cup and European Cup treble, the Reds finally established themselves as the dominant force in domestic and European football. Playing an irresistable brand of pass-and-move football, Liverpool raced into the lead in the championship, advanced to the FA Cup final, disposing of Everton in a replayed semi, and honed in on a European Cup final date in Rome after seeing off St Etienne in a game that has gone down as one of the most memorable ever seen at Anfield. Trailing by a goal from the first leg of the quarter-final, Liverpool were twice behind on aggregate before David Fairclough sprang from the bench and set off on a 40-yard run that would cement his place in the history of the club. There were just eight minutes left on the clock when that run ended with a deftly-placed shot into the top corner before a heaving Kop.

Liverpool went on to beat Zurich to reach their first European Cup final before wrapping up the title at home to West Ham. The treble was on and just five days before facing Borussia Mönchengladbach in Rome, Liverpool walked out at Wembley to play Manchester United in the FA Cup final. Two soft goals gave Tommy Docherty's young side a surprise victory and wrecked dreams of the treble, leaving Paisley just a few days to pick his players off the floor in preparation for the greatest night in the club's history. From Wembley, advance parties of Kopites, from an estimated travelling contingent of 30,000, headed across Europe for their date with destiny in Rome.

On a sultry night at the Olympic Stadium, one of the most glorious chapters in the club's history was written. When the players emerged from the tunnel to inspect the pitch before the game they were greeted by a huge bank of red and white at one end of the stadium. The spectacle of this vast and vociferous army of fans convinced Paisley's men they could not lose and from the start they played like a team possessed. Terry McDermott gave Liverpool the lead, Borussia equalised but Keegan was in inspired form throughout, giving German skipper Bertie Vögts the runaround. Second-half goals from Tommy Smith and Phil Neal completed a well-deserved victory and the celebrations went on long into the night. Only Bob Paisley remained sober, determined to savour the moment and his team's remarkable triumph.

At the start of the victorious 1976/77 campaign the Liverpool hierarchy knew it was to be Keegan's last at Anfield. The England international had been persuaded to spend one final season trying to land the European Cup before moving on to test himself on the Continent. Typically, Paisley was well ahead of the game and having lined up Keegan's replacement well in advance, he unveiled Kenny Dalglish, the greatest signing in the history of Liverpool FC, at a press conference in the summer of 1977.

Dalglish joined Alan Hansen, recruited from Partick Thistle that April, and later a third Scot, Graeme Souness, would sign from Middlesbrough. They would go on to form a Scottish backbone to the side that had echoes of the club's first team, known affectionately as 'the team of macs'. Dalglish made an immediate impact, scoring within seven minutes of his league debut, but his goals and ingenuity could not prevent Nottingham Forest from winning the title and foiling the Reds in their first League Cup final. Thankfully, Europe was a different matter and in a dour final against Bruges at Wembley, the new Caledonian combo came up trumps with Souness playing Dalglish in to break the deadlock with a deft finish.

Liverpool's most decorated							
	League	FAC	R/up	LC	R/up	Euro	R/up	Total
Phil Neal	8	0	1	4	1	5	1	20
Alan Hansen	8	2	1	3	1	3	1	19
Ian Rush	6	3	1	4	1	1	1	17
Kenny Dalglish	6	1	0	4	1	3	1	16
Bruce Grobbelaar	6	3	1	3	1	1	1	16
Ray Clemence	5	2	1	1	1	5	0	15
Ronnie Whelan	6	3	0	3	1	1	1	15
Phil Thompson	7	1	0	2	1	3	0	14
Ian Callaghan	5	2	2	0	1	3	1	14
Ray Kennedy	5	1	1	1	1	4	0	13
Alan Kennedy	5	0	1	4	0	2	1	13
Graeme Souness	5	0	0	4	0	3	0	12

A second consecutive European Cup triumph confirmed Liverpool as the Continent's undisputed heavyweight.

A season later, Liverpool and Forest swapped trophies with the Reds cantering to a 10th league championship and conceding a miserly 16 league goals all year. The 1979/80 season followed along similar lines with early disappointment in Europe, swept away by an 11th league title in May after semi-final exits in the League and FA Cups, the latter against Arsenal after three replays. Liverpool were dominant domestically but during the summer Paisley, as ever looking to the future, took the advice of scout Geoff Twentyman and signed a young Welsh striker named Ian Rush from Chester City.

Liverpool 1978
The European Cup final team vs Bruges
Ray Clemence
Phil Neal
Phil Thompson
Alan Hansen
Ray Kennedy
Emlyn Hughes
Kenny Dalglish
Jimmy Case
(Steve Heighway)
David Fairclough
Terry McDermott
Graeme Souness

Too many draws cost Liverpool a hat-trick of titles in 1980/81, but silverware was easier to come by in other competitions as the Reds won their first League Cup, beating West Ham after a replay. That success began an unbeaten four-year sequence that would see the club awarded the trophy outright. Paisley's men also qualified for a third European Cup final in Paris, having overcome Alex Ferguson's Aberdeen in a 'battle of Britain' and famously upset the odds in Munich to down Bayern in the semis. Alan Kennedy, signed the season before, lit up a tense final with Read Madrid by scoring the decisive goal in the 82nd minute. Victory reserved Bob Paisley a place in the history books as the first manager to win the trophy three times.

Like Shankly, whom a city mourned on his sudden death in September 1981, Paisley knew when change was required. Ray Clemence, Phil Thompson, Jimmy Case and Ray Kennedy, all loyal and decorated servants of the club, were eased out as the manager began rebuilding. Recent recruit Ronnie Whelan handed Paisley a second consecutive League Cup, by then known as the Milk Cup, when he equalised two minutes from time against Tottenham before goals from Craig Johnston and Ian Rush made the game safe in extra time.

Meanwhile, having been written off by the critics at the halfway stage in the title race, Paisley's thoroughbreds stormed through the pack to

275

clinch yet another title with 11 straight wins at the death. Ominously for the opposition, the Dalglish-Rush strike partnership had started to click.

After 43 years loyal service as a player, physio, coach and manager, Bob Paisley's last season in charge finished in appropriate style with the Reds winning the League by a country mile and taking a third straight League/Milk Cup at Wembley. It was fitting that after defeating Manchester United, the most successful manager in the history of English football should be sent up by his players to collect the trophy – the 13th he'd won during a quite staggering nine-year reign as boss.

Evolution of Anfield

From toilet to fortress
The paddock section of the Main Stand was seated in 1980, expanding the ground's seating capacity to over 17,500. Two years later the Anfield Road end was seated, which lowered capacity from 50,000 to around 45,000. The 80s also saw the arrival of one of Liverpool's most distinctive landmarks, the Shankly Gates. Nessie Shankly unlocked the memorial to her late, great husband in August 1982.

The torch is passed

Fagan and Dalglish

While Joe Fagan was a newcomer to management, he was certainly no Anfield novice, having spent 26 years as part of the fabled Boot Room set-up. Ian Rush was by now a goalscoring phenomenon and the Welshman scored 45 goals in all competitions as Fagan led the club to still greater heights. A hat-trick of league titles was secured, yet another Milk Cup came thanks to a victory over Everton in an historic first all-Merseyside cup final and the Reds marched back to their spiritual home, Rome, for a fourth European Cup final. There, against the longest possible odds, Liverpool defeated Roma on their own ground, in front of their own fans, on penalties, to win a fourth European Cup and land an unprecedented treble in Fagan's first season.

Following the success of his debut season proved a tall order for Fagan. Everton effected a shift in the balance of power on Merseyside, while Spurs and Manchester United did for Liverpool's cup ambitions, but the campaign still appeared destined to end in triumph when Liverpool progressed to the 1985 European Cup final in Brussels. Disaster struck, however, as before kick-off Liverpool fans rioted at one end of the crumbling, inadequate Heysel Stadium. The resulting stampede left 39 Juventus fans dead and the previously untarnished reputation of Liverpool supporters abroad in tatters. The game was played out in mute disbelief with Juve winning through a Michel Platini penalty. Fagan, who had revealed to Anfield insiders he would step down after the final, walked away from what should have been a glorious farewell, a tired and broken man.

Heysel proved another watershed, both for Liverpool and the domestic game. English clubs were banned from Europe, with a further one-year exile for Liverpool, Joe Fagan walked into grief-tinged retirement and Graeme Souness signed for Sampdoria. Kenny Dalglish was a surprising if popular appointment as Fagan's heir and aided by the back-room wisdom of Bob Paisley, Ronnie Moran and Roy Evans, the Scot set about restoring Liverpool's reputation as the club's first player-manager.

Like Shankly, Paisley and Fagan before him, Dalglish was unafraid of taking unpopular decisions: Alan Kennedy and Phil Neal, the most

Top scorers in all competitions			
	League	Others	Total
Ian Rush 1980-96	229	117	346
Roger Hunt 1959-69	245	41	286
Gordon Hodgson 1925-36	232	8	240
Billy Liddell 1938-60	216	13	229
Kenny Dalglish 1977-90	118	54	172
Robbie Fowler 1993-01	117	50	167
Harry Chambers 1919-28	135	16	151
Jack Parkinson 1899-14	123	5	128
Sam Raybould 1899-07	120	8	128
Dick Forshaw 1919-27	117	7	124
Ian St John 1961-71	95	23	118
Michael Owen 1997-	83	28	111*
Jack Balmer 1935-52	98	12	110
John Barnes 1987-97	84	24	108
* and still counting			

decorated player in the club's history, being the first of the old guard to disappear from the first-team picture. Jan Molby, Paul Walsh and Steve McMahon all began to feature and after a runaway Man United were caught and overhauled, Dalglish put the icing on the cake with a title-clinching goal at Stamford Bridge. 'Hand it over Everton!' rang round west London as 12,000 Kopites reflected on a 15-game unbeaten run to close out the League, and looked ahead to an all-Merseyside FA Cup final against Everton to clinch the Double.

For the second time in as many years, Wembley became an enclave of Merseyside for the day, with fans mingling on the journey south and at either end of the ground. Everton took the lead through Gary Lineker but failed to capitalise on their superiority. Jan Molby gradually took charge in midfield, Ian Rush found his range and a 3-1 victory gave Dalglish a historic first League and FA Cup Double – a maiden managerial season to rate alongside that of his predecessor.

Ian Rush signed for Juventus the following close season but would not leave Anfield until the end of a see-saw league campaign that saw the Reds relinquish their title to Everton and lose the Littlewoods Cup to Arsenal – the first defeat in a game where Ian Rush scored. If 1986/87 had been a disappointment, the following season would witness some of the finest football ever played by a team representing Liverpool. In the close season Dalglish landed John Barnes, Peter Beardsley and, soon after, Ray Houghton.

Liverpool 1986

The FA Cup final team
vs Everton
Bruce Grobbelaar
Mark Lawrenson
Jim Beglin
Steve Nicol
Ronnie Whelan
Alan Hansen
Kenny Dalglish
Craig Johnston
Ian Rush
Jan Molby
Kevin MacDonald

Concerns about a future without Ian Rush were shelved in an opening to the campaign that signalled Liverpool's intent. With Barnes, Aldridge and Beardsley on a footballing charm offensive, Dalglish's team swept opponents aside and were still unbeaten when 1987 drew to a close. After a record-equalling 29 league games without defeat, a goal from Everton's Wayne Clarke stopped Liverpool setting a new record. It was a minor blip in an all-conquering campaign in which the 5-0 victory over Nottingham Forest at Anfield set new standards for total football. An off-key display against Wimbledon in the FA Cup

The way we wore

Football hasn't always been trendy but Liverpool's fashion leaders have consistently led the way in the sartorial league table...

1940s Flat caps, overcoats, rattles and rosettes
1960s Merseybeat-inspired suit and tie
Early 1970s Ben Shermans, Dr Martens and crombies vs feather cuts, stack heels and scarves on wrists
Late 1970s Adidas Samba, snorkel parkas, Lois jeans, floppy fringes
Early 1980s Stan Smith trainers, bubble jackets, Mash hats
Mid 1980s Bobble hats, Barbour jackets, old man cardigans
Late 1980s Mountaineering boots, Russian hats, all-in-one ski suits
1990s Shellsuits, Argyle socks, Rockport boots, Stone Island jackets

final, including a disallowed effort from Peter Beardsley and the first missed penalty in a final from John Aldridge, was all that stopped Liverpool from crowning a champagne season with another double.

Hillsborough and beyond

The 1988/99 season dawned brightly with the news that Ian Rush was on his way back to Anfield after an unsuccessful year at Juventus. Liverpool overcame a series of early-season injuries to go 24 games without defeat and finally overhaul Arsenal at the top of the League in April. Now closing in on yet another double, the 17th FA Cup semi-final in the club's history was to end in tragedy on 15 April at Hillsborough. It was an event that changed the club forever (see overleaf).

The season was put on hold as funerals were attended and the club rallied round, becoming the focal point for a community's grief. The road back began with a friendly at Celtic to raise funds for the disaster fund, one of the most emotional Goodison derbies ever and the replayed semi-final against Forest at Old Trafford. A 3-1 victory set up the potential catharsis of another all-Merseyside Cup final. The 1989 Cup final will live long in the memory of every fan who was there. Merseyside's football tribes were united and on a day when the occasion almost mattered more than the scoreline, John Aldridge gave Liverpool the lead before Ian Rush (who else?) settled the outcome with two goals

Hillsborough

The deaths of 96 supporters as a result of what happened at Hillsborough on 15 April 1989, and the circumstances surrounding them, is a wound that will never heal for fans of Liverpool Football Club. The families of the victims and their many supporters, are still campaigning for justice more than a decade after an FA Cup semi-final turned into the worst crowd disaster in British footballing history.

For those who survived the fatal crush in the central pen of the Leppings Lane terrace, the sights, sounds and smells of that fateful afternoon are indelibly printed on the mind. The pen behind the goal was already filled to capacity an hour before kick-off and was dangerously overcrowded when Peter Beardsley hit the crossbar with a header just six minutes into the match.

The game was eventually stopped when a policeman, alerted to the screams of panic and fear behind Bruce Grobbelaar's goal, ran on to the pitch and spoke to the referee. What most didn't know at that time was that an exit gate had been opened to alleviate congestion behind the stand, allowing thousands of fans to swarm into the ground. In the absence of adequate stewarding and policing, many of those fans made for the tunnel leading to the central pen.

A crush barrier buckled under the weight of the crowd and with nowhere to go, those already on the terrace were pushed helplessly towards the metal fences at the front. Within minutes, the pitch was awash with overwhelmed first-aid teams and fans carrying makeshift stretchers. It became apparent very quickly there had been serious loss of life.

On the long, silent walk away from Hillsborough, fans listened on radios as the death toll rose – first four, then 16, 20, 50 and more. It was the worst day in the history of the club and a tragedy that defined much of what was wrong in football at that time. It also united a city and the nationwide football community, in grief. Sadly, while justice has yet to be done, there can be little hope of closure for those affected.

Hillsborough

Support and campaign groups
The Hillsborough Justice Campaign
134 Oakfield Road, Anfield, Liverpool L4 0UG
Tel/fax: 0151 260 5262
email: info@hillsboroughjustice.org.uk
website: www.contrast.org/hillsborough

Hillsborough Families Support Group
First Floor, Central Buildings, 41 North John Street, Liverpool L2 6RR

in extra-time. His first strike broke Dixie Dean's Merseyside derby scoring record.

Three days later, a 5-1 win over West Ham left Arsenal requiring a two-goal winning margin in the delayed last game of the league season to lift the title at Anfield. It was the Reds' third game in six days and the tiredness and emotion of recent weeks took its toll. The Liverpool players were desperate to close a traumatic, tragic year with a second double, but a goal from Alan Smith and a second from Michael Thomas with almost the last kick of the season gave the Gunners the spoils.

Liverpool bounced back a year later, winning the title thanks to a spurt of goals from new signing Ronny Rosenthal near the end of the season. The club's record 18th league championship featured some scintillating football, including a 9-0 thrashing of Crystal Palace at Anfield.

After 10 successive wins to start the following season, Kenny Dalglish emulated Bill Shankly by shocking the world with his decision to resign. The news came hard on the heels of a breathless and unforgettable 4-4 FA Cup draw with Everton at Goodison two days before. Alan Hansen announced his retirement a week after Dalglish's exit and Ronnie Moran became caretaker manager before Graeme Souness was tempted to leave Ibrox to return to Anfield.

Sadly, for all Souness' desire and endeavour, it was not a happy reunion. In truth, Dalglish's vintage side was growing old and injury deprived the new manager of many experienced performers so it was no surprise when the title was relinquished to Arsenal. At Rangers, Souness had rebuilt the Glasgow club from top to bottom. He tried to do the same at Anfield, but a combination of ill-advised transfers – both in and out – disrupting the

The badge

The Liverpool FC crest consists of different elements that relate to important events in the club's history.

The Liver Bird is a mythical cross between an eagle and a cormorant. When Liverpool was granted city status by King John in 1207, the Liver Bird was first used as an official seal. Ever since, it has been the symbol of the city.

Kopites first sang You'll Never Walk Alone before games in 1963, when local group Gerry and the Pacemakers' version was number one. Shortly afterwards the song was adopted as the club's anthem. The song's title now adorns the top of The Shankly Gates located at the entrance to the Main Stand. The ironwork at the top of the gates forms the top part of the club crest.

The year of the club's formation, 1892, also features on the ribbon below the main crest.

The burning flames honour the 96 Liverpool supporters who lost their lives at Hillsborough in 1989.

tradition of continuity behind the scenes and the need to blood youngsters before they were ready, led Liverpool into a downward spiral that was to last the best part of a decade.

An FA Cup final win over lower division Sunderland in 1992 was all Souness had to show for his time in charge. Hereditary heart problems meant he need open-heart surgery directly following the Cup semi-final win over Portsmouth but he committed the cardinal sin of selling his exclusive to The Sun, the reviled rag that propagated lies about Liverpool supporters at Hillsborough. To compound the error, the story appeared on the third anniversary of the disaster and although Souness donated all the proceeds to a local charity, it was a mistake for which he was never truly forgiven.

The autumn of 1992 saw knives being sharpened as a team without the likes of McMahon, Houghton, Steve Staunton, Beardsley and Barry Venison (all sold) stuttered and shrank. The undoubted promise of Jamie Redknapp, Steve McManaman, Mike Marsh and Don Hutchison was not

Fans tied scarves to the Shankly Gates following the Hillsborough tragedy in April 1989

enough to compensate for big-money flops like Paul Stewart, Dean Saunders and Mark Walters. Liverpool finished the season in an outwardly respectable sixth but had spent much of the campaign battling to avoid a relegation fight. To make matters worse, Manchester United won the first in a long sequence of league titles.

When the board met at the end of the 1993 season, it was decided not to oust Souness when it became clear how expensive it would be but they insisted on Roy Evans being promoted to assistant manager – the first in the club's history. Nigel Clough and Neil Ruddock were brought in for the start of the following campaign but they could do little to prevent Souness from being sacked. After all the rumours about training methods being responsible for the endless injury list and dressing-room bust-ups wrecking team unity, things reached a head when Bristol City knocked Liverpool out of the FA Cup at Anfield. Within days, Souness became the first Reds manager to be sacked since Don Welsh in 1956.

Roy Evans was the obvious replacement – a return to the Anfield philosophy of promotion from within – but improvement was anything but rapid. A crowd of 44,000 turned up to bid farewell to the standing Kop on the last day of the 1993/94 season, but Liverpool turned in another lacklustre display, losing 1-0 to Norwich City to finish a dismal eighth. In 1994/95 new signings improved matters, the Reds hung on to the coat tails of the League leaders and won the Coca-Cola Cup, beating Bolton Wanderers 2-1 thanks to an inspired display from Steve McManaman. A return to the glory days appeared to be just round the corner.

It was not to be. While the teams assembled by Roy Evans undeniably played some exhilarating football –

Liverpool's managers	
1892-1896	W Barclay & J McKenna
1896-1915	Tom Watson
1920-1923	David Ashworth
1923-1928	Matt McQueen
1928-1936	George Patterson
1936-1951	George Kay
1951-1956	Don Welsh
1956-1959	Phil Taylor
1959-1974	Bill Shankly
1974-1983	Bob Paisley
1983-1985	Joe Fagan
1985-1991	Kenny Dalglish
1991-1994	Graeme Souness
1994-1998	Roy Evans
1998-1999	Roy Evans & Gérard Houllier
1999-present	Gérard Houllier

Evolution of Anfield

Farewell to the Kop

In 1992 a new tier was added to the Kemlyn Road Stand, coinciding with the club's centenary. The smart, new double-decker structure was rechristened the Centenary and boasted an all-seated capacity of 11,000.

Hillsborough brought about new attitudes towards terracing. The tragic deaths of 96 Liverpool fans in Sheffield led to the Taylor Report on the safety of stadia, and it was important Liverpool led the way, despite muted protests from long-standing Kopites. The Kop terrace was demolished and replaced with an all-seated Kop stand in 1994. This new stand was faithful in design to the old structure, but with a capacity reduced from 27,000 in its prime to 10,000, there can be no surprise that the atmosphere has been affected.

An upper tier was added to the Anfield Road end in 1998, taking the ground's capacity to 44,000, and a year later the Paisley Gateway was opened outside the Kop to commemorate the life and achievements of Liverpool's most successful manager.

witness the two 4-3 victories over Newcastle United, there was a lack of the steel that characterised sides from previous eras. Defeat in the 1996 FA Cup final to Manchester United, made famous by the white Armani suits that seemed to define Liverpool's 'Spice Boy' mentality, encapsulated the truth that while the Reds were good, they were not good enough. Not even the goals of Robbie Fowler, the pace and running of McManaman or the emerging genius of Michael Owen could reverse that trend. When Gérard Houllier was appointed joint-manager 1998 the writing was on the wall for one of the club's Boot Room legends.

Houllier and the modern Liverpool

The Evans-Houllier partnership was dissolved in November 1998 when Evans resigned, leaving the man who laid the foundations for France's World Cup victory that summer, to become the first foreign manager of Liverpool.

The Frenchman had once been a teacher in the city and was steeped in the history of Anfield. Like Bill Shankly, he inherited a club in decline on the field of play. And like Shankly he set out a plan and stuck to it, building a young team in his own image that would restore pride in the club and deliver trophies to the Anfield sideboard.

Houllier's first two seasons in charge saw the Reds finish seventh and fourth, with a disappointing end to the 1999/00 campaign robbing him of the chance to lead Liverpool into the Champions League for the first time. But in 2000/01 Houllier's signings began to gel and the team, and how he wanted it to play, emerged from the shadows. With Sami Hyypia and Stephane Henchoz imperious in defence, the mighty Steven Gerrard defying his tender years to boss the midfield and the irrepressible Michael Owen scoring for fun upfront, Liverpool became more than the sum of their cosmopolitan parts.

While the championship still remained out of reach, the modern Reds set off on a cup crusade that rekindled memories of the glory days. First Birmingham City were beaten in a penalty shootout in the Worthington Cup final at the Millennium Stadium. Then Arsenal paid the ultimate price for their profligacy in the FA Cup final when Michael Owen confirmed his status as Europe's deadliest striker by scoring twice in the last eight minutes. And finally, on to Dortmund for the Uefa Cup final and a campaign that had accounted for Porto, Roma and Barcelona

Most appearances in all competitions		
	Appearances	Years
Ian Callaghan	857	1959-78
Emlyn Hughes	665	1966-79
Ray Clemence	665	1968-81
Ian Rush	660	1980-96
Phil Neal	650	1974-85
Tommy Smith	639	1962-78
Bruce Grobbelaar	628	1981-94
Alan Hansen	620	1977-91
Chris Lawler	549	1962-76
Billy Liddell	537	1945-61
Kenny Dalglish	515	1977-91

along the way. On a rain-soaked night in Germany, Houllier's young side turned back the clock to give a new generation of Kopites their first taste of European glory, beating Alavés 5-4. They returned to England to wrap up qualification for the Champions League, consigning a period in the doldrums to the history books. Liverpool were back. Allez les Rouges, indeed.

Liverpool 2001

The UEFA Cup final team vs Alavés

Sander Westerveld
Markus Babbel
Stephane Henchoz
(Vladimir Smicer)
Sami Hyypia
Jamie Carragher
Steven Gerrard
Dietmar Hamann
Gary McAllister
Danny Murphy
Emile Heskey
(Robbie Fowler)
Michael Owen
(Patrik Berger)

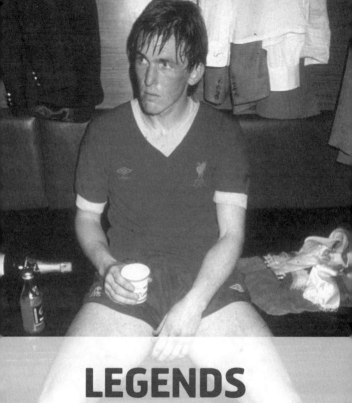

LEGENDS

LEGENDS

Liverpool FC has always been about teamwork, but along the way there've been more than a few heroes who've stood out as the best of the best. Whether you're five or 95, you're bound to have worshipped at the altar of a Michael Owen or a Billy Liddell. You sang their name, you put their poster on your wall and you copied their goal celebration/Herbert's perm. In this section, we profile some of the greatest players who've pulled on a Red shirt and made Saturday afternoon the best bit of the week.

John Aldridge
Striker 1987-89

Ace marksman in the dream team of 1987/88 that swept all before it to claim a 17th league title in irresistible style. Signed from Oxford United to replace the Juventus-bound Ian Rush, the Republic of Ireland forward scored 63 goals in 104 games for the Reds, finding the net in a record 10 consecutive top-flight matches.

Best remembered for scoring with his first touch in the 1989 FA Cup final – at the same end where he'd missed a penalty with his last touch in the previous year's final.

In his own words "Every time I went out I felt I was going to score. With the likes of Barnesy and Ray Houghton out wide, Peter Beardsley tucked in behind and Steve McMahon and Ronnie Whelan in midfield, we were just scoring for fun."

John Barnes
Midfielder 1987-97

The jewel in Kenny Dalglish's late-80s crown, Barnes' mesmerising flair put thousands on the gate wherever the Reds played. Signed from Watford for £900,000, he enjoyed five fabulous seasons before a ruptured

Achilles tendon, sustained while playing for England, changed his game and finally gave Liverpool's opponents a fighting chance.

Best remembered for gliding through the QPR defence in the late autumn sunshine to score at a delirious Kop end, October 1987. Rangers were title pretenders. Digger was the real deal.

In his own words "I never considered myself a winger at Liverpool. I was more of a left-sided player although the attacking instincts I had as a player certainly helped. To me, Liverpool didn't play wingers so I had to fit into the way the team played."

Peter Beardsley
Striker 1987-91

An established England international by the time he joined Barnes in August 1987 as a £1.8million signing from Newcastle United, Pedro took a little longer to settle, but it was worth the wait. Quick feet, shimmying hips and a great football brain marked him as the best inside forward at Anfield since King Kenny before his shock move across the park to Everton.

Best remembered for a brilliant chip against Arsenal, half-volleyed thunderbolt against Everton and man-of-the-match performance in the seminal 5-0 win over Nottingham Forest.

In his own words "I played in a great side, there's no doubt about that. Had we played in Europe I'm sure we would have added to Liverpool's European success."

Gerry Byrne
Full back 1957-69

Rock-solid defender in the no3 shirt and one of the most ferocious but fair tacklers of 1960s football. He must have been tough – he once broke Tommy Smith's nose on the training ground. He won two championship medals and played a mythical part in the club's first-ever FA Cup success.

Best remembered for playing for 117 minutes in the 1965 FA Cup final against Leeds United with a broken collar bone.

In his own words "I was actually on the transfer list until Bill Shankly arrived. He played me at left back when Ronnie Moran got injured, then switched me to the right. I owed him everything."

Ian Callaghan
Winger/midfielder 1959-78

Toxteth-born and an ever-present throughout the 1960s and 70s, making 843 appearances and winning five league championships, two FA Cups and one European Cup. Oh, and an MBE. He was also a member of England's 1966 World Cup squad. Spent a decade storming down the right flank before reinventing himself as a central midfielder.

Best remembered for his astonishing disciplinary record – he was booked just once, in virtually his last game for Liverpool, against Nottingham Forest in the 1978 League Cup final replay.

In his own words "One season we used just 14 players, an unbelievable feat. Squad rotation is the one thing I wouldn't like now. Playing every week you develop an understanding."

Jimmy Case
Midfielder 1973-81

Signed from South Liverpool. Signed off with four league titles, three European Cups, one Uefa Cup and one League Cup. Possessing limitless energy and a degree in advanced free-kick ballistics, he was one quarter of the awesome 1970s midfield that also featured Graeme Souness, Terry McDermott and Ray Kennedy, his best mate.

Best remembered for his equaliser against Manchester United in the 1977 FA Cup final, and a screamer against Borussia Mönchengladbach in the 1978 European Cup semi.

In his own words "When you had the artillery we had, you always felt comfortable going out to play. It was built into the team that you'd have three players to pass to, within two seconds on the ball."

Ray Clemence
Goalkeeper 1967-81

In his 14 years wearing Liverpool's no1 jersey, he won every domestic honour, keeping a staggering 323 clean sheets in 665 appearances and playing an indispensable part in five glorious European campaigns. To many, in his hey day he was the greatest keeper in the world, winning 61 England caps despite stiff competition from Peter Shilton.

Best remembered for crucial saves against St Etienne's Dominique Rocheteau and Borussia Mönchengladbach's Uli Stielike in the 1977 European Cup quarter-final and final respectively.

In his own words "People ask about your best-ever save and expect you to pick something spectacular, but that's not always the case. Great saves are the ones that win matches, they don't have to be flash."

Stan Collymore
Striker 1995-97

Signed from Nottingham Forest by Roy Evans for a club record £8.5million, his attitude was often exasperating but his first season still brought 17 goals – the first on his home debut – and a lethal partnership with Robbie Fowler. The following year the Reds cut their losses and sold him to Aston Villa, and he retired prematurely at 30.

Best remembered for his injury-time winner against Newcastle United in the first epic 4-3 between the two sides at Anfield.

In his own words "I never really felt fulfilled at Liverpool. I could've been the out-and-out goalscorer, but Robbie Fowler was already established there and being in and out of the team didn't give me the confidence I needed."

Peter Cormack
Midfielder 1972-76

Signed from Nottingham Forest as the final piece in the jigsaw of Shankly's second great team. The intelligent Scot's midfield play added a new dimension to Liverpool's game and his precision passing, deft touches, fondness for the tackle and opportunist goalscoring endeared him to the Kop.

Best remembered for scoring the winner with a soaring header against Everton in his first derby, October 1972, and an immaculate performance in the 1974 FA Cup final.

In his own words "It was a privilege to be at Liverpool during the same time as Shankly and players like Tommy Smith, Cally and Keegan. Guys like these played for the love of the club. It wasn't about money in those days. We'd have played for nothing."

Kenny Dalglish
Striker 1977-90

The Supreme Being, as one fanzine correctly dubbed him. Signed from Celtic for a British record £440,000 to replace Kevin Keegan, he scored 172 goals and won 14 medals and 55 of his record 102 Scotland caps while playing in red. Liverpool's greatest-ever player, no argument.

38 legendary nicknames

Albert Kevin MacDonald	**God** Robbie Fowler
Andy McDaft Kevin Keegan	**Jocky** Alan Hansen
Anfield Iron Tommy Smith	**Little Bamber** Brian Hall
Barney Rubble Alan Kennedy	**Mighty Mouse** Kevin Keegan
Big Bamber Steve Heighway	**Omar** Ian Rush
Bionic Carrot David Fairclough	**Pedro** Peter Beardsley
Chico Steve Nicol	**Quoz** Peter Beardsley
Choccy Graeme Souness	**Rambo** Jan Molby
Champagne Charlie	**Razor** Ray Kennedy, Ray Houghton,
Graeme Souness	Neil Ruddock
Cheswick Terry McDermott	**Rowdy** Ron Yeats
Colossus Ron Yeats	**Shaggy** Steve McManaman
Crazy Horse Emlyn Hughes	**Silent Knight** Chris Lawler
Dex Jim Beglin	**Sir Roger** Roger Hunt
Digger John Barnes	**Skippy** Craig Johnston
Doc David Johnson	**Stan** Steve Staunton
Dog's Kenny Dalglish	**Tonka Toy** Phil Thompson
Dusty Ronnie Whelan	**Tosh** Ian Rush
Flying Pig Tommy Lawrence	**Trigger** Rob Jones, Jason McAteer
Fraggle Alan Irvine	**Zico** Phil Neal

Best remembered for the volleyed title-clincher at Chelsea in 1986. The little chip against Bruges in 1978. Shielding the ball. Turning his marker. The eye-of-the-needle assists. Puffed-out cheeks. Beaming smile etc, etc
In his own words "Just play. That's all they said. Absolutely nothing was pre-planned. The quality of the pass, the movement off it – everything came in training. The players were all intelligent so they all knew when to go, when to stay. And never one of them put themselves before the team."

David Fairclough
Winger/striker 1975-83

A shock of red hair earned him the nickname 'Bionic Carrot', but it's as Supersub that's he best remembered. Brought up within earshot of Anfield, he developed a habit of coming on as substitute and scoring vital goals, beginning with the 1976 Merseyside derby and most famously in the European Cup quarter-final the following year.

Best remembered for his legendary strike against St Etienne in the 1977 European Cup – the goal that changed Liverpool's destiny.

In his own words "The Supersub thing doesn't annoy me now. All the time I played I hated it. It was the suggestion I couldn't play for 90 minutes. But I proved many times that it was unfair and untrue."

Robbie Fowler
Striker 1993-01

To see him in his incorrigible youth was to witness a phenomenon at work. He hit his first hat-trick in his fifth league game and was the club's top scorer for four seasons running. In the late 90s injury began to take its toll, but his record of 171 goals in 330 games speaks for itself.

Best remembered for his hat-trick in four minutes and 32 seconds against Arsenal at Anfield in 1994 – still a Premiership record.

In his own words "I always had a great rapport with the fans. They could relate to me because I'm a local lad and they knew I wanted to win things for them. It made me so proud to play for Liverpool, and also to captain them as well."

Gary Gillespie
Centre half 1984-91

Joe Fagan's first signing, nominally as cover for the flawless duo of Hansen and Lawrenson, he made the breakthrough under Kenny Dalglish and eventually clocked up 212 games. A classy, commanding defender with a presence in both boxes and a sight for goal.

Best remembered for a hat-trick, incredibly, against Birmingham City in April 1986. And a headband Jane Fonda would've been proud of in the 1988 FA Cup final.

In his own words "I can't remember a single occasion when I was coached on technique. It was simple stuff. A warm-up, then lots of games. Everyone was so technically gifted anyway, they barely needed to work on it."

Bruce Grobbelaar
Goalkeeper 1981-94

Eccentric Zimbabwean showman, signed from Vancouver Whitecaps, who succeeded Ray Clemence between the posts and made more than 600 appearances in 13 years. He was branded a bungling clown by Evertonians, but it was a small price to pay for 13 major medals.

Best remembered for walking on his hands after the 1982 Milk Cup final, his wobbly legs during the 1984 European Cup final penalty shoot-out and his wonder save from Graeme Sharp's header in the 1986 FA Cup final.

In his own words "Whenever I got any stick, it acted as a spur to me. And the Kop were brilliant. There was no question of them getting on my back – they always gave me a lift."

Alan Hansen
Centre half 1977-91

British football's answer to Franz Beckenbauer and second only to Phil Neal in the club's all-time pantheon of medal-winners. In an era of 'stoppers' he was a gloriously elegant exception. And cool with it – while others bit their nails, he'd spend the build-up to a match flicking through the programme in the dressing room. Absolutely no problem.

Best remembered for his flawless positional play and countless surges upfield with the ball at his feet.

In his own words "Whenever a new player arrived, especially a defender, Ronnie Moran would point to me and say, 'Don't watch Big Al play – don't try to do what he does because he's a one-off.'"

Steve Heighway
Winger/striker 1970-81

The heir to Peter Thompson's touchline-scorching throne, this graduate in politics and economics actually spent as much time upfront as he did on the flanks. A joy to behold in his exhilarating heyday, tearing down the wing, skipping hideous tackles, winning penalties or crossing for others to score. Now director of the club's Academy.

Best remembered for inspiring a 3-2 comeback on his derby debut, November 1970.

In his own words "One of the first people to make me feel at home was Peter Thompson. I had something to follow because, with the possible exception of George Best, Peter was the most skilful player I'd seen."

Ray Houghton
Midfielder 1987-92

Glasgow-born Irish international whose childhood love of Celtic meant there was only one answer when Kenny Dalglish asked him to be the fourth big signing for the legendary 1987/88 season. He was the final piece in the jigsaw – skilful, determined and the perfect right-wing foil to John Barnes on the left.

Best remembered for heading the winner in the FA Cup fifth-round derby at Goodison Park.

In his own words "It was simple. At most clubs when you get the ball you only have one or two options, but all of a sudden I had eight or nine. When you look at that team, everyone was quality."

Emlyn Hughes
Full back/centre half 1967-79

Shrill-voiced stalwart signed from Blackpool when Shanks dismantled and rebuilt his team in the late 1960s. He became a mainstay of the team for 13 years, making over 600 appearances and winning nine medals. Replaced Tommy Smith as captain and later skippered on A Question Of Sport.

Best remembered for his notorious 1977 chant, "Liverpool Are Magic, Everton Are Tragic!" Gumph…

In his own words "The secret of our success was the team and I was a good player in a great team. I had very little ability but tons of enthusiasm and desperation by the bucket loads."

Roger Hunt
Striker 1959-69

Before Owen, Fowler, Rush, Dalglish and Keegan, there was sir Roger. Top marksman in nine of his 10 full seasons at the club, he scored more league goals for Liverpool (245) than anyone else and was knighted by the Kop. His belated testimonial in 1972 was watched by a lock-out 56,000 crowd. A World Cup winner, too, in 1966.

Best remembered for his half-volleyed goal against Inter in the 1965 European Cup semi-final – "one of my sweetest ever".

In his own words "In the mid 60s the happiness on people's faces had to be seen to be believed. It was all part of a fantastic period in the city of Liverpool. Whichever way you looked there was something happening."

David Johnson
Striker 1976-82

Halewood-born England striker who partnered Kenny Dalglish and became the first man to score a winning goal in a Merseyside derby for both Liverpool and Everton. Missed the 1977 and 1978 European Cup finals through injury but finally picked up a winner's medal in 1981.

Best remembered for the vital, headed away goal at Mönchengladbach in the 1978 European Cup semi and the kit bag full of pills and remedies that earned him the nickname Doc.

In his own words "When you're pushing for top honours, unless you've got the release that comes from humour the tension can get to you. You've got to have that blend of hardmen, characters and idiots. We had a fantastic dressing-room banter."

Craig Johnston
Midfielder 1981-88

Volatile. Ambiguous. Infuriating. But above all irrepressible. The hyperactive Aussie midfielder spent seven years careering down the right flank, cutting inside and out before delivering good cross after bad. At just 27 he retired to look after his sick sister Down Under.

Best remembered for Riverdancing in mid air after scoring against Everton in the sun-drenched 1986 FA Cup final. Inventing the Adidas Predator boot. Penning The Anfield Rap.

In his own words "I used to run around the field winning the ball and making things happen. You didn't know whether it was going to be good or bad, but things always happened."

Joey Jones
Full back 1975-78

Three short of 100 appearances in the no3 shirt for the fist-clenching Welshman with the never-say-die attitude. He won two league titles and one European Cup and inspired the world's best-ever football banner. Measuring 24ft by 8ft, it earned top billing at the 1977 European Cup final in Rome…

Best remembered for 'Joey Ate The Frogs Legs, Made The Swiss Roll, Now He's Munchen Gladbachs'.

In his own words "Like all the people who go on the Kop, they're supporting Liverpool because they'd love to play for them and that's exactly what happened to me. It actually happened to me. And I felt that when I signed, I was representing the supporters."

Kevin Keegan
Striker 1971-77

Five feet eight inches of explosive energy, his 100 goals have earned him 15th place on the all-time list of top Reds marksmen – Michael Owen recently overtook him. A self-made footballing superstar, he turned in a man-of-the-match performance in the 1974 FA Cup final against Newcastle, the club he would later manage.

Best remembered for terrorising Bertie Vögts in the 1977 European Cup final. And wearing rather deafening trousers in photo-shoots.

In his own words "I was never easily overawed, but I'll never forget the first time I ran on in front of the famous Kop. The ovation was deafening, the red and white scarves having a life of their own. The whole scene got through to me."

Alan Kennedy
Full back 1978-85

Pacy, energetic Wearsider nicknamed 'Barney Rubble' by the Kop. He was never the most accurate shooter – after his mishit shot knocked a policeman's helmet off on his Anfield debut Bob Paisley told him, "I think they shot the wrong Kennedy" – but he had a real sense of occasion and the uncanny knack of scoring important goals.

Best remembered for being the only British player to score winning goals in two European Cup finals, 1981 and 1984.

In his own words "I wasn't a hardman type, but when that red shirt went on I was prepared to give it everything. I was a swashbuckling player, not the most skilful but determined and dedicated."

Ray Kennedy
Midfielder 1974-82

Left-footed midfielder whose languid, almost Brazilian gait and effortless finishing were unique to English football. He scored 72 goals in 389 appearances at home and in Europe, often ghosting into the penalty area on the blind side to connect with instinctive, diagonal passes from fellow midfielders.

Best remembered for the vital equaliser away at Bayern Munich that sent the Reds through to the 1981 European Cup final in Paris on away goals. **In his own words** "People would say I was lazy, which I was, but I could read where the ball was going so what was the point of running for it? I wasn't the best or the fastest, but I thought a good game."

Chris Lawler
Full back 1963-75

One of five brothers, all Liverpool supporters, he was nicknamed 'Silent Knight' because he was so quiet. His regular charges down the flank plus an ability to pop up in the box made him the first top-flight full back to score more than 50 times without the aid of penalties, 11 of them in European ties. As sturdy as they come.

Best remembered for blasting the winner with six minutes left after Liverpool had been 2-0 down in the 1970 derby at Anfield – just as the Kop was belting out You'll Never Walk Alone. Aw yes…

In his own words "There weren't many who got the better of me and Tommy Smith down the flanks. Best, Charlton, yes, they were good. But we usually had the beating of them."

Tommy Lawrence
Goalkeeper 1962-71

Dubbed 'the Flying Pig', he spent a decade between the sticks, missing just a handful of games and in one season conceding a mere 24 goals and keeping 21 clean sheets to set a top-flight record that was bettered just once – by his successor Ray Clemence. On Shankly's orders, he also set the trend for rushing out of the area to beat opposing forwards to the ball.

Best remembered for having the ball kicked out of his hands by an Inter forward in the infamous 1965 European Cup semi-final second leg.

In his own words "Courage was vital. You had to be prepared to dive at feet, go where the boots and elbows were flailing. I broke the odd finger, but that was par for the course."

Mark Lawrenson
Centre half 1981-88

Arguably a better defender in the truest sense than Alan Hansen, his partner at the back. He was snatched from under the noses of Manchester United and Arsenal for a club record £900,000 and won five

They coulda been contenders...

Jack Charlton

During his first season as boss, Bill Shankly made an £18,000 bid for the giant centre half, then struggling with Leeds United at the bottom of the table. Leeds wanted more, so Liverpool bought Ron Yeats instead.

Luis Figo

Admitted three years ago that he'd had the chance to go to Liverpool in 1995. Roy Evans reportedly tabled a £1.4million bid for the Portuguese international, but Sporting Lisbon sold him to Barcelona instead for twice as much.

Tim Flowers

In 1993 the would-be England keeper wanted to follow pal Alan Shearer from Southampton to Kenny Dalglish's Blackburn. Saints boss Ian Branfoot tried to flog him to Liverpool instead – Graeme Souness even offered David James in part-exchange – but Flowers eventually got his move to Ewood Park.

Paul Gascoigne

When Gazza joined Tottenham from Newcastle in 1988, he wanted a clause in his contract ensuring that if Liverpool ever made a bid for him, he'd be free to go. Terry Venables quickly put the kibosh on it.

Michael Laudrup

Chief scout Tom Saunders visited the 17-year-old Danish striker in 1982, but Laudrup's dad wanted a two-year deal rather than the proposed four. Michael joined Juventus the following season. Five years later he declared further interest in joining the Reds but signed for Barcelona.

Denis Law

No sooner had Bill Shankly joined Liverpool in 1959 than he went back to Huddersfield for Law, whom he'd blooded in the Yorkshire side as a 16-year-old. Shanks was furious when the Liverpool board refused to sanction the deal. The following year Law joined Manchester City for a British record £65,000. In 1964 he was European footballer of year.

They coulda been contenders...

Lou Macari
In 1973 Bill Shankly invited the Celtic striker to watch Liverpool at Anfield and eventually made a £200,000 offer. But the wee Scot opted for Manchester United, for whom he scored 96 goals in 400 games.

Charlie Nicholas
A straight choice between Liverpool and Arsenal in 1983 for the wedge-haired Scot, who'd just scored 46 goals for Celtic. The Gunners, however, were prepared to pay him five times what he was on at Parkhead. "Charlie would have been great for us," said Kenny Dalglish. "But he was frightened he wouldn't get a game."

Gary Pallister
Rumoured to be a target in 1988, effectively to replace Alan Hansen in the long term. When a press conference was called at Anfield that summer, many assumed it was to unveil the Boro defender. Instead it was to announce the return of Ian Rush from Juventus.

Ian Snodin
Both Liverpool and Everton tabled £800,000 offers for the Leeds skipper, who was widely regarded as one of the finest midfielders around. To Kenny's chagrin he picked the Blues, but a long-term injury effectively ended his top-flight career.

Frank Worthington
The flamboyant striker actually put pen to paper in a £150,000 deal in 1972, but he was diagnosed with high blood pressure so Bill Shankly sent him on holiday. Upon his return his blood pressure was even higher, and Shanks pulled out.

titles, one European Cup and the Double in 1986. At 30, his career was brought to an untimely end by a snapped Achilles.

Best remembered for his title-clinching header against Tottenham at Anfield in the last game of his first season. And ill-advised hair tints.

In his own words "Neither me nor Alan Hansen were fantastic communicators on the pitch, but we just seemed to know what each other was doing. And if we made a mistake we both had enough pace to rectify it."

Sammy Lee
Midfielder 1979-86

At 5ft 7in, what he lacked in height he made up for in heart. He broke through in the early 1980s as a replacement for Jimmy Case, with whom he shared a cannonball shot – current Reds reserve coach and former Manchester City keeper Joe Corrigan was twice beaten by long-range Lee drives at Maine Road. Ten major honours in five full seasons and now Liverpool's first-team coach.

Best remembered for marking Bayern Munich's strutting skipper Paul Breitner out of the second leg of the 1981 European Cup semi-final.

In his own words "Time and time again it was drummed into us – football is a simple game, so why complicate it?"

Billy Liddell
Winger/striker 1938-60

Accountant, RAF navigator, university bursar, Justice of the Peace, Scottish international and Anfield's first superstar – so much so the team was dubbed Liddellpool. He's still fourth in the club's all-time scoring charts with 229 goals in 537 games. A true gentleman, he never shirked a tackle but hardly ever committed a foul. He died in 2001.

Best remembered for putting Liverpool on the map, pre-Shankly. "His name is like a neon sign on Merseyside," says Ian Callaghan.

In his own words "At Anfield when we were a goal down it was invariably the signal for the Kop to go into action with their famous roar. The cheers almost literally forced us back into the game."

Terry McDermott
Midfielder 1974-82

An integral part of arguably the club's greatest-ever team, he was the dynamic goalscorer in an all-star late-70s midfield and the first player to win both the PFA and Football Writers player of the year awards in the same season. Five League titles, three European Cups.

Best remembered for The perm, the tache, the sovereign rings, the bandy legs, the public inconvenience at the 1977 European Cup homecoming. But most of all, the brilliant, brilliant goals.

In his own words "The players Bob Paisley bought were winners. We all wanted to win. It was simple – get it, give it, move. That's what was drummed into us. Don't stand and admire."

Steve McMahon
Midfielder 1985-91

Kenny Dalglish's first signing and still the only player to skipper both Liverpool and Everton, his first club. Exhibiting bite and subtlety in equal measure, he became Liverpool's new midfield soprano, restoring it to an opposition no-go area with bone-crunching tackles and defence-splitting passes.

Best remembered for an unbelievable assist against Arsenal in 1988 – racing to keep the ball in, beating two men and crossing for Aldridge to score.

In his own words "I used to have some great tussles with Peter Reid. Derbies were great games to play in. You tackle him, he tackles you, you get up. None of this off-the-ball stuff."

Steve McManaman
Winger/midfielder 1990-99

Raised in Kirkdale and a Goodison Park regular, he was lured to Anfield by Kenny Dalglish and the promise of a pair of new boots. Graeme Souness gave him his debut, Roy Evans handed him a free role. 'Shaggy' illuminated the often bleak mid 90s with his amazing stamina and long, dribbling runs.

Best remembered for his 60-yard solo goal against Celtic in the 1997/98 Uefa Cup, and a brace against Bolton in the 1995 Coca-Cola Cup final.

In his own words "Dribbling came naturally to me. As a kid I was small and thin and didn't have much of a shot. The only way I could compete was to run with the ball."

Jan Molby
Midfielder 1984-96

Liverpool's first European import, signed as a 21-year-old from Ajax by Joe Fagan as a replacement for Graeme Souness. But Molby was always more of an artist than a destroyer. Beneath that bulky exterior lay an engine that positively purred – the finesse and unmistakable pedigree of an Aston Martin lurking in the body of a Sherman tank.

Best remembered for his thunderbolt shot – especially the one that whizzed past Manchester United's Gary Bailey in a 1985 Milk Cup tie at Anfield. And that preposterously natural Scouse accent.

In his own words "Everyone assumed I was going to be a 'breaker' but that's never what my game was about. Only in the 1985/86 season when I played just behind the front two did the fans see the real Jan Molby. I loved that."

Phil Neal
Full back 1974-86

Bob Paisley's first signing and a fixture at full back right throughout the glory years of the 1970s and 80s, clocking up 635 games, including 417 consecutively, and winning eight titles and four European Cups – in all he picked up a club record 20 medals. Reliable, versatile and a team player.

Best remembered for his arch penalty-taking, bounteous perm and swerving shots – the Kop whimsically dubbed him 'Zico'.

In his own words "Once I was given my chance in the team, I took it with both hands. I didn't want to give up the red shirt. I'd risk myself to hang on to my place and I never missed a day's training."

Steve Nicol
Full back/midfielder 1982-95

A modern-day master of all trades, he played in every outfield position for Liverpool, tormenting opponents down the flanks and scoring goals as both defender and midfielder. Brought to Anfield from Ayr United as a £300,000 teenager, he won a European Cup medal at 22 and was voted PFA player of the year in 1989. Now see Ripping Yarns.

Best remembered for his televised hat-trick at Newcastle United, 1987.

In his own words "I felt most comfortable as a full back, but I'd play anywhere for Liverpool and I got my chance in several positions. Wherever I played, there was so much quality in the side it was never too difficult."

Jamie Redknapp
Midfielder 1991-02

British football's most expensive teenager when signed by Kenny Dalglish from Bournemouth for £350,000, he also became the youngest player to represent Liverpool in Europe. Injury dogged his Anfield career, but he still managed over 300 appearances and was appointed club captain by Gérard Houllier for his courage and loyalty.

Best remembered for the brilliant free-kick that beat Kenny Dalglish's title-winning Blackburn Rovers at Anfield in 1995.

In his own words "I had some incredible times at Liverpool and will never forget them. I may have left Liverpool, but Liverpool will never leave me. I love the club to bits."

Michael Robinson
Striker 1983-84

Irish international and England's first £750,000 teenager when he joined Manchester City from Preston, at Anfield he was a one-season wonder in the most affectionate sense, forging an adoring relationship with the fans and leaving with League, European Cup and Milk Cup honours.

Best remembered for patting his stomach in the pre-match warm-up when the Kop chanted 'One Fatty Robbo!'

In his own words "I still consider it an honour to have played for Liverpool, especially as I was chunky and not too skilful. On my first day they gave me the red shirt and I didn't know whether to put it on or ask the other players to autograph it!"

Ronny Rosenthal
Striker 1990-93

Explosive Israeli international whose arrival originally on loan from Standard Liège was likened to a fistful of Alka Seltzer hitting a bucket of water. Against Charlton he became the first Liverpool player since Bobby Graham to score a hat-trick on his first full start, and seven goals in his first eight games hauled the Reds over the championship finishing line.

Best remembered for scoring the winner in the derby... and a dreadful miss at Villa Park in 1992, a fixture on every video of sporting howlers.

In his own words "The side I played in was the last one to win the title for Liverpool. So whenever I go back to Anfield I always get a tremendous reception. It's an honour to be remembered with such affection."

King Kenny – a snip at £11m

What would yesterday's Liverpool stars be worth today? You can get a good idea by dividing the average Premiership admission price in 2002 (£20) by ticket prices at the time of each transfer (eg 2s 6d in 1961 = 12.52p) and multiplying the result by the fee that was paid...

John Barnes
Then £900,000 (July 1987 from Watford; admission £3)
Now £3million

Graeme Souness
Then £352,000 (January 1978 from Boro; admission 80p)
Now £8.8million

Kenny Dalglish
Then £440,000 (July 1977 from Celtic; admission 80p)
Now £11million

Alan Hansen
Then £100,000 (May 1977 from Partick Thistle; admission 80p)
Now £2.5million

Kevin Keegan
Then £35,000 (May 1971 from Scunthorpe United; admission 20p)
Now £3.5million

Ron Yeats
Then £30,000 (July 1961 from Dundee United; admission 2s 6d)
Now £4.8million

Ian St John
Then £37,500 (May 1961 from Motherwell; admission 2s 6d)
Now £6million

Ian Rush

Striker 1980-87; 1988-96

The hard facts are barely believable. He scored 346 times in 658 appearances – more than a goal every other game – over two spells at Anfield interrupted by his short sojourn in Italy with Juventus. Began as King Kenny's apprentice, ended as Robbie Fowler's mentor.

Best remembered for his goals against Everton. All 25 of them. Including a fabulous four in the 5-0 win at Goodison in November 1982.

In his own words "What Bob Paisley gave me was confidence. I was never afraid to miss. I might miss eight chances, but I knew I'd score two. That was the belief he gave me."

Ian St John
Striker 1961-71

A landmark signing by Shankly in 1961, his darting, all-action style perfectly complemented Roger Hunt in what was a bludgeon-and-rapier combination. When the Kop began to clap and sing in the early 1960s, it was St John's name they sang to the tune of the Routers hit, Let's Go.

Best remembered for the headed goal that brought the FA Cup to Anfield after a 73-year wait.

In his own words "Those early days were memorable. It was the start of a surge. We led the Second Division from start to finish and had a great rapport with the Kop. We needed them to lift us, and they needed us."

Tommy Smith
Full back/centre half 1963-78

'The Anfield Iron' was certainly hard as nails but by no means the archetypal clogger – over 600 first-team appearances and a glittering array of medals are ample proof of that. He progressed from first-team rookie to club captain and in 1973 became the first Liverpool skipper to hold aloft a European trophy – the Uefa Cup.

Best remembered for his crashing header that made it 2-1 against Borussia Mönchengladbach in the 1977 European Cup final.

In his own words "You had to be hard in those days. The game was a lot more aggressive and this was drummed into us very early on at Liverpool. Training was always very competitive, the boss encouraged it, and once or twice it would explode."

Graeme Souness
Midfielder 1978-84

Scottish skipper and the most complete British midfielder of his era. For him, a football match was a floor exercise in power and grace amid the red blur of his team-mates and indeterminate grey of the opposition. His fearsome elegance yielded five championships, three European Cups and three League Cups in six seasons. Left to try his luck in Serie A.

Best remembered for tossing the League championship trophy to Ronnie Whelan at Anfield, May 1982. Seminal.

In his own words "I was with the best club in the world. We knew at the start of each season when we were photographed with the trophies there was a fair chance they were going to be in the same picture the following year."

Albert Stubbins
Striker 1946-53
Geordie centre forward and Liverpool's first post-war superstar. Described during his playing days as "a sizeable boy with boxer's features", he signed from Newcastle for a club record £13,000, scored 83 goals in 180 games, won the championship and played in an FA Cup final. Everton wanted him, too, but he tossed a coin and spoke to the Reds first.

Best remembered for being on the Sgt Pepper's cover, and his spectacular diving header in an FA Cup quarter-final win over Birmingham City at a snow-covered Anfield in 1947.

In his own words "When I was last in Liverpool a taxi driver beeped his horn and shouted, 'Albert, have you brought your boots?' There's always someone who remembers me when I come back."

Peter Thompson
Winger/midfielder 1964-73
Flying winger signed from Preston for a club record £40,000 – Shankly later described it as "daylight robbery" – who became one of the game's great entertainers during his decade at Anfield, inspiring the Reds to the First Division title within nine months of arriving and winning an FA Cup medal the following season.

Best remembered for scoring a brilliant solo goal against Chelsea in the 1965 FA Cup semi at Villa Park in his first season as a Red.

In his own words "Bill Shankly made me believe I was the greatest winger in Europe, and he made Ian Callaghan think he was better than I was! We went on to the pitch genuinely believing we were the greatest."

Phil Thompson
Centre half 1972-82
Kirkby boy who graduated from the Kop to the first team and became the first Scouser to skipper England. His frail-looking physique belied often abrasive defending which, allied with fierce pride and determination, earned him 13 major honours. Played alongside Emlyn Hughes, whom he succeeded as captain, then Alan Hansen, to whom he ultimately relinquished the armband.

Best remembered for pleading for the European Cup from a Uefa official after he skippered the Reds to victory over Real Madrid in the 1981 final.

In his own words "I never had a big frame and people thought they could take advantage of me. But that's where the heart took over. Kirkby people are like that."

John Toshack
Striker 1970-78

Welsh target man and self-styled bard of Anfield, he formed an almost psychic partnership with Kevin Keegan upfront and is the only man to have scored a winning goal for an English club against Barcelona in the Nou Camp.

Best remembered for being drafted into the side by Bill Shankly and terrorising Borussia Mönchengladbach when the first leg of the 1973 Uefa Cup final was abandoned and played the following evening.

In his own words "A golden night and what a thrill, it's Liverpool 1 Barcelona 0. One away goal will suit us fine, and I'm so pleased it was mine."

Paul Walsh
Striker 1984-87

Tousled-haired striker who took Kenny Dalglish's no7 shirt and combined impish skill with electric pace to twist and turn past defences. He arrived from Luton Town as the PFA young player of the year, but a succession of injuries prevented the popular Londoner from fulfilling his enormous potential.

Best remembered for scoring 14 seconds into his debut against West Ham, equalising in extra time against Manchester United in the 1985 FA Cup semi-final and, ahem, flooring Southampton's Kevin Bond with a sweet right hook after the big defender had been fouling him all night.

In his own words "Joining Liverpool was everything I'd wanted – a massive club, success and fantastic support. But whatever happened it was always fish and chips on the coach home. I loved it."

Ronnie Whelan
Midfielder 1981-94

Precocious Dubliner who inherited Ray Kennedy's no5 shirt and won a championship medal and PFA young player of the year award in his first full season. He gravitated from left to central midfield and matured into the reliable fulcrum of the great 1980s sides. Liverpool's last great Irishman.

Best remembered for scoring against Man United in the 1982 Milk Cup final and 1985 FA Cup semi-final – and netting *for* them, lobbing unintentionally but exquisitely over Bruce Grobbelaar at Old Trafford in 1990.

In his own words "I never felt more at home than in the middle, I loved it. I was the sitting midfielder and the defensive side was natural to me because I had to do it so often when I played on the left."

Ron Yeats
Centre half 1961-73

One of Bill Shankly's earliest signings and the rock upon which the modern-day Anfield empire was built. Within a year he'd led the Reds to the Second Division title. Two league championships followed and in 1965 he became the first Liverpool captain to lift the FA Cup. Fondly remembered as 'Rowdy' and 'the Colossus', now chief scout at the club.

Best remembered for his sheer size. When he signed, he was described by Shankly as "Six feet tall and strong as an ox." It was upon Yeats that Shanks experimented with the intimidating all-red kit.

In his own words "People ask me what was the highlight of my career. In terms of the club's history it was winning promotion from the Second Division in 1961/62. Without that, nothing else could have followed."

Ripping yarns

In football, the past is not such much another country as another solar system. Throughout the 1970s and 80s Liverpool somehow managed to reconcile a phenomenal run of success with Sunday league slapstick and camaraderie. Usually with Steve Nicol as the fall guy…

Michael Robinson

"When I was first discussing my transfer with Bob Paisley and Joe Fagan they were baffled when I asked how I should play if I signed. *'How should I play?'* I remember them echoing the question and looking at each other amazed. 'If you don't know how to play football, we're spending an awful lot of money badly here.' And I said, 'No, no, no. I mean, according to the system.' 'Ah, the system,' they went. 'Now listen, Michael. We always put 11 players on the pitch so we don't start off at a disadvantage and then this is what we try to do. In midfield we always give the ball to a red shirt, and you upfront, if you can possibly kick it in the net that'll be great. If you can't, knock it to

Ripping Yarns

somebody else who can. And at the back we're going to try very hard not to let a goal in. Now if we can do that all the time – and we normally do – we'll most often win. What do you think about the system?' And I said, 'Yes, but is there any more?' And they replied, 'Is there any more to football?'"

Paul Walsh

"The medical facilities were unbelievable in those days. The treatment room was like a museum. I remember in the 1986 double-winning season I was going along nicely until I picked up an ankle injury against Manchester United. There's a picture on my wall at home of me in the dressing room with Roy Evans dabbing my ankle with a cold sponge. I've ruptured my ligaments and I've got Roy giving it a dab and wiggling it about saying, 'It'll be all right.' I was hobbling around for months. The funny thing is, eventually this fella comes round to test the ultra-sound machine and it turns out it's not even working. I'd been having the ultra-sound on my ankle religiously three times a day for three months and it wasn't even working. Looking back it was a joke, but at the time that's just how things were."

Ronny Rosenthal

"There was one incident I'll never forget. We were warming up on the training field the morning after the Christmas party. Bruce Grobbelaar was leading the pack with Roy Evans behind him as we jogged round the pitch. Without warning Bruce broke wind and as Roy was right behind him, he was the first to run into it. It was so bad Roy keeled over and actually started vomiting. All the other players then ran into it and keeled over or tried to escape the poisonous gas. It really was the most incredible sight I've ever seen on a training field."

Phil Neal

"Terry McDermott once got us hysterical in the dressing room, laughing at Bob Paisley's expense. The boss had a habit of saying the word 'doings' all the time. He'd refer to opposition players as 'doings' instead of naming them. So Bob comes into the dressing room and starts a talk. Terry is stood behind him with a big grin on his face and every time Bob says 'doings' he holds a finger up. By the time he gets to six, Terry is starting to titter and we're desperately trying not to laugh. Ray Kennedy is kicking me and when Terry

Ripping Yarns

gets to 10, Ray just turns and flees into the toilet, he's in absolute fits. We were like a bunch of schoolkids."

Terry McDermott

"I was 46 before I got rid of my perm. Kevin Keegan was the first to get it done, then came the two Phils, Thompson and Neal, before I followed suit. Thommo looked like Shirley Temple. I remember going to get my first perm with him in Kirkby. We didn't want people watching us so we sat upstairs in the attic with our curlers in. We had them done on the Friday and we had to go to the hotel before the home game on a Saturday. We used to get on the coach just outside Kirkby and when I got on the lads absolutely slaughtered me. If it was any consolation my perm was definitely better than either of the two Phils because of the colour. I'd definitely put myself in the top 10 of British perms alongside Keegan and Leo Sayer."

David Hodgson

"It was in Israel just before the European Cup final in 1984 and we'd been playing fizz-buzz, one of those drinking games. There was Alan Hansen, Kenny, Bruce Grobbelaar, Stevie Nicol, myself, Ronnie Whelan, Ian Rush, Sammy Lee, all drinking in this square in Tel Aviv. Things got said and a fight started. Me and Rushie were quite close, we travelled in together. So it's us, back to back, against everybody else. Unbelievable. Somehow it calmed down and I remember coming back to the hotel with Rushie and Alan Kennedy, who fell on the ground and couldn't get up.

"There was an old Liverpool director, Mr Moss. Always away with the team on the big trips. Well, he was coming out of the hotel just at that moment. So I've got down to pick up Alan Kennedy and I couldn't get up either. And Mr Moss is stood above us, frowning. He says, 'Gentleman, this is Liverpool Football Club.' So I grabbed hold of his trousers and pulled myself up his body. As I'm pulling myself up, I'm pulling his trousers down. And I put my arm round him and said, 'Mossy, you old bugger, you might be a director but I think you're a great fella!'

"So the next morning, Bob Paisley collars us when we come down for breakfast. He knew what had gone on and there were three empty chairs next to him at the front of the table. I come down first and he says, 'You, sit there.' Then Rushie comes down. 'You, sit there.' Then Alan Kennedy. 'And you, sit

Ripping yarns

there.' Bob turns to me and Rushie and says, 'So you think you're hard, youse two, fighting?' Then they call this big meeting and around the table there's Bob, Joe Fagan, Moran, Evo… and Mr Moss, who stands up. 'I've been at this football club for over 20 years,' he says. 'And I have never, ever witnessed anything like last night in my life. I've had many accolades passed on to me but never have I received one so touching than from David Hodgson.' Then they lift up the tablecloth – and underneath it's piled high with beer!"

Graeme Souness

"I remember that night in Tel Aviv. We were in our beds. And Hansen's come banging on the door. 'Get up! Get up!' Why? 'They're all fighting each other down there!' So Kenny and I got up and got in the lift. Coming up the lift shaft, for about 10 feet, was a chorus of Suicide Is Painless. What they'd done, a dozen or so of them, they'd all got in the lift and jumped up and down and it'd got stuck halfway up. Call it team spirit. Call it madness. Call it drink. But that was how we were back then. Great times."

Alan Hansen

"We're in Israel preparing for the European Cup final. We're out having a drink but Kenny is nae there, he's nae drinking. Nicol turns to me and says, 'Is there something wrong with Kenny?' Off the top of my head I say, 'He's got six months to live, he's dying.' So Nicol goes like this *(puts hands on head)*. He says, 'Nooo… Nooo… You're kidding?!' I say, 'It's true. He's in his room. But don't tell anybody.'

"Anyway, he's goes to the toilet. Souness has clocked this and says to me, 'What did you say to him?' I say, 'Kenny's dying. Incurable disease, right?' So Graeme says, 'Take him back to see him. I'll phone Kenny and tell him you're coming.' So I say to Nicol, 'I'm going back to see Kenny, do you fancy coming?' He says, 'Aye, aye.' So we get in the taxi. Nicol's staring out of the window and suddenly turns to me and says, 'See when we get there, show him no pity. That's the worst thing you can do.'

"We get back to the hotel and take up two beers and a lemonade for Kenny. We get in there, sit down and Nicol's going, 'I just can't believe this .' Kenny's going, 'Alan, I thought I told you not to tell anyone.' I say, 'Well, he was upset and wondering what was wrong, so I told him.' So Nicol's sat there, shaking his head and talking away to himself. Then he suddenly turns to Kenny and says, 'Here I was wondering why you were playing so badly.' He goes out of the room with tears in his eyes and me and Kenny are in fits on the floor."

Jan Molby

"Steve Nicol was legendary for being the fall guy and Alan Hansen loved telling us the story where he was in a minibus with Steve and Graeme Souness driving through Scotland. Souness was at the wheel, driving through a blizzard on the motorway and it really was bitterly cold. Suddenly Souness announces that the windscreen wipers had broken. They're stuck at the side of the motorway, you could hardly see for the snow, so Souness says, 'Steve, you're going to have to nip out and wipe the windscreen, else we can't go on.' So poor Stevie Nic leaps out in just a Scotland T-shirt and shorts to clear the windscreen. No sooner has he leapt out than Souness has roared away leaving Nicol stranded in a blizzard. At first they were really laughing then they got a bit concerned because they'd misjudged the proximity of the next exit. They had to go on for another 10 miles before they could come off the motorway to drive back. By the time they reached Nicol, Hansen said he looked like a snowman sat shivering by the side of the motorway.

"The thing was, poor Steve was so easy to wind up he became the butt of most of the jokes in the dressing room. I remember Alan Hansen winding him up about a Puma contract. Steve was complaining that he hadn't heard from the guy at Puma so Alan says, as casual as you like, 'Oh yeah, they asked me to pass on a message for you to meet him on Sunday morning at this service station on the motorway.' So Alan gives him directions and tells him to dress smartly to make a good impression. I never thought he'd fall for it but apparently Steve got dressed in a suit and tie, took the whole family to this motorway service station on a Sunday morning and sat there for four hours waiting for this fictitious bloke to turn up. He took some stick for that, all right."

Kenny Dalglish

"We'd been due to play Luton in an FA Cup replay at Anfield. In those days the team would stay in a hotel before a match, relaxing before the coach took us to the ground. Alan Irvine, who we'd just signed from Falkirk, was staying in the hotel anyway, but the boys were all on the same floor. Roy Evans went round waking them up at five with tea and toast. Then Alan left his room to go

Ripping yarns

down to get ready. Roy came back round then. He said, 'Look, the game's off. Luton cannae get up here because of snow.'

"So we've all got to go back to Anfield to get our cars. We've got on the bus in our tracksuits. Alan's walked on the bus, collar and tie on. So Big Al Hansen says to me, 'He thinks the game's on. Go on, wind him up.' So I gave him a shout down the bus. I said, 'Look, we're a wee bit short. Y'know, for players, a few injuries. Can you play centre back?' 'Aw,' he went. 'I cannae play centre back.' I said, 'Why not? It's just the reverse of what you do when you're upfront. You're a big lad. You can run. No problem.' He's shaking his head. I said, 'What about midfield then? Could you fill in there?' 'Aw Jesus,' he goes. 'I dunno.' I said, 'Look, I'll take full responsibility. Just do your best. If it doesnae work out, it's my fault. But eh – when you go back down the bus, don't you tell anyone you're playing. Right?' It's a certainty. He goes down the bus. He's smiling. Big Al goes to him, 'What'd he say?' 'Ach no, I cannae tell ye.' 'What'd he say?!' 'I'm playing. Centre back.'

"So we get to Anfield. Players' entrance where we leave the tickets. Into the dressing room. And the lads are all sitting down. He's sitting there with his suit on. The tactics board was always there, with the numbers. And I said, 'Look, there's nae point going through the meeting at the moment. Leave your tickets at the door and come back in. Right? Then we can have a chat.' 'Course, that was the cue for the boys to get out the dressing room and go.

"So I come back in the dressing-room 10 minutes later, and he's in his kit in the shower area. We used to call him Fraggle, after the guy out of Fraggle Rock. So he's going to the loo and I says, 'Fraggle, the game's off.' 'What?' 'The game's off.' And he shrugs like he knew all along and goes, 'Aye, I know…'"

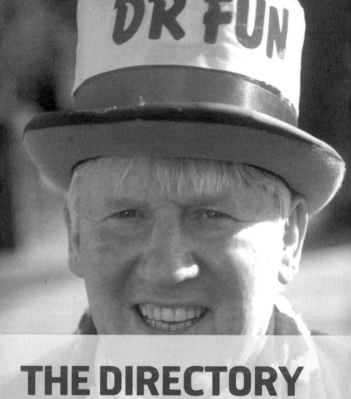

THE DIRECTORY

THE DIRECTORY

Supporters' organisations | Reds in the community | The board | Songs | Talking Scouse |
Liverpool media | Reds in the media | On the Net | Books and videos

Anfield is a broad church. From shaven-headed scalls in Lacoste shellies to daytripping Norwegians in bizarre, customised boiler suits and jester's hats, Liverpool FC draws its congregation from far and wide. You only have to bump into the legendary Dr Fun, and faithful puppet Liverpool Charlie, pictured on the cover of this section, to understand that devotion to the cause manifests itself in many ways in many people. But all those on the march with Gérard's Army, whether from Kirkdale or Killarney, Norris Green or Novosibursk, share one thing in common – an undying love for the club. And this is the chapter for all devout Reds, both practising and exiled...

Supporter Organisations

The LFC Official Supporters Club

The club launched its revamped official supporters club in 2000 and membership for last season cost **£23 +p&p** for adults, **£14 +p&p** for juniors. The scheme offers many advantages, including free admission to reserve matches, sizeable discounts at the club store (or on museum and stadium tours) and entry to the special pre-season event at Anfield, when fans get the unique opportunity to watch the squad train. There are a host of additional goodies on offer for adult and junior members, making the official supporters club good value for money. Fans can use their credit or debit cards to join by ringing **08707 02 02 07 (UK residents)**, or **+44 151 702 8859 (others)**.

LFC Association of International Branches

It's hardly surprising Liverpool's unparalleled success over the years has attracted admirers from all over the world. Up until the early 1990s, Reds in locations as diverse as Mauritius, Malta and Milton Keynes usually got together with other like-minded souls to form satellite LFC supporters clubs, with little involvement from Anfield. In May 1992, the club formed the LFC International Supporters Club (ISC) – an Anfield-based organisation to provide assistance to what had become a sizeable global network of supporters branches. In 2002, the Association of International Branches (AIB) replaced the ISC to give an even better service and almost 130 worldwide branches are now signed up. For a small fee, joining the scheme brings official recognition and with it access to the invitation-only pre-season fans' day and other social events, exclusive merchandise and advice on travel and accommodation. However, since the days of the ISC, the main selling point has been access to tickets. The club does grant block allocations to many branches, but due to the massive demand for tickets some branches are not as fortunate.

Why join an LFC AIB branch?

It can take the hassle out of travelling to games and save money. UK-based branches frequently run subsidised coaches to matches, which works out cheaper and means you don't have to worry about driving after a pre or post-match bevvy. Members from beyond the UK have their flights and accommodation sorted out by a branch travel liaison officer and block bookings can often mean discounted rates. Branches usually run social events throughout the year and if you can't make it along to matches, members usually meet up in a local pub to watch televised games with other Reds. Membership fees are reasonable and for any Liverpool fan who lives beyond Merseyside and wants to get to Anfield for games regularly, joining a local branch is recommended. Even if you live in Liverpool, joining the Merseyside branch offers superb value for money (annual fee £3), especially for the monthly meetings where members get the chance to take part in Q&A events with top names from the current side and legends from the past. Call the **AIB** on **0151 261 1444** to find your nearest branch. There are a very limited number of non-AIB affiliated Liverpool supporters associations which can be found by surfing the net.

Reds in the community

In an average week the club is inundated with charity and community-based requests. Most letters ask for autographed items for auctions, the club's endorsement of a wide range of community initiatives, or special visits to Anfield or the club's training HQ at Melwood. For obvious reasons the club can only agree to a tiny percentage of visits requested and tend to grant them to the terminally ill, fans recovering from extreme illnesses, or those with obvious special needs. Nevertheless, throughout the course of a season many hundreds of fans do get to meet their Red heroes by writing to the club's community department. The Community Department can be reached on **0151 260 1433.**

Useful numbers	
Anfield switchboard 0151 263 2631	**Liverpool Supporters Club** 0870 702 0207
Ticket office 0870 2202345	**Association of International Branches**
Liverpool clubcall 09068 121184	**of the Supporters Club**
Credit-card hotline 0870 2202151	0151 261 1444
24-hour info line 0870 4444949	**Reds in the community**
Liverpool ticket information line 09068 121584	0151 260 1433
Priority membership scheme 0151 261 1444	**Anfield club store** 0151 263 1760
	Williamson Square club store 0151 330 3077
Liverpool FC text messages 0871 2200 045	**Corporate sales department** 0151 263 9199
	Reduc@te 0151 263 2361

Reduc@te

Liverpool FC's Study Support Centre stands adjacent to the club museum at the Kop end of Anfield and was opened in February 2000. Its aim is to provide a fun learning environment for after-school study, where children from the Liverpool area are able to improve their core educational skills. Reduc@te is the result of a partnership between the club, Department of Education and Employment and the Local Education Authority. Using football as a motivational tool and to compliment school-based learning, 323 staff use players' stats to improve numeracy, literacy, computer skills and independent learning, while hoping to build pupils' self esteem in the process. You can contact Reduc@te by calling **0151 263 2361** or email your enquiry to **reducate@liverpoolfc.tv**

Who's in charge of Liverpool?

The board of directors

David Moores chairman since 1991 and a member of the Liverpool board since 1990. A true Kopite, he has witnessed the great events in the club's history from the 1960s onwards and owns 51 per cent of shares in the club.

Rick Parry chief executive since July 1998. He played a decisive role in shaping football in this country during his six-year spell as chief executive of the FA Premier League. He oversaw the development of the Premier League into one of the world's top professional competitions, thanks largely to the series of massive television deals he brokered.

Noel White co-owner of the White & Swales chain of TV and hi-fi shops who was Altrincham chairman throughout the club's cup runs of the late 1970s. He joined the Liverpool board in the early 80s and was chairman when Kenny Dalglish resigned as manager. An FA Councillor, White became chairman of the international selectors committee in the early 1990s.

Other board members **TD Smith**, **KEB Clayton**, **J Burns**

Liverpool songs

A brief history of singing at Anfield

As early as 1905/06, Liverpool fans sang en masse to celebrate the club's second title and for the next 50 years, limited and sporadic chanting became popular at Anfield. However, influenced by televised coverage of South American fans during the 1962 World Cup finals in Chile, the early 1960s saw singing really take off at Anfield and the simple 'Liverpool' (clap, clap, clap) became one of the first terrace chants. As the new Merseybeat phenomena swept the city, suit-wearing, mop-topped Kopites were only too willing to play their part in the new cultural revolution. Below we feature three of the longer songs from Liverpool's vast repertoire...

The anthem

Appropriated since by many clubs, eternally sacred to just one. You'll Never Walk Alone was written by Rogers and Hammerstein for their 1945 Broadway musical Carousel, and Merseybeat band Gerry and The Pacemakers recorded their own version in 1963. It became their third consecutive British number one and nowhere was it more popular than on the Kop. As the chart-topper, it was the final record played over the PA system at Anfield before kick-off and struck a deep chord with the crowd. Fans swayed and sang along to lyrics that captured what it is to support the team through good times and bad. Marsden recalls Shankly saying to him, "Gerry son, I've given Liverpool a team – you've given us a song." It's been played and sung prior to kick-off ever since and the title has been incorporated into the club crest since the early 1990s. Musician and Reds fan Elvis Costello calls it, "a mighty, mighty song, a hymn for Liverpool. Other football songs just pale in comparison."

When you walk through a storm
Hold your head up high
And don't be afraid of the dark
At the end of a storm
There's a golden sky
And the sweet silver song of a lark

Walk on through the wind
Walk on through the rain
Though your dreams be tossed and blown
Walk on, walk on, with hope in your heart
And you'll never walk alone

Walk on, walk on, with hope in your heart
And you'll never walk alone
You'll never walk alone

Scouser Tommy

Written by fans, Scouser Tommy is the Kop's second anthem and the ability to sing every word is one of the marks of a true Kopite. The verse is sung to the tune of 19th-century American folk song Red River Valley, the chorus to the melody of The Sash, an Orange Order song. After a memorable four-goal performance against Everton in 1984 at Goodison, the Ian Rush sign-off was added.

Let me tell you the story of a poor boy
Who was sent far away from his home
To fight for his king and his country
And also the old folks back home
So they put him in a highland division
Sent him off to a far, foreign land
Where the flies swarm around in their thousands
And there's nothing to see but the sand

Well the battle it started next morning
Under the Arabian sun
I remember that poor Scouser Tommy
He was shot by an old Nazi gun

As he lay on the battlefield dying, dying, dying
With the blood gushing out of his head, of his head
As he lay on the battlefield dying, dying, dying
These were the last words he said…

Chorus
Oh I am a Liverpudlian
I come from the Spion Kop
I love to sing, I love to shout
And I go there quite a lot (every week!)

We support the team that's dressed in red
It's a team that you all know
It's a team that we call Liverpool
And to glory we will go

We've won the League
We've won the Cup
We've conquered Europe too

And we played the Toffees for a laugh
And we left them feeling blue – 5-0!

1, 2
1, 2, 3
1, 2, 3, 4
5-0!

Rush scored one
Rush scored two
Rush scored three
And Rush scored four
La-la, la-la
La, la-la, la-a

The Fields Of Anfield Road

The original Fields Of Athenry was written by an Irish folk singer in 1979 and was soon adopted by Celtic fans, but arguably the first time it was sung at Anfield was December 1995 when the Republic of Ireland's fans invaded L4 for their Euro 96 play-off with Holland. The Liverpool version is believed to have originated in The Oakfield pub, home of the Liverpool Away Supporters Club, about five years ago. Like all great Liverpool songs, the lyrics have been adapted from the original and the emotional lament of the music gives it the same 'us against the world' quality as YNWA. Promises to be very big in 2002/03.

Outside the Shankly Gates
I heard a Kopite calling :
Shankly they have taken you away
But you left a great eleven
Before you went to heaven
Now it's glory round the fields of Anfield Road.

Chorus

All round the fields of Anfield Road
Where once we watched the King Kenny play (and he could play)
We had Heighway on the wing

327

We had dreams and songs to sing
Of the glory round the fields of Anfield Road

Outside the Paisley Gates
I heard a Kopite calling

Sound La

Liverpool fans from the world of music

Gerry and The Pacemakers A close friend of Shankly, Dingle's finest balladeer is still as staunch as ever. One singer, one song…

The Beatles Post-war Reds legend Albert Stubbins appeared on the Sgt Pepper's cover at the request of John Lennon

Cast Stevie Heighway's stylish 1970s wing play dazzled the young John Power. The former La's bass player usually sits in the Main Stand

Elvis Costello Gérard's Army is here to stay. London-born, Liverpool-bred Dec McManus was a Kopite in the early 1970s and is still an Anfield regular

Echo and The Bunnymen Super cool Scouse singer Ian 'Mac' McCulloch's love for the boys in Red has never waned

Lightning Seeds More Liver Bird than three Lions on a shirt for singer-songwriter Ian Broudie. Marvellous…

The Farm Former lead singer and fervent Kopite Peter Hooton is a dedicated follower at home and abroad. All together now…

John Peel The legendary DJ has supported Liverpool since Billy Liddell terrorised the opposition in the 1950s

Space The quirky Scouse popsters' front man Tommy Scott has made pilgrimages to Anfield since the early 1970s

Mel C Has been a fan since long before the press dubbed our mid-1990s side the Spice Boys. Widnes wannabe Sporty wore a Liverpool shirt in early publicity shots. Needs to work on that plazzie Scouse accent, though…

Other music-related Reds include **Pete Wylie** (formerly of Wah, his dog's called Shankly), **DJ Spoony** (Radio One DJ and mate of Emile Heskey) and **Mark Morriss** (of Hounslow Britpoppers The Bluetones). Former NWA gangsta rapper (and Eminem homie) **Dr Dre** fell in love with John Barnes' silky skills in the late 1980s and still watches the Reds on the box whenever he's on tour in the UK. And there's always, ahem, **Chris De Burgh**.

Paisley they have taken you away..
You led the great eleven
Back in Rome in 77
And the redmen they're still playing the same way

Chorus
All round the Fields of Anfield Road
Where once we watched the King Kenny play (and he could play)
We had Heighway on the wing
We had dreams and songs to sing
Of the glory round the Fields of Anfield Road

Talking Scouse

Liverpool has long considered itself an independent state and it's fitting therefore it should have its own language. Though far from exhaustive, these useful Scouse phrases should enable out of towners to understand the locals

'Ardface cheeky person
'Ardknock ruffian
Case, Head the ball larger than life or unhinged personality
Bluenose Evertonian
Beaut, Blairt, Divvy, Gobshite, Loon, Ming, Melt, Nugget, Soft lad idiot
Bairst urination
Bullet head
Bizzies police (also see 'feds')
Brewsted rich
Bombhead ugly person
Boss, Custy, Gear, Sound excellent
Do one get lost, let's go
Dead very (as in 'dead good')
Go'ed go on or go ahead
Half-a-tart visiting player who indulges in histrionics
Hard lines unlucky
Jarg, Lowcost false, fake
Joey taxi

Kecks trousers
Kidder mate, brother or friend
Kip personal appearance, state
La boy, young man
Mickey pigeon
Mingebag tight, miserly person
Meff/Meph tramp
No-mark insignificant individual
Owl old (as in owl fella)
Queen female (term of endearment)
Scran food
Shitehawk noisy person, dissembler
Spec place or seat
Trainees trainers
Wack Liverpudlian gent
Wildies diarrhoea
Woollyback out of towner
Yard dog clumsy footballer, precursor to the cart horse

Celebrity Liverpool fans

Mike Myers Austin Powers
Sue Johnston Barb from the
Royle Family
Angus Fraser ex-England pace
bowler
Phil Middlemiss Corrie's Des Barnes
Gail McKenna TV presenter and
ex Page-3 stunna

Robert Carlyle Scottish thespian
Michael Howard shadow cabinet
minister
Adam Woodyatt Albert Square's
Ian Beale
Aleksandar Hemon novelist
Phil Redmond TV soap guru
Peter Sissons newsreader

Liverpool media

Matchday Magazine

330   For decades, it was the traditional Anfield Review. Then, at the start of season
2000/01, the 68-page Official Liverpool Matchday Magazine burst on to the
scene, scooping publishing awards and dragging the football programme

kicking and screaming into the 21st century. Written by fans for fans, its passion, tone and quality of writing and photography put it in a different league to the pre-match reads at every other Premiership club – a fact grudgingly conceded by even Evertonians and Mancs. However, the magazine will not be produced by the same team in 2002/03 after the contract was poached by the Trinity Mirror Group that publishes the Liverpool Echo. They've got a hard act to follow.

Fanzines

Through The Wind And Rain

Healthily sceptical take on all matters Red on and off the field, edited by Steven Kelly and the longest-running of the current trinity of Liverpool fanzines. TTWAR comes out just four times a season, but it's worth waiting for. Perceptive and intelligent with a nicely cynical eye on the press, the Blues and the Mancs.

Red All Over The Land

First hit the streets of Anfield in November 1995 and comes out pretty much every month throughout the season. Sharp and irreverent in its tone but lacking the militancy of TTWAR. Essential purchase nonetheless. Proud to celebrate the club's unique heritage at every opportunity and big on epic ballads about Bill Shankly. It's the RAOTL crew who are behind the now trademark Kop mosaics. Sellers dotted around the ground on matchdays. Go talk to them, they're good skins.

The Liverpool Way

The scatological little brother of TTWAR and RAOTL and arguably the most Scouse of the three, The Liverpool Way was first published by Dave Usher in August 1999. Front cover proclaims 'not suitable for children and Evertonians' which gives you a pretty good idea of the contents. Frequently hits the mark, though, especially on the travails of our brethren across the park. Big on the Academy too – Dave regularly watches the reserves and youth teams. In short, The Liverpool Way's definitely worth buying – but don't let yer mam catch you reading it.

Liverpool on the net

Official site

www.liverpoolfc.tv

Unbelievably, Liverpool were the last Premiership club to go officially online, but since then they've embraced cyberspace in a big way and can now claim to have the most popular club site in Britain with 22million hits a month. It makes the most of its official access and boasts plenty of video interviews and match action – but most of this is only available if you fork out for an e-season ticket. In January 2002 the site featured the first ever 90-minute webcast of a Premiership match when subscribers were able to watch the now traditional victory at Old Trafford.

Kop Talk

www.koptalk.co.uk

Reds news resource, comprehensive but fails to capture the unique spirit of the club (it's been dubbed Krap Talk by the fanzines). Boasts columns from Jan Molby, Tommy Smith, Barry Venison and Irish fringe winger Richie Partridge. For just over a tenner you can sign up to The Insider, a subscribers-only email newsletter containing "exclusive" news and gossip.

LFC Online

www.lfconline.com

Decent site featuring all the usual Anfield news, forums and ritual abuse of Phil Neville. It's elevated above the norm by some well-written, pertinent and passionate think pieces and retro articles from regular contributing fans. A must-read for the discerning Red. Plus there are song clips, including 1996's majestic Pass And Move (It's The Liverpool Groove), to download, as well as ringtones and nifty desktop icons.

Red And White Kop

www.redandwhitekop.net

Proclaiming itself as the Independent LFC website, this is a testament to the articulacy and fervour of the Anfield crowd. Impassioned articles on the club's deeds from a hardcore of devoted writers, along with a song archive (essential if for some reason you don't know all the words to A Scouser In Gay Paree) and the usual messageboards. Plus if you find yourself with or without spares, the site runs an invaluable ticket exchange service.

Shankly Gates

www.shanklygates.co.uk

Excellent mix of news, opinion, speculation and interviews with a Red hue. Home of The Boot Room, a lively LFC messageboard where you can discuss the merits of Vladimir Smicer to your heart's content. The site also features a compendium of classic Shanks quotes. Tom O'Connor has even contributed some gags – what more could any self-respecting Red wish for?

Houllier

www.leboss.org.uk

Le Boss is a site devoted to the words and deeds of Gérard Houllier, featuring hundreds of quotes from and about the great man, on such topics as his footballing philosophy, favourite players, club culture or just sounding off, where you can relive Ged slagging off referee Graham Poll one more time. Plus there's Houllier's complete career CV from Le Touquet to L4, as well as tributes and features on the man. Allez, allez…

Shankly

www.shankly.com

A labour of love and a more than fitting tribute. The site delves deep into the great man's life but laudably avoids the usual 'more important than that' soundbite approach. Exclusive interviews with those who knew him, fresh anecdotes, quotes and a remarkable database of Liverpool's 784 matches with Shanks in charge make this an essential bookmark.

The Alan Hansen Appreciation Society

members.tripod.com/~Unitybel/index.html

Unbelievable. A site dedicated to Jocky and, as the cool one himself might say, it's got the lot. Career stats, interviews, book reviews and a section called Alan Spotting, featuring fans' sightings of Hansen at large, including an appearance in a pet shop in Childwall. Plus a transcript of Alan's spot on The Frank Skinner Show (the infamous Ribena incident). The site's been visited by Jocky himself, who only rates it 95%. Diabolical.

Liverpool Programmes

www.liverpool-programmes.co.uk

Essential destination for the proey-obsessed. Dealing exclusively in Liverpool, the site has thousands of old and new, home and away Reds programmes for sale. Even if you're not in a position to buy, it's worth a look just for a browse, as they're all illustrated, from the simplicity of the 1940s to the magnificent Matchday Magazines of last season. There's also a guide to forthcoming programme fairs if you're that way inclined.

Terrace Retro
www.terraceretro.com

Not strictly a Liverpool website, but worth a mention as the internet's spiritual heir to The End fanzine, with musings on the latest Red deeds alongside pieces on music, fashion and, inevitably, trainers.

Partizan Media
www.partizanmedia.com

And while we're at it, welcome to the world (and elsewhere) of "a collective of musicians, writers, DJs, designers and gobshites formed during a Guinness and Jamesons bender." Its aim? "To champion Merseyside street culture in all its diversity." Protean. Gaminish. Scouse.

Players' websites

Footballers have been prime movers in the dot.com boom, with scores of famous and not-so-famous players launching their own sites. Or rather, getting someone else to do it for them – we don't imagine Stephane Henchoz has an intimate knowledge of HTML coding. Still, they've proved pretty popular – so much so that icons.com which hosts sites for Jerzy Dudek, Vladimir Smicer and John Arne Riise among others, has obliged users (ie journos) to declare they won't nick the content. Most of which is, predictably, fairly bland. Still, Markus Babbel's site is worth a look, if only for the revelation that his favourite temperature for playing football is 20°C, but turn down your PC speakers for the blaring, unreconstructed Teutonic metal of his favourite band, Krokus. And Dietmar Hamann remarkably offers up some shooting tips on his site. "Don't break too many windows!" warns the midfield kingpin. A bit rich from someone who, judging by current striking form, must have single-handedly kept the German equivalent of Everest in business as a teenager.

334 Dietmar Hamann www.bigfanof.com
Markus Babbel www.mbabbel.com/
Icons www.icons.com

Home to sites of Pegguy Arphexad, Patrik Berger, Jerzy Dudek, Vegard Heggem, Stephane Henchoz, John Arne Riise and Vladimir Smicer

Merseyside media

Liverpool Echo

"Eeeeeeyechoooooo!" The Liverpool Echo is a city institution, selling 400,000 copies a night, but Anfield regulars mutter darkly about its alleged Blue leanings. For all that, it's still a vital source of information about the Reds without the sensationalist taint of the nationals. On Wednesdays, the Echo hosts the legendary letters pages where Tommy Smith and now Howard Kendall answer your letters on matters Red and Blue, although they usually respond to criticism by toeing the club line all too readily. The addition of Kendall sadly robbed the pages of the Anfield Iron's comforting Fair Tackle, Over The Top and Bounce Ball responses, depending on the validity of your argument. Saturday nights aren't the same without the Footie Echo, which is published just minutes after the final whistle, featuring reports on Liverpool's match, plus more of Smithy and Howard, and those all-important Zingari League tables.

Reds on the radio

Liverpool boasts two big radio stations, both following the Reds home and away with live coverage and updates. BBC Radio Merseyside can be located on 95.8FM and 1485AM and broadcasts commentary on practically every Liverpool match from sports editor Ian Kennedy, followed on Saturday at 5.15pm by the legendary moan-in, moderated by superannuated local hack John Keith. Beware of whining Blues and scalls who pretend to make valid points before cussing down the blower at poor old JK. On week nights the station transmits a surfeit of football shows from around 7pm. If the Reds aren't in action there'll still be plenty of chat plus Red Alert, the Friday night show presented by Nigel Reed. Twiddle the knob to the right and you'll find Radio City on 96.7FM, broadcasting from the tower of power that is St John's Beacon. Radio City provides commentary on every Liverpool match from Steve Hothersall and pundit John Aldridge and also broadcasts a Saturday night post-match phone-in with the mighty Aldo and his Blue counterpart Ian Snodin. There's also Century Radio, broadcasting across the north west on 105.4 FM, which carries regular live Reds commentaries, presented by Elton Welsby – yep, that's where he's got to – with analysis from Alan Kennedy, and the Legends football phone-in at 6pm on week nights.

Reds in the media

There's something about pulling on the Red shirt that doesn't just make you play a good game but talk a good one, too. Usually. Press boxes and commentary gantries up and down the land are crammed with ex-Reds carving out new careers as pundits on television or radio…

Alan Hansen BBC The consummate panellist, if perhaps a touch self-regarding these days, with the knack of pointing out something in his analysis you didn't spot in the match. Seems personally affronted by bad defending.

Mark Lawrenson BBC Hansen's defensive partner in the 1980s and now his accomplice on the BBC's coverage of England and the FA Cup, as well as Football Focus' expert in residence. Tends to view everything in black and white ("I just can't see it, Ray") but pithy and astute.

Jim Beglin ITV and BBC Radio Five Live Incisive, dry and fast becoming the best commentator's sidekick around. Excellent on ITV's coverage of the Champions League.

Barry Venison ITV Little less high-profile than a few years back when a reference to his lurid locks and suits was part of every football wag's armoury. Of the 'tell you what you can already see' school of punditry.

John Barnes ITV Regular member of ITV's Champions League team, and as smooth a performer on the box as he was in a no10 shirt. Sometimes lacks a cutting edge (season 1996/97 all over again, then).

Reds in the media

Kevin Keegan ITV Seen and heard less frequently these days, but bound to return soon. Check out www.geocities.com/SouthBeach/Palms/6687/keggy.html for some of his punditry gems.

Ray Houghton Channel 5 Decent enough expert when called into action to cover C5's portfolio of early-season Uefa Cup ties in the Lower Dnieper Basin or the occasional big international.

Graeme Souness Sky Sports Still as fearless as ever, Souey can frequently be found spending his Sunday afternoons in a pitchside studio in the company of Richard Keys. Uncompromising, as you'd expect.

Nigel Spackman Sky Sports Frequent pundit and summariser on Sky's live coverage and a regular reporter for Soccer Saturday, the network's strangely compelling live results programme. Pronounces Henchoz as 'Henchkov'.

John Aldridge Radio City Aldo provides perceptive co-commentary on every Reds match for the city's biggest commercial station. He helps present a lively post-match phone-in too, when the moaners and mings come out to play.

Alan Kennedy Century Radio Barney provides punditry on Liverpool matches for the north west station and takes part in its nightly Legends phone-in alongside Mickey Thomas, Gary Owen and Graeme Sharp.

Michael Robinson Canal Plus Yes, Fatty Robbo is Spain's top football presenter and pundit, hosting the channel's Monday night highlights programme 'El Día Después' (The Day After) boasting a mix of trenchant analysis and humour.

Plenty more Reds regularly turn up on radio or TV, including Davie Fairclough on local radio, Five Live and the now defunct ITV Digital, Paul Walsh on ITV2's The Goal Rush programme, Steve McMahon on Sky Sports, Kenny Dalglish on Sky and C5, Ray Clemence on C5, Phil Neal and Peter Beardsley on Five Live, Gary Gillespie on Radio Merseyside and Ian Rush on BBC Wales.

Liverpool books

Reference and history

Anfield Voices David Paul (Tempus)

Oral history from the fans, compiled under headings like Around Anfield, Travelling to Games, European Matches and inevitably, Shankly. And, you'll be relieved to hear, you won't have heard or read most of them before. Some evocative pictures of the fans on their travels, too.

The Best Official Liverpool Quiz Book Ever Dave Ball and Ged Rea (Carlton)

No arguing with the title, really. Some 1,500 Red questions to liven up those long drives to away games and get your mates arguing. Compiled by the doyens of Liverpool statisticians, to boot.

Better Than The Brazilians Darren Phillips (Carnegie)

Think 1987/88. Barnes and Beardsley. Twenty-nine games unbeaten. Finney purring at the annihilation of Forest. Stevie Nic scoring left, right and centre. Classic Adidas kits. And a hole in the Kop. It's all recalled in this match-by-match diary of a season and a team that'll probably never be emulated. Recollections from players, opponents and fans feature. And unafraid to tackle the racism directed at Digger upon his arrival.

The Boot Room Boys Stephen F Kelly (Collins Willow)

Oral history of the Boot Room itself, tracing the history of Anfield's mythological war room through the words of players, journalists, fans, opponents and the Boot Room boys themselves. In among the predictable and occasional stale anecdotes there are a few gems, like Joe Fagan's supply of extra-strong African beer for post-match entertaining, and the unsung heroes like Tom Saunders, Geoff Twentyman, John Bennison get their due, too.

Cup Kings 1965 Mark Platt (Bluecoat Press)

Round-by-round history of the season Liverpool went to Wembley and beat Leeds to win the FA Cup for the first time. Beautifully compiled, featuring fresh insight from the likes of Ian St John, Ron Yeats and Sir Roger Hunt.

Everton v Liverpool Brian Barwick and Gerald Sinstadt (BBC)
The story of the derby as told by players Red and Blue. It's all here –
Gordon West's handbag, Sandy Brown, Clive Thomas, McDermott and
Stanley's brawl, Rush scored four, 'Mer-sey-side' at Wembley…
Published in 1988 so you might have to hunt to find a copy.

Hillsborough The Truth Phil Scraton (Mainstream)
Detailed, harrowing account of the afternoon of 15 April 1989, and an
aftermath that is still going on. Exposes the contradictions between the
findings of the Taylor Report and the result of the seven-week trial that
followed the disaster. A recommended read, if for all the wrong reasons.

The Kop Stephen F Kelly (Mandarin)
An oral history of the Kop, compiled in 1993 just before the demise of its
legendary terraced incarnation. Features anecdotes and memories of
classic matches from Kopites, players and ground staff, and if you can grit
your teeth through the 'Scousers and their unique chirpy sense of humour'
stuff then you'll find some brilliant, funny and moving tales in here.

Liverpool FC The Historic Treble Liverpool Matchday Magazine (Carlton Books)
Stats-packed record of the unforgettable 2000/01 campaign with match
reports and images from every step of the Treble, assembled by the team
behind that season's Official Matchday Magazine. If you were in Cardiff
or Dortmund this is essential. If you weren't, buy it anyway.

Liverpool In Europe Steve Hale and Ivan Ponting with Steve Small (Carlton)
Magnificent and utterly comprehensive, this lavish book tells the story of
Liverpool's glorious history in Europe, from Reykjavik in 1964 to
Dortmund in 2001, using the evocative black and white photographs of
legendary snapper Steve Hale, along with an account of every match
Liverpool have played in Europe, interviews with players and managers
and all the stats, too. Worth buying a coffee table just to put this on.

Liverpool's Greatest Players David Walmsley (Headline)
Excellent compendium of pen portraits of Anfield's greatest names,
imaginatively written with a keen awareness of tactics and footballing 339
attributes. Admirably up to date, too, so Robbie Fowler and Jamie
Redknapp rub shoulders with Callaghan and Liddell.

Liverpool Player By Player Ivan Ponting (Hamlyn)
Published in 1990 and reissued in 1997, this large-format book profiles at length every footballer to run out in the Red shirt since Bill Shankly became manager in 1959. Classy photography and full stats make this a good reference point as well as a book to dip into for hours. Another volume just waiting for an update very soon.

The Official Illustrated History Of Liverpool Stephen F Kelly (Hamlyn)
Well-illustrated and comprehensive account of the club's first century. The season-by-season format makes it a chore to wade through but useful as a reference source.

Supporter books

Extra Time Kevin Sampson (Yellow Jersey)
A season in the life of a football fan, the Red in question being Upper Centenary regular and author of Away Days and Powder, Kevin Sampson. And the season in question being 1997/98 means there's not a lot of great football, but arguably that, along with a frequently eccentric supporting cast, makes this book the engaging read it is. And nails the irritating Man United trait of singing "champione" without a hard c along the way.

Faith Of Our Fathers Alan Edge (Mainstream)
Evocative account of one devout fan's life growing up as a Red. Edge recounts resisting childhood attempts to make him turn to the dark side across Stanley Park, the glory of the 1960s and 70s and the first seeds of hooliganism, the 80s and the media reaction to Hillsborough, and the 90s and the football boom and Liverpool's uncomfortable decline. Funny, honest and moving. If this book was a goal it'd be Kenny's chip against Bruges in the 1978 European Cup final.

Into The Red John Williams (Mainstream)
Astute excursion through the Treble season in the company of the Kop's football professor, as he's dubbed by a bunch of Reds on the train home from the Millennium Stadium. Thoughts on the action on the pitch month by month are interspersed with perceptive analysis of Gérard Houllier's Anfield revolution and a detailed examination of the reasons behind the club's decline of the 1990s. Sometimes threatens to drift into right-on territory, but by and large an intelligent critique of football and big business

in the Sky/Bosman era. And Williams' account of being trapped in the company of Emlyn Hughes at Anfield is both hilarious and depressing.

Facts and stats

Liverpool: A Complete Record Brian Pead (Breedon)

Ah, the venerable Pead. Essentially, the total statistical history of Liverpool FC – every line-up, scorer and attendance in every competition from the first match against Higher Walton in 1892, along with the history of Anfield, profiles of great players and managers, international caps, head-to-head records and leading scorers and appearances. Just begging for an updated edition.

The Reds: Day To Day Life At Anfield Richard Lerman and David Brown (Mainstream)

A day-by-day history of Liverpool FC, compiling what's happened on every day of the year from 1 January to 31 December – results, signings, debuts, glory nights. Not the most thrilling of reads, as the incessant lists of results utterly fail to bring the club's history alive, but probably useful if you like that kind of thing.

The Ultimate Book Of Stats And Facts Dave Ball and Ged Rea (Bluecoat Press)

If you only buy one Liverpool stats book – and frankly if you buy two, you worry us – this is the one to get. Everything you really need to know about the club – top scorers, record appearances, most expensive transfers, head to heads and so on, all laid out in a clear, easy-to-use format. Best thing about this book is the compilers have shown some imagination, so you get interesting lists like Substituted Substitutes, take a bow Howie Gayle, a complete guide to Liverpool's squad numbers since 1993 (no3 has changed hands six times) and the revelation that Tony 'Bonus' Warner sat on the bench 89 times without playing a game. Essential.

Biographies

My Story John Aldridge (Hodder and Stoughton)

Readable, no-frills biog featuring the inside word on a successful if sometimes turbulent time at Anfield, including an absorbing chapter on Hillsborough by someone more moved by the tragedy than most. Plus the story of his Ireland career, including that touchline bust-up at USA 94.

John Barnes The Autobiography **John Barnes (Headline)**
Stimulating and candid autobiography, in which Digger not only discusses life at Anfield but also reflects on racism and Hillsborough, the Anfield Rap, kung-fu DVDs and, er, European integration.

Out Of His Skin **Dave Hill (WSC)**
Much-praised account of John Barnes' momentous arrival at Anfield in 1987, entwining his effect on the pitch with analysis of racism in football and society as a whole, and the brutal effect of the 80s on Merseyside itself. Plus an absorbing account of Barnes' youth in Jamaica, and it has to be said, some fantastic football recalled. The 2001 edition includes a new chapter.

Dalglish My Autobiography **Kenny Dalglish with Henry Winter (Coronet)**
The glorious life story of the King. Glasgow housing estate, watching Rangers, playing for Celtic, World Cup failures, joining the Reds, lifting silverware by the barrowload, becoming manager, the shock resignation, on to Blackburn and Newcastle. Adroitly ghosted by the Telegraph's Henry Winter. Read, absorb, worship.

A Matter Of Opinion **Alan Hansen (Partridge)**
Intelligent and stylish. Just like the man himself. Jocky reflects on his career on the pitch and on the box, and muses on the influx of money into the game, success in Europe and inevitably, golf. And why Hansen winces every time he hears the name Billy Whitehurst.

My Autobiography **Kevin Keegan (Time Warner)**
Published in 1998, this is a decent, readable, honest account of Kev's career up to that point, therefore it's engaging on his tenure at Anfield in tandem with Tosh, plus his time at Newcastle, but without the rain-sodden misery of that England stewardship cut short by Dietmar Hamann.

Ray Of Hope **Ray Kennedy and Dr Andrew Lees (Pelham)**
Not just one amazing tale but two. The story of Ray Kennedy, the son of a north-east mining town who became Liverpool's guileful midfield genius of the 1970s gives way to the story of Ray Kennedy, sufferer of Parkinson's Disease. Moving and engagingly told.

Jan The Man **Jan Molby** and Grahame Lloyd (Orion)

Quite simply one of the finest passers of a ball ever to pull on a Red shirt, Rambo is undeniably a Liverpool legend and this is his story, which includes an uncompromising chapter on his spell behind bars.

In Person **Michael Owen** (HarperCollins Willow)

The story so far of the striking genius who's already racked up a century of Red goals. There's little insight here in this book aimed at kids. In fact there's none, to be honest. But lots of big colourful pictures. Isn't he nice?

Bob Paisley's Liverpool Scrapbook **Bob Paisley** (Souvenir Press)

If you ever come across a copy of this in a jumble sale or second-hand shop, buy it immediately. Published in 1979, it's 144 pages of classic photographs and personal memories from Sir Bob's tenure at Anfield as player and manager. Instantly evocative, with snaps of card schools and foreign excursions, post-victory celebrations and classic match action.

Bob Paisley Manager Of The Millennium **John Keith** (Robson)

Comprehensive if workmanlike account of the life of football's most successful manager of all time, from his home village of Hetton-le-Hole to the domination of European football.

This Is Anfield Calling **George Sephton** (Red Rag)

Possibly the only example in the history of literature of a football club PA announcer penning his memoirs, but then, there are few in-ground DJs quite like George Sephton. Best read by imagining the dulcet tones of the mighty George himself. "Some interesting half-time scores for you…"

It's Much More Important Than That **Stephen F Kelly** (Virgin)

Detailed and dense biography of the legend. Particularly good on Shankly's early days mining in Glenbuck. The section on Liverpool inevitably suffers from the fact you've heard all the stories before, but a good read.

Shankly **Bill Shankly** (Mayflower)

The man's official biog from 1977. If it was ghosted, the writer has done a magnificent job evoking Shankly's unique delivery. It recalls his upbringing in Glenbuck, immortal career, favourite players and bosses and those 'devious' continentals. Seek out a second-hand copy. Biblical.

343

Shanks For The Memory **John Keith** (Robson)

Forget the terrible name, this book's worth reading for the transcripts of Shankly's 1975 Radio City interview with prime minister Harold Wilson. Some other good stuff on Shankly's playing days, too.

Over The Top **Tommy Smith with Ken Rogers** (Breedon)

Shanks was a complete one-off. Paisley quiet but a genius. Emlyn Hughes a pain in the arse. They were as hard as nails in the 60s but they could play a bit too. Like sitting through an after-dinner speech without the cigars.

Toshack **Chris Hughes** (Virgin)

Tosh enjoyed a magnificent decade at Anfield, forming a deadly spearhead with Kevin Keegan and he has since carved out a successful if sometimes stormy career as a manager at home and abroad. This tells his story from Ninian Park via Anfield to Iberia. Compelling.

Coaching

Michael Owen's Soccer Skills **Michael Owen** (HarperCollins Willow)

If you want to play just like the mercurial no10, and we mean for real, not just netting another hat-trick before the alarm clock goes off, then this colourful and accessible book might help you get there.

Liverpool videos

Needless to say, Liverpool fans are well-served on the video front, with shelf upon shelf of classic games, season reviews, profiles and highlights packages available. Some are better than others and we've tried to pick our way through the quality minefield. Not all are still readily available but if you can't find them at your local megastore, you should be able to track them down relatively easily through car boots, second hand shops and websites Ebay **www.ebay.co.uk** and Blackstar **www.blackstar.co.uk**

Historic

201 Great Goals (Video Collection)

344   Does exactly what it says – 80 minutes of volleys, long-rangers, free-kicks, pass-and-move strikes from Fowler, Rush, Hunt, Owen, Dalglish and co.

300 Glorious Goals (Video Collection)

Earlier collection of an hour-and-half's worth of classic Red strikes.

Beating The Blues (Video Collection)

One hour of classic derby footage from 1969 to 1989. Some satisfying action that'll have you punching the air for old time's sake.

Classic Matches (Video Collection)

Highlights from six memorable Reds encounters, including the demolitions of Tottenham, Southampton, Nottingham Forest and Manchester United, plus the first 4-3 defeat of Newcastle and 2001's 3-2 beating of the Blues.

The Greatest Ever Liverpool Team (Video Collection)

Brian Moore comperes, Ian St John compares, as the ever-chortling Saint selects his perfect Reds XI in this 1989 release.

Greatest Games Volumes One to Three (Quantum Leap Group)

Tape one recalls the 1965 FA Cup triumph and the 4-4 draw with Everton in 1991. Tape two features the 1982 title clincher against Spurs and Fowler's demolition of Villa in 1996. Tape three includes Keegan's return with Newcastle in 1984 and Steve McManaman destroying Leeds in 1996.

Liverpool FC The Centenary (BBC)

Celebrating 100 years of the mighty Reds, in the company of the man Motson, with classic footage from the BBC's bulging archives and contemporary interviews with Kop heroes.

Liverpool In Europe (BBC)

In this 1991 production, Motty tells the story of how Liverpool became Britain's most successful team in Europe. Sixty matches, 150 goals.

Liverpool's Greatest FA Cup Victories (Castle Home Video)

Two separate volumes of unforgettable Cup action featuring the Reds. Both only an hour-long, mind.

The Pride And The Passion (Universal)

Two compilations produced in the early 1990s recalling Liverpool's best victories over Everton and Manchester United. Rush, Dalglish, Beardsley in action. Nuff said.

Team Of The Decade (Castle Home Video)

Series of three tapes, determining the greatest Liverpool XI s of the 1970s, 80s and 90s, with plenty of classic action thrown in.

Team Of The Eighties (BBC)

The best action from the best team of a decade that saw the Reds win six titles, two European Cups and the Double. The action comes from the BBC archives so the best commentators too. And yours for about £6.

This Is Anfield (Video Collection)

Go behind the Shankly gates, featuring backstage footage of Anfield, plus interviews and classic memories from the supporters and the likes of Graeme Souness, Ian Rush and Michael Owen.

The Top Ten Strikers (Video Collection)

Hour-long production counting down the club's 10 finest marksmen since the 60s. We won't give away number one… suffice to say he had a muzzie.

Walk On (PT Video)

Formidable production entwining excellent footage from the Granada archive, with contemporary interviews. Narrated by Jim Beglin.

Classic Games

FA Cup Final 1974 (Revelation Films)

"Goals pay the rent! And Keegan does his share!" Newcastle's Supermac gets his comeuppance, Shanks orchestrates from the bench, David Coleman gets overexcited, and Frank Clark swears loudly at a linesman.

FA Cup Final 1986 (Revelation Films)

Rewind to 10 May 1986. Red and Blue together at Wembley, Lineker slips Hansen to give Everton the lead, Brucie throws a wobbler before Rambo and Rush take control of the show to seal the Double. Halcyon.

FA Cup Final 1989 (BBC)

The emotional post-Hillsborough Cup final against Everton, sealed in extra time by a couple of goals from a returning Rushie.

The Greatest Cup Tie Ever (Telstar)

Everton 4, Liverpool 4. That extraordinary FA Cup tie from 1991.

Liverpool League Cup Winners Again (Video Collection)

The cup that kickstarted Houllier's Red revival on a fantastic afternoon at the Millennium Stadium in 2001. Stunning goal from Robbie and a nerve-wracking penalty shootout starring Sander Westerveld.

European Cup Final 1977 (Revelation Films)

The glory that was Rome. Paisley's greatest night, Keegan's last match, Smithy gets on the scoresheet and Joey's munchen' Gladbachs. The BBC coverage in full with commentary from Barry Davies.

Uefa Cup Final 2001 (Video Collection)

Featuring 119 minutes of nailbiting, rollercoaster action from the 5-4 Dortmund defeat of Alavés, plus all the goals from the previous rounds.

Are You Watching Manchester (Video Collection)

Ignore the awful, clueless title and concentrate on the action from our two victories over Manchester United from the 2000/01 season, with crackers from Murphy, Fowler and Gerrard to savour.

Season by season

Liverpool FC The Mighty Reds (Revelation Films)

The BBC-produced review of the 1987/88 season, featuring the memorable defeats of QPR and Arsenal, as well as all 90 minutes of the annihilation of Nottingham Forest. Utterly essential and yours for a fiver.

The Official 1988/89 Season Review (20th Century Fox)

The first Reds season review tape featuring every goal of the League campaign, from a season blighted by the tragedy at Hillsborough, when the Reds came within seconds of an incredible title win.

The Official 1989/90 Season Review (20th Century Fox)
Champions! Every goal from our 18th title win, with Barnes, Rush and friends in prime form.

The Official Story Of The 1990/91 Season (Telstar)
Dalglish out, Souness in. All the goals, including the record 7-1 victory over Derby County, the 5-4 win over Leeds United and Peter Beardsley's hat-trick against the Mancs.

The Official Story Of The 1991/92 Season (Telstar)
Back in Europe, and every goal from the Uefa Cup campaign features on this tape, along with all the netbusters from Division One.

The Official Story Of The 1992/93 Centenary Season (Telstar)
All the highlights from our inaugural Premiership season, although how they managed to find 90 minutes worth is beyond us.

The Official Story Of The 1993/94 Season (Telstar)
The main action from all 42 Premiership matches, plus interviews with players and new boss Roy Evans.

Official Review 1994/95 (Telstar)
Fowler and McManaman in their prodigious pomp winning the Coca-Cola Cup in Roy Evans's first season as manager. Plus Premiership goals.

Official Season Review 1996/97 (Video Collection)
Ninety-minute production featuring every single goal from a season that promised much but ended with the Reds empty-handed. Interviews and analysis too.

Official Season Review 1997/98 (Video Collection)
Not the most classic of seasons, but worth reliving for Michael Owen's extraordinary arrival on the English football stage. Goals and usual chat.

Back To The Future – Houllier's Way 1998/99 (PT Video)
All the Premiership goals from 1998/99, plus interviews with Redknapp, Gerrard, Riedle and co, and a feature on the opening of the Academy.

Liverpool FC Season Review 1999/2000 (Video Collection)
Every goal from Houllier's first season in sole charge at Anfield, along with interviews with the boss, Stevie G, Owen and Jamie Redknapp.

Liverpool The Treble Season Review 2000/01 (Video Collection)
Bringing together every strike from the Treble of FA Cup, League Cup and Uefa Cup as well as the Premiership, plus interviews with players, management and fans. Also available on DVD.

Liverpool FC Season Review 2001/02 (Video Collection)
Second in the League and the Champions League quarter-finals. Proof the club is going places. Every goal from an eventful season. On DVD, too.

The Record (Telstar)
Liverpool started the 1990/91 season in blistering form, winning their first eight games, so how we ended the campaign in second is anyone's guess. But here's the action from that record-breaking streak.

Back To The Bootroom (Telstar)
This 1995 vid records Liverpool's renaissance under Roy Evans, including interviews with lieutenants Ronnie Moran, Sammy Lee, Steve Heighway and Doug Livermore..Plus Robbie Fowler's hat-trick against Arsenal, and trebles from Rush and McManaman.

Never Walk Alone (Video Collection)
Produced every two months between 1995 and 1997, these tapes feature every goal from league and cup, plus backstage footage and exclusive interviews, including a guided tour of Jamie Redknapp's fridge. A good laugh if you can track them down.

Profiles

Fowler's Hot 100 (Video Collection)
Still mourning the departure of God to the wilds of West Yorkshire? Relive the good times with this video issued after Robbie hit his century for the Reds. God's job's a good 'un…

Ray Of Hope (Chrysalis)
Excellent documentary about the masterful midfielder with plenty of footage of Ray Kennedy at his creative best, alongside a profile of his battle with Parkinson's disease. Narrated by James Bolam.

Michael Owen Close Up (Video Collection)
Sky One's officially-stamped behind-the-scenes documentary about the mercurial menace, hence lots of footage of Michael playing golf. However, it does feature the mythical Maltesers trick. Kids only, really.

Michael Owen The Scoring Sensation (Video Collection)
From Selhurst Park in 1997 to Upton Park in 2001, the boy wonder's first century of goals replayed, plus interviews with Owen and team-mates, and his hat-trick against Germany, to boot.

Michael Owen Young, Gifted And Red (PT Video)
Hour-long profile of the prodigious predator, tracing his career from Flintshire schoolboys to the World Cup.

Shankly (Telstar)
The story of a legend, featuring brilliant archive footage from his myriad triumphs and interviews with those who played for him. Narrated by Clive Tyldesley.

DIARY

5 Monday

6 Tuesday

7 Wednesday

8 Thursday

9 Friday

10 Saturday
1977 Kenny Dalglish signs for Liverpool for £440,000 from Celtic

11 Sunday
Liverpool vs Arsenal FA Community Shield, Cardiff 2pm

12 Monday

13 Tuesday

14 Wednesday

15 Thursday

16 August
1992 Liverpool play in the first live Premiership match on Sky at Nottingham Forest

17 Saturday

1964 The Reds play their first match in Europe, a 5-0 victory at Reykjavik

18 Sunday
Aston Villa vs Liverpool Premiership 2pm (PPV)
1988 Ian Rush returns to Anfield after one season with Juventus for £2.8m

19 Monday

20 Tuesday

21 Wednesday

22 Thursday
1964 Liverpool vs Arsenal is the first game shown by the BBC's new Match Of The Day programme. Ken Wolstenholme commentates on the Reds' 3-2 win

23 August

24 Saturday
Liverpool vs Southampton Premiership

25 Sunday

26 Monday Bank holiday UK (not Scotland)

....

27 Tuesday
1973 Dietmar Hamann is born in Waldasson, Germany

....

28 Wednesday
Blackburn Rovers vs Liverpool Premiership
1994 Robbie Fowler scores the fastest Premiership hat-trick in just 4minutes 30seconds against Arsenal at Anfield.
....

29 Thursday
Uefa Champions League first group stage draw Friday August 30

....

30 August

....

31 Saturday
1954 Alan Kennedy is born in Sunderland

....

1 Sunday
1892 Liverpool play their first ever game at Anfield, beating Rotherham 7-1 in a friendly

....

2 Monday
Liverpool vs Newcastle United Premiership, 8pm (SKY)
1978 The Reds tear apart newly-promoted Tottenham Hotspur 7-0

....

3 Tuesday
1898 After playing in blue and white for the previous five years, Liverpool change their strip to red

....

4 Wednesday

....

5 Thursday

....

6 Friday

....

7 Saturday
1974 Stephane Henchoz is born in Billens, Switzerland

Euro 2004 qualifiers include Finland vs Wales, Faroe Islands vs Scotland, Russia vs Republic of Ireland

....

8 Sunday
1972 Markus Babbel is born in Munich

....

9 Monday

....

10 Tuesday

....

11 Wednesday
Liverpool vs Birmingham City Premiership

....

12 Thursday
1989 John Aldridge comes on as sub to score a farewell penalty in 9-0 rout of Crystal Palace

....

13 Friday

....

14 Saturday
Bolton Wanderers vs Liverpool Premiership

....

15 Sunday

....

16 Monday
1969 Gérard Houllier watches his first match at Anfield, a 10-0 defeat of Dundalk in the Fairs Cup

. . . .

17 Tuesday
Uefa Champions League first group stage, match 1 [or Weds 18th]
1974 The Reds record their biggest ever win, 11-0 vs Stromsgodset in the Cup Winners Cup

. . . .

18 Wednesday
1991 Liverpool return to European competition after six-year ban with a 6-1 win over Kuusysi Lahti

. . . .

19 Thursday

. . . .

20 Friday

. . . .

21 Saturday
Liverpool vs West Bromwich Albion Premiership
1985 Kenny Dalglish scores after just 20 seconds of the Merseyside derby at Goodison Park

. . . .

22 Sunday
1993 Robbie Fowler scores on first-team debut against Fulham in the League Cup

. . . .

23 Monday

....

24 Tuesday
Uefa Champions League first group stage, match 2 [or Weds 25th]
1983 Phil Neal plays the last of a record 365 consecutive-game run that stretches back to 1974

....

25 Wednesday
1961 Ronnie Whelan is born in Dublin

....

26 Thursday

....

27 Friday

....

28 Saturday
Manchester City vs Liverpool Premiership

....

29 Sunday
1981 Bill Shankly dies of a heart attack at the age of 67

....

30 Monday
1981 Ian Rush scores the first of 346 goals for Liverpool, against OPS Oulu in the European Cup

....

1 Tuesday
Uefa Champions League first group stage, match 3 [or Weds 2nd]

....

2 Wednesday

....

3 Thursday

....

4 Friday

....

5 Saturday
1993 Robbie Fowler scores five against Fulham in the League Cup

....

6 Sunday
Liverpool vs Chelsea Premiership, 4.05pm (SKY)

....

7 Monday
1973 Sami Hyypia is born in Porvoo, Finland

8 Tuesday

9 Wednesday

10 Thursday

11 Friday

12 Saturday
Euro 2004 qualifiers include Slovakia vs England, Iceland vs Scotland, Spain vs Northern Ireland

13 Sunday
2001 Gérard Houllier undergoes emergency heart surgery after falling ill during Leeds match

14 Monday

....

15 Tuesday

....

16 Wednesday

Euro 2004 Qualifiers include England vs Macedonia, Wales vs Italy, Northern Ireland vs Ukraine, Republic of Ireland vs Switzerland

....

17 Thursday
1987 John Aldridge scores in 11th consecutive League match, a 4-0 defeat of QPR

....

18 Friday

....

19 Saturday
Leeds United vs Liverpool Premiership 12noon (PPV)

....

20 Sunday
1961 Ian Rush is born in St Asaph

....

21 Monday

22 Tuesday
Uefa Champions League first group stage, match 4 [or Weds 23rd]

23 Wednesday

24 Thursday

25 Friday

26 Saturday
Liverpool vs Tottenham Hotspur Premiership
1981 Steve Nicol is signed from Ayr United for a fee of £300,000

27 Sunday European summer time ends

28 Monday Bank holiday Republic of Ireland

. . . .

29 Tuesday
Uefa Champions League first group stage, match 5 [or Weds 30th]
1983 Ian Rush scores five goals against Luton Town in 6-0 League victory

. . . .

30 Wednesday
1957 Floodlights are switched on at Anfield for first time in a friendly against Everton

. . . .

31 Thursday
1963 You'll Never Walk Alone reaches no1 for Gerry And The Pacemakers

. . . .

1 Friday

. . . .

2 Saturday
Liverpool vs West Ham United Premiership

. . . .

3 Sunday
1998 Paul Ince and Steve McManaman sent off in Uefa Cup tie at Valencia

. . . .

4 Monday

5 Tuesday

6 Wednesday
Worthington League Cup **third round**
1982 Rush scores one. Rush scores two. Rush scores three and Rush scores four. La la-la, la-la-la, la-la…

7 Thursday
1963 John Barnes is born in Jamaica

8 Friday

9 Saturday
Middlesbrough vs Liverpool **Premiership**

10 Sunday
1973 Patrik Berger is born in Prague

11 Monday

. . . .

12 Tuesday
Uefa Champions League **first group stage, match 6** [or Weds 13th]
1998 Roy Evans quits as joint manager, Gérard Houllier takes sole charge of the team

. . . .

13 Wednesday

. . . .

14 Thursday

. . . .

15 Friday
Uefa Champions League **second group stage draw**

. . . .

16 Saturday
Liverpool vs Sunderland **Premiership**

. . . .

17 Sunday

. . . .

18 Monday
1997 Michael Owen scores his first hat-trick for the club against Grimsby in the League Cup

. . . .

19 Tuesday

. . . .

20 Wednesday
Euro 2004 qualifiers include Azerbaijan vs Wales. International Friendlies (to be arranged)

. . . .

21 Thursday
1970 Reds fight back from two-goal deficit to beat Everton 3-2 at Anfield

. . . .

22 Friday
1952 Ronnie Moran makes his debut for the club

. . . .

23 Saturday
Fulham vs Liverpool Premiership
1946 Jack Balmer scores a hat-trick for Liverpool for the second weekend running

. . . .

24 Sunday

. . . .

25 Monday

....

26 Tuesday
Uefa Champions League second group stage, match 1 [or Weds 27th]
1986 Jan Molby scores a hat-trick of penalties against Coventry in the League Cup

....

27 Wednesday
1942 Peter Thompson is born in Carlisle

....

28 Thursday

....

29 Friday

....

30 Saturday
1972 Abel Xavier is born in Mozambique

....

1 Sunday
Liverpool vs Manchester United Premiership,12.15pm (SKY)

....

2 Monday

3 Tuesday

4 Wednesday
Worthington League Cup fourth round

5 Thursday

6 Friday

7 Saturday
Charlton Athletic vs Liverpool Premiership

8 Sunday
1951 Terry McDermott is born in Kirkby

9 Monday
1984 Liverpool lose 1-0 to Independiente in the World Club Championship in Tokyo

....

10 Tuesday
Uefa Champions League second group stage, match 2 [or Weds 11th]

....

11 Wednesday
1962 Steve Nicol born in Irvine

....

12 Thursday

....

13 Friday

....

14 Saturday
1996 Robbie Fowler scores four goals against Middlesbrough, the first coming after 28 seconds

....

15 Sunday
Sunderland vs Liverpool Premiership, 4.05pm (SKY)
1990 Steve McManaman makes his league debut as substitute vs Sheffield United at Anfield

....

16 Monday

. . . .

17 Tuesday
Worthington League Cup fifth round [and Weds 18th]

. . . .

18 Wednesday

. . . .

19 Thursday
1958 Bill Shankly's first match as Liverpool boss, a 4-0 defeat at home to Cardiff City

. . . .

20 Friday

. . . .

21 Saturday

. . . .

22 Sunday
Liverpool vs Everton Premiership, 4.05pm (SKY)

. . . .

23 Monday

....

24 Tuesday

....

25 Wednesday Christmas Day
1964 Gary McAllister is born in Motherwell

....

26 Thursday Boxing Day
Liverpool vs Blackburn Rovers **Premiership**

....

27 Friday

....

28 Saturday

....

29 Sunday
Arsenal vs Liverpool **Premiership, 4.05pm** (SKY)

....

30 Monday

31 Tuesday

1 Wednesday New Year's Day
Newcastle United vs Liverpool Premiership, 7.45pm (SKY)

2 Thursday

3 Friday

4 Saturday
FA Cup third round
1994 Liverpool come back from three goals down to draw 3-3 with Man United at Anfield

5 Sunday
1957 David Fairclough is born in Liverpool

6 Monday

7 Tuesday
Worthington League Cup semi-final first leg [and Weds 8th]

8 Wednesday

9 Thursday
1962 Ray Houghton is born in Glasgow

10 Friday

11 Saturday
Liverpool vs Aston Villa Premiership
1978 Emile Heskey is born in Leicester

12 Sunday

13 Monday

14 Tuesday

15 Wednesday

16 Thursday

17 Friday

18 Saturday
Southampton vs Liverpool Premiership

19 Sunday
1969 Steve Staunton is born in Dundalk

20 Monday

21 Tuesday
Worthington League Cup semi-final second leg [and Weds 22nd]
1954 Phil Thompson is born in Liverpool

22 Wednesday

23 Thursday
1919 Bob Paisley is born in Bishop Auckland

24 Friday
1900 Battle of Spion Kop during Boer War, which lends its name to Anfield's legendary terrace

25 Saturday
FA Cup fourth round

26 Sunday

27 Monday

28 Tuesday
1994 Graeme Souness departs manager's chair at Anfield

29 Wednesday
Liverpool vs Arsenal Premiership

30 Thursday

31 Friday

1 Saturday
West Ham United vs Liverpool Premiership

2 Sunday
1952 Record attendance of 61,905 at Anfield to see FA Cup victory over Wolves

3 Monday

4 Tuesday

5 Wednesday

6 Thursday

7 Friday
1959 Sammy Lee is born in Liverpool

8 Saturday
Liverpool vs Middlesbrough Premiership

9 Sunday

10 Monday

11 Tuesday
1998 Michael Owen becomes the youngest player this century to play for England

12 Wednesday
International Friendlies (to be arranged)

13 Thursday

14 Friday
1996 Bob Paisley dies aged 77

15 Saturday
FA Cup fifth round

16 Sunday

17 Monday

....

18 Tuesday
Uefa Champions League second group stage, match 3 [or Weds 19th]

....

19 Wednesday

....

20 Thursday

....

21 Friday

....

22 Saturday
Birmingham City vs Liverpool Premiership
1991 Kenny Dalglish resigns as manager of Liverpool

....

23 Sunday

....

24 Monday

....

25 Tuesday
Uefa Champions League second group stage, match 4 [or Weds 26th]

....

26 Wednesday

....

27 Thursday

....

28 Friday
1934 Ronnie Moran is born in Liverpool

....

1 Saturday
Liverpool vs Bolton Wanderers Premiership

....

2 Sunday
Worthington League Cup final, Cardiff

....

3 Monday

....

4 Tuesday
1951 Kenny Dalglish is born in Glasgow

....

5 Wednesday

....

6 Thursday

....

7 Friday

....

8 Saturday
FA Cup sixth round [and Sun 9th]

....

9 Sunday

....

10 Monday
1997 Liverpool beat Newcastle United 4-3 at Anfield for the second season running

. . . .

11 Tuesday
Uefa Champions League second group stage, match 5 [or Weds 12th]
1967 40,149 at Anfield to watch FA Cup tie at Everton live on giant screens

. . . .

12 Wednesday

. . . .

13 Thursday

. . . .

14 Friday
1936 Matt Busby makes his first-team debut for Liverpool

. . . .

15 Saturday
Tottenham Hotspur vs Liverpool Premiership
1969 Anfield hosts first colour edition of Match Of The Day – Liverpool vs West Ham

. . . .

16 Sunday
1977 Reds stage amazing fightback to beat St Etienne on one of Anfield's greatest nights

. . . .

17 Monday

18 Tuesday
Uefa Champions League second group stage, match 6 [or Weds 19th]

1977 Danny Murphy is born in Chester

19 Wednesday
2002 Gérard Houllier makes emotional return to Anfield after heart surgery for Champions League clash with Roma

20 Thursday
1988 Everton beat Liverpool 1-0 at Goodison Park, which means the Reds must share with Leeds the record of 29 matches unbeaten from the start of a season

21 Friday
Uefa Champions League knockout stages draw

22 Saturday
Liverpool vs Leeds United Premiership

23 Sunday
1991 Caretaker boss Ronnie Moran leads Liverpool to record away win, 7-1 at Derby County

24 Monday

....

25 Tuesday
1984 First all-Merseyside League Cup Final ends goalless at Wembley

....

26 Wednesday
1986 Kenny Dalglish is awarded the freedom of Glasgow after winning his 100th Scotland cap

....

27 Thursday

....

28 Friday

....

29 Saturday

Euro 2004 qualifiers include Liechtenstein vs England, Scotland vs Iceland, Wales vs Azerbaijan, Armenia vs Northern Ireland, Georgia vs Rep of Ireland

....

30 Sunday
1976 Liverpool become first English club to beat Barcelona at Nou Camp

....

31 Monday

1 Tuesday
1979 Billy Butler tells Radio Merseyside listeners the Kop is on fire

2 Wednesday

**Euro 2004 qualifiers include England vs Turkey, Lithuania vs Scotland,
Yugoslavia vs Wales, Northern Ireland vs Greece,
Albania vs Republic of Ireland**

3 Thursday
1996 Liverpool 4 Newcastle United 3 in an extraordinary match at Anfield

4 Friday

5 Saturday
Manchester United vs Liverpool Premiership
1987 For the first time Liverpool lose when Rush scores to Arsenal in League Cup final

6 Sunday

7 Monday

8 Tuesday
Uefa Champions League quarter-finals first leg [or Weds 9th]

9 Wednesday
1975 Robbie Fowler is born in Liverpool

10 Thursday

11 Friday

12 Saturday
Liverpool vs Fulham Premiership

13 Sunday
FA Cup semi-finals

14 April

---

15 April
1989 Ninety-six Liverpool fans die in Hillsborough disaster

---

16 Wednesday
1991 Graeme Souness announced as new manager in succession to Kenny Dalglish

---

17 Thursday

---

18 Friday
Good Friday Bank holiday UK

---

19 Saturday
Everton vs Liverpool Premiership

---

20 Sunday
Easter Day

---

21 Monday
Easter Monday Bank holiday UK & Republic of Ireland (not Scotland)
Liverpool vs Charlton Athletic Premiership

....

22 Tuesday
Uefa Champions League quarter-finals second leg [or Weds 23rd]

....

23 Wednesday

....

24 Thursday

....

25 Friday
1914 Liverpool lose first FA Cup final, to Burnley by a single goal at Crystal Palace

....

26 Saturday
West Bromwich Albion vs Liverpool Premiership

....

27 Sunday

....

28 Monday

....

29 Tuesday
1901 Liverpool beat West Brom 1-0 at the Hawthorns to clinch first league title

....

30 Wednesday
International Friendlies (to be arranged)

....

1 Thursday
1965 Ee-ay-addio, we won the Cup! Reds beat Leeds 2-1 at Wembley to win FA Cup for first time

....

2 Friday

....

3 Saturday
Liverpool vs Manchester City Premiership

....

4 Sunday

....

5 Monday Bank holiday UK & Republic of Ireland

---

6 Tuesday
Uefa Champions League semi-finals first leg [or Weds 7th]
1997 Michael Owen comes on as a substitute debutant in the 57th minute at Wimbledon and takes just 13 minutes to score

---

7 Wednesday

---

8 Thursday
1988 The Anfield Rap enters the UK charts, eventually reaching no3

---

9 Friday
1973 Uefa Cup final vs Borussia Mönchengladbach is postponed due to torrential downpour

---

10 Saturday
1986 Liverpool beat Everton 3-1 to win the Double in Kenny Dalglish's first season in charge

---

11 Sunday
Chelsea vs Liverpool Premiership (final game of season)

---

12 Monday
1984 Goalless draw at Notts County secures third league championship in as many seasons

13 Tuesday
Uefa Champions League semi-finals second leg [or Weds 14th]

14 Wednesday

15 Thursday

16 Friday
2001 Golden own goal wins Reds the Uefa Cup for the third time against Alavés

17 Saturday
FA Cup final, Cardiff 3pm

18 Sunday
1954 Jimmy Case is born in Liverpool

19 Monday

....

20 Tuesday
1989 Liverpool beat Everton 3-2 after extra time to win emotional post-Hillsborough FA Cup final

....

21 Wednesday

....

22 Thursday

....

23 Friday

....

24 Saturday
1973 Vladimir Smicer is born in Degin, Czech Republic

....

25 Sunday
1977 Liverpool defeat Borussia Mönchengladbach 3-1 to lift European Cup for the first time

....

26 Monday Bank holiday UK & Republic of Ireland

....

27 Tuesday
1981 Liverpool beat Real Madrid in Paris to complete a hat-trick of European Cup triumphs

....

28 Wednesday
Uefa Champions League final, Old Trafford, 7.45pm

....

29 Thursday

....

30 Friday
1984 Reds beat Roma on penalties to win the European Cup and complete treble

....

31 Saturday

....

1 Sunday

....

2 Monday
1957 Mark Lawrenson is born in Preston

....

3 Tuesday

....

4 Wednesday

....

5 Thursday

....

6 Friday

....

7 Saturday

Euro 2004 qualifiers include Scotland vs Germany and Republic of Ireland vs Albania

....

8 Sunday

....

9 Monday

....

10 Tuesday

....

11 Wednesday

....

12 Thursday
1943 Anfield stages world featherweight boxing championship, won by American Freddie Miller

....

13 Friday
1955 Alan Hansen is born in Alloa

....

14 Saturday
1947 Liverpool become League champions at the end of a season heavily disrupted by freezing winter conditions

....

15 Sunday

....

16 Monday

17 Tuesday

18 Wednesday

19 Thursday

20 Friday

21 Saturday

22 Sunday

23 Monday

....

24 Tuesday
1967 Ray Clemence signs from Scunthorpe United

....

25 Wednesday

....

26 Thursday

....

27 Friday

....

28 Saturday

....

29 Sunday

....

30 Monday
1998 Michael Owen scores wonder goal against Argentina in the World Cup in St Etienne

....

1 Tuesday
1986 Ian Rush is sold to Juventus in a £3.6m deal that saw him loaned back to Liverpool for the 1986/87 season

....

2 Wednesday

....

3 Thursday

....

4 Friday
1963 Jan Molby is born in Kolding, Denmark

....

5 Saturday
1960 Gary Gillespie is born in Stirling

....

6 Sunday

....

7 Monday

....

8 Tuesday

....

9 Wednesday

....

10 Thursday

....

11 Friday

....

12 Saturday
1974 Bill Shankly stuns Merseyside by announcing his retirement as Liverpool manager

....

13 Sunday

....

14 Monday
1984 American evangelist Billy Graham begins a week of services at Anfield

....

15 Tuesday

....

16 Wednesday
1998 Gérard Houllier arrives at Anfield as joint manager alongside Roy Evans

....

17 Thursday

....

18 Friday

....

19 Saturday
1981 Grégory Vignal is born in Montpellier, France

....

20 Sunday

....

21 Monday

. . . .

22 Tuesday
1999 Dietmar Hamann signs for Liverpool from Newcastle United for a club record £8m

. . . .

23 Wednesday

. . . .

24 Thursday
1978 Liverpool become the first Football League club to wear sponsored shirts after signing a deal with electronics firm Hitachi

. . . .

25 Friday

. . . .

26 Saturday
1974 Bob Paisley is confirmed as manager of Liverpool in succession to Bill Shankly

. . . .

27 Sunday

. . . .

28 Monday

....

29 Tuesday

....

30 Wednesday

....

31 Thursday

....

1 Friday

....

2 Saturday

....

3 Sunday

....

4 Monday

....

5 Tuesday
1948 Ray Clemence is born in Scunthorpe

....

6 Wednesday

....

7 Thursday

....

8 Friday

....

9 Saturday

....

10 Sunday

....

11 Monday

. . . .

12 Tuesday

. . . .

13 Wednesday

. . . .

14 Thursday

. . . .

15 Friday

. . . .

16 Saturday

. . . .

17 Sunday

. . . .

STOP PRESS

WORLD CUP REDS

Dietmar Hamann Germany

Dubbed at the start of the competition as Germany's worst national side ever Rudi Völler's men proved the critics wrong with a well-organised, determined passage to the final. While it's easy to see it as a triumph of traditional Teutonic efficiency, such broad generalisations conceal the contribution made by key individuals. Oliver Kahn lived up to his billing as the world's best keeper, Miroslav Klose emerged as an unlikely contender for leading goalscorer and the timely interventions of Michael Ballack confirmed him as one of Europe's very best midfielders. Völler insisted the team ethic made up for the lack of superstars and nowhere was this better exhibited than in the meanest defence of the tournament, shepherded by our very own Dietmar Hamann.

Throughout, Didi's ability to shield his defenders, pick up the scraps and set the ball rolling upfield contributed to a burgeoning belief within German ranks. These understated, and often under-rated skills, will have come as no surprise to those who have watched him become such an influential player at Anfield, and they enabled Germany to soak up significant amounts of pressure before attacking with pace. Only Tortsen Frings, who played a game more, made more tackles for Germany and both were ranked in the top-five defensive players of the tournament. Didi also made it on to most pundits' teams of the tournament.

Unfortunately for Hamann, his most memorable contribution in the final, after an otherwise peerless performance, was losing possession to Ronaldo on the edge of his own box, an error compounded when the hitherto reliable Kahn spilt Rivaldo's shot for Ronaldo to open the scoring. Didi and co put up a valiant display but ultimately, not even the tightest defence in the finals could cope with the Brazilians' attacking genius. On a bright note, in reaching the final, Didi can now reclaim bragging rights from his English colleagues at Anfield after the 5-1 defeat in Munich.

Matches 6 **Goals** 0 **Rating** 8

A top-class tournament for Didi, one of Germany's best players

Michael Owen England

Like England's overall World Cup campaign, there was a sense of what might have been about Michael Owen's tournament. It was always going to be hard to emulate the impact of 1998 and in a team that failed to provide its main scoring outlet with the right service Owen often looked frustrated. But even in flashes, the European footballer of the year demonstrated why he is one of the most feared strikers in the world. Twice he took on the Argentine defence, first hitting a post and then showing there are now tricks to go with the pace to win the decisive penalty. A similar run from 25 yards out against Nigeria ended with a goal-bound shot being deflected wide. Against Denmark, he latched on to his first clear chance of the tournament, swivelled and found the side panel of Sorensen's net. Then, in the country's most important game for 12 years, he rose to the challenge by punishing Lucio's mistake with a chip over Marcos for the opening goal. The way the Brazilian keeper went down prematurely suggested he too knew Owen would score on the big occasion.

Michael Owen pushes the ball past Lucio to score against Brazil

It is no surprise that so many of England's hopes rest on the uncanny ability of Michael to find the net. What is surprising, is that he is substituted so regularly when not given the opportunity to do so. The highlights of what was a moderately successful tournament for him illustrate how few chances he needs to score. Still only 22, there is every reason to believe Owen will go on to play and score in at least two more World Cups. He proved himself once again on the biggest stage and with better service, principally one suspects from Steven Gerrard, the England scoring record held by Bobby Charlton should still be in sight.

Matches 5 **Goals** 2 **Rating** 7

Emile Heskey England

Heskey bashing has become a favoured pastime for media pundits and armchair critics alike so the big man's goal against Denmark will have been particularly sweet. Much of the way Heskey plays for England is governed by the system favoured by Eriksson and while his reluctance to frighten defenders with his strength and pace remains frustrating, it is hard to get your head down and run when you are playing most of the game with your back to goal. Against Argentina, Heskey's ability to drop back into midfield and nick possession was utilised almost as much as his threat to the opposition goal. This contribution was overlooked somewhat because the man who replaced him after 54 minutes, Teddy Sheringham, almost scored what would have been the goal of the tournament. In the pedestrian match against Nigeria, Heskey again showed his strength by holding the ball up while also supplying a wonderful cross that Owen narrowly failed to convert. Denmark saw glimpses of the real Heskey when he burst past Martin Laursen in the opening exchanges before scoring England's third goal with a well-struck shot. Like most of his team-mates, Heskey had a disappointing afternoon against Brazil prompting the same critics to peddle their familiar lines. Unfortunately, this looks set to continue unless Heskey can up his scoring rate for England.

Matches 5 **Goals** 1 **Rating** 6

El Hadji turns on the style against Turkey in the World Cup quarter-final

El Hadji Diouf Senegal

Normally a striker who fails to score a single goal would not be considered one of the stars of the World Cup but this was no ordinary tournament, and the Serial Killer is no ordinary striker. Dazzling against France in the opening game, Diouf demonstrated his ability to float across the frontline and pick up positions that make him hard to defend against. The former bad boy showed glimpses of petulance in the draw with Denmark and failed to trouble the scorers again in the six-goal thriller with Uruguay but he was undoubtedly the shining jewel in Senegal's crown. El Hadji drifted wide to make space for Henri Camara to score, beat opponents at will and showed he will be competing for the ball at set pieces this season with a deftly taken free-kick that almost broke the deadlock against Turkey. It is unlikely we will see the £11million man used as an out-and-out striker although his pace, trickery and strength could well make him the perfect foil for Michael Owen.

Matches 5 **Goals** 0 **Rating** 7

Salif Diao Senegal

The leggy midfield enforcer drew favourable comparisons with Patrick Vieira after a World Cup that saw him excel in one of the greatest upsets of all time, give away a penalty, score one of the goals of the tournament, get sent off, dropped and then knocked out by a golden goal in the quarter-finals. When the tall Senegalese star settles in at Anfield, Liverpool look set to profit from his athleticism and ability to adapt to different situations during a match. Senegal proved themselves to be anything but a stereotypical African team – they were disciplined, tactically astute and consistent, and Diao looks set to give another of Liverpool's World Cup successes, Didi Hamann, a strong battle for his place this season.

Matches 3 **Goals** 1 **Rating** 7

Diao, our new man in the middle and scorer of one of the goals of the summer

Jerzy Dudek Poland

A thoroughly disappointing tournament for Liverpool's number one reached its nadir when he was dropped for Poland's consolation win over the United States. There were question marks against Dudek's name over a couple of the goals Poland conceded on the way to finishing bottom of Group D although Jerzy pointed out that his country had not prepared properly for the tournament by playing friendlies against weak opposition. We trust a well-earned summer holiday will restore his confidence in time for a new campaign between the sticks for the Reds.

Matches 2 **Goals conceded** 6 **Rating** 3

The new season starts here for Jerzy

THE ROUGH GUIDE TO

Videogaming

Informed, independent advice
on the major gaming platforms

Punchy reviews
of the top games in every genre

Hints, tips and cheats
to crack each game

Directories
of the best Web sites and gaming resources